FILM REVIEW

1979–80

FILM REVIEW
1979-80

edited by F. Maurice Speed

W. H. Allen · London
A Howard & Wyndham Company
1979

This book or parts thereof may not be
reproduced in any form whatsoever without
permission in writing from the publisher.
Printed in Great Britain by
Fletcher & Son Ltd, Norwich, and bound by
Richard Clay (The Chaucer Press) Ltd,
Bungay, Suffolk, for the publishers,
W. H. Allen & Co. Ltd,
44 Hill Street, London W1X 8LB

ISBN 0 491 02169 0

CONTENTS

INTRODUCTION

Last year I began these introductory notes, news and comments about the year in the cinema by expressing an opinion that while we appeared to be approaching the end of a cycle of the more outrageously pornographic sex and/or violence movies, we were moving into a new and almost equally offensive era of films which for no valid reason were exploiting foul language. Events have proved me happily right in the first forecast, and unhappily correct, too, in the second.

In fact the considerable numbers of the more objectionable sex and violence films, which for far too long a period degraded the whole cinema business, have tapered off to practically nothing,* and of those that do still from time to time reach the screen many had been made or planned before it became obvious to the producers that, public curiosity about these examples of 'new-frontiers' movies having been satisfied (and realisation and boredom at the same old dreary pornographic content having set in), good taste had reasserted itself at least to the extent of making this kind of production a very dubious commercial proposition.

The moviegoing public showed that now, as ever, it is in the long run Entertainment which they ask for in the cinema and they rewarded the producers who provided this kind of film fare with record profits. Sex and violence are still very much a part of cinema, of course—as indeed they are of life—but both are now being used more wisely as only a part of a film and not as its entire motivation. In this way, both can be justified, as, for instance, they were in this year's outstanding Australian film *The Chant of Jimmie Blacksmith*, in which the sudden outbursts of bloody violence, were a key to the whole film, forcefully underlining its implied social warning.

Of course the more blatant kind of sex films are still made, but the great majority of these are small and shoddy affairs destined for the back-alley sex shops and small club cinemas catering for the simple, the curious and the kinky, and as such do little real harm to either the industry or the public at large.

But as this problem begins to grow small, the other looms more threateningly large. The use of foul words and gutter expressions in films is an increasingly unpleasant trend—one to be found not only in a few minor movies but in some first feature films, written by screenwriters of some repute and made by directors, producers and companies who should know and show a greater sense of their social responsibilities.

Starting with the occasional swear-word slipped into the dialogue, quite justifiably in many cases, such words have proliferated until in some extreme cases in recent movies one gets the impression that take out all the four-letter (and allied) words and you'd have a pretty thin script left! You may well feel that I am making something of the proverbial mountain out of a molehill in regard to this matter, but as it is a fashion which is likely to get more and more outrageous as one producer tries to go further than another (as always seems to happen in the movie business) I think right now is the time for anyone with the opportunity to stand up and cry: '*Enough!*' After all, there can be no justification for this kind of thing; *in excess* such words debase the language, degrade the characters and encourage the wider use of such ugly and basically meaningless words among youngsters, who may well be persuaded that their use is essential in adult conversation, which, thankfully, is just not so.

Added to the now all too familiar 'natural' sound backgrounds (an irritation to which I'll return later) this proliferation of foul words and gutter expressions has in some extreme cases made some of the year's movies almost unintelligible to me, and accordingly, I presume, to many others too.

An American film called *Blue Collar* was a pretty good example of the

*With regard to films of extreme violence, there have still been shown some unpleasant examples during the period under review, such as the 1979 release *The Hills Have Eyes*, in which an American Family on holiday in a remote desert location are besieged by a collection of freaks who rape the daughter, burn the father alive, shoot the mother and run off with the baby with the intention of making a tasty meal of it—after having killed and eaten (apparently raw) the family's Alsatian dog as a sort of *hors-d'œuvre*!

kind of production I am condemning. It had so many of the foulest words and equally unpleasant expressions peppering the dialogue (at times there seemed to be little else), and so much mumbled and garbled dialogue spoken against strident background noise, that I soon lost all interest in the apparently moronic leading characters and the film as a whole, although I am well aware that beneath these blemishes were some fresh and interesting ideas and, indeed, a pretty good movie.

Now I assure you I am not writing all this from some Cloud-Cuckoo-land. I am as well aware as the next man that many rougher, less educated characters do in fact converse in this dismal way. My early experience in a printing and publishing house taught me this; it taught me, too, how utterly banal and boring such conversation becomes. I certainly don't want this kind of thing served up to me in a movie, where life should at least be tempered, and illuminated, by art.

Now back, for just a few lines, to those 'natural' sound backgrounds. (I may as well get all my grumbles off my chest before I settle down to less controversial matters.) By this I mean the apparently casual, or 'realistic', recording of conversations in the streets, factories and elsewhere where background noise all but drowns the voices: allowing, or perhaps even encouraging, the characters to speak with their mouths full or with their heads turned away from the camera, and the use of uncomfortably intrusive background music. Such features help to make it a strain to catch all the dialogue and sometimes make it necessary for you to puzzle out the words for yourself.

Maybe it is time for the pendulum to swing back towards the period when players were expected to have a reasonable standard of elocution and due homage was paid to the microphone, so that every carefully enunciated word could be easily recorded and then clearly heard by the audience?

When I tackled a director, who shall be nameless, about this some months back, his cheerful riposte was: 'Oh, I wouldn't worry too much about it, old chap, if I were you, I don't suppose any of those lines you missed were important anyway.' I don't know what your reactions are to this, but mine were little short of disbelief. If any lines are so unimportant that they can be lost without effect, and are inserted merely as padding, then they should be edited out at some point before the film is completed because they can only be helping to stretch it out to a needless length. And it happens far too often these days that a naturally-paced ninety-minute movie is spun out laboriously to some two hours, turning what might have been a crisp-moving, say, thriller into a heavy-footed bore.

All this is, I appreciate, a sour note on which to start this review of the movie year but I honestly believe I am only voicing feelings of irritation felt by many moviegoers about these subjects, and which they have so often expressed to me. My own gripe springs from my great affection for the movies and my desire that they should be as good as they can be made, so attracting, rather than alienating, an increasing number of moviegoers.

Now, on a happier note, some cheering facts and figures about the year just ended—by which I mean the latter half of 1978 and the early part of 1979. In spite of all the depressing signs and portents evident at about this time last year, the second half of 1978 and the first part of 1979 have been a good period for the cinema both in terms of production and projection.

Attendances were up, often surprisingly so, in both Britain and America. As an example, taking just one of the months for which I have definite figures, October 1978 saw a rise in cash taken at the US box-offices of some 17% over the same period of the previous year. If you eliminate the actual rise in seat prices over that period (something which often distorts statistics) the figure does admittedly fall, but still only to 13%. The final total of admission during 1978 in America was very near to 73 millions, an increase over 1977 of around 16%.

In Britain the figures were even more spectacular, with a rise in admissions during the same period of 40%! This is despite the fact that even with the various twinning and tripling, and whatever, of cinemas that has been going on, the actual number of cinemas has fallen.

As a matter of interest, the films which took the most money at British cinemas during 1978 were: 1. *Star Wars*; 2. *Grease*; 3. *Close Encounters of the Third Kind*; 4. *Saturday Night Fever*; 5. *Revenge of the Pink Panther*; 6. *The Rescuers*; 7. *ABBA—The Movie*; 8. *The Gauntlet* and *Herbie Goes to Monte Carlo* (sharing); 9. *The Stud*; 10. *The Deep*; 11. *Annie Hall*; 12. *Convoy*; 13. *The Wild Geese*; 14. *Warlords of Atlantis*; 15. *Candleshoe*; 16. *The Goodbye Girl*; 17. *Spiderman*; 18. *Heaven Can Wait*; 19. *Julia*; 20. *International Velvet*.

Some interesting points about this list is that it includes no less than three Disney features and a number of critically panned movies like *Convoy*.

With regard to film production, film studios on both sides of the Atlantic had a very good year too, even if we always have to take into account the fact that without the production of the ever-increasing number of television films and series the situation would be pretty grim, if not actually disastrous.

It is reckoned, for instance, that at any one time about 75% of all film production is for the small screen, and though at one time during 1978 this figure became more favourable (at about 60% to 40%) it was expected that at the year's end a tally would show that, overall, it was back to about this average.

Though by far the greater proportion of the films made in Britain were American financed, nobody seemed inclined to grumble too much about this, appreciating that if it were not for such movies there would be a very great deal more unemployment right through the industry.

Not so long ago fears were being expressed that the British studios were likely to become a disaster area, but all that has swiftly changed. The studios in operation have all been so busy that in some cases extensions are being carried out, or are planned. For instance, the Lee Brothers, who took over the old Rediffusion Studios at Wembley, brought forward by about a year the operating of their refurbished five stages and by early 1979 four of the five were already occupied.

At the Elstree EMI Studios,* they built a large new silent stage to which the *Star Wars* sequel of *The Empire Strikes Back* was quickly moved. Pinewood studios started its year with three productions on the floor and with plenty more promised to follow, among them such major movies as *Nijinsky, Raise the Titanic, Bear Island, Flash Gordon* and at least some of the sequences of the new James Bond film *Moonraker*. In America, Universal announced that they were to spend something like £14 million on extending and refurbishing their Studio City. Though all the major American film companies appear to have done extremely well financially recently, none has done better than Disney, who go on solidly proving that the policies initiated by the late, astute Walt of sticking to the production of 'U'-certificated family films was the right one, at least for them. 1978 brought a rise of 20% in Disney's profits, with rentals of their cinema and television films up from the 1977 total of £118 millions to a new record of £147 millions.

One of the more interesting and possibly important aspects of recent film production has been the emergence of an increasing number of young men, and women, to take over the major seats of celluloid power. The strong current feeling in the industry that it is essential that films must appeal to the younger members of the community (those with the most spare spending-power of any age-group now) has given greater opportunities to the young

*On 24 January 1979, a fire on Stage 3 of these studios caused damage estimated at £1¼ million. This stage was at the time occupied, as it had been since the midsummer of 1978, by Stanley Kubrick's *The Shining* (in all, the film had been in production for about a year when the fire occurred) which at that point needed only about two weeks' shooting for completion. Fortunately, as it happened, most of the set was no longer required and only some minor rebuilding was needed to shoot the final scenes.

In connection with Kubrick's painstaking methods of production, when Shelley Duvall explained to Robert Altman, who makes his films on *very* different schedules, that she had been working a year on her part in the movie his comment was: 'Jesus! I couldn't do that. I see these people taking two years to make a film, and waiting for the weather to change for every scene. It may be all right for them but my films are more an exercise in style, and content is something I don't impose, but something which is already there.'

Jerzy Skolimowski explains to the cameraman what he wants in *The Shout*.

Ingmar Bergman explains a scene in his ITC film *Autumn Sonata*.

Mel Brooks directs a scene in *High Anxiety*, the comedy in which he also played the leading role.

executives. The average age of film directors, for instance, has taken a quite dramatic turn-down in the past few years with comparative youngsters like Francis Ford Coppola (39), Martin Scorsese, John Carpenter and George Lukas (all of a similar age, or even younger) getting chances to make big movies on budgets of a size which only the old and proved directors would have been trusted with a few years ago. Donald Simpson, Paramount's Vice-President in charge of production is only 32; Paula Weinstein, who holds down a like position at Fox, is the same age. Tom Mount, doing a similar job across at Universal Studios, is only 29; and Claire Townsend, Vice-President of Fox's Creative Department, is 26. At Warners 30-year-old Mark Rosenberg has taken over the Vice-President's chair and has now been placed in charge of production there. Most of these youngsters have come into the industry from college (and most of them, incidentally, are politically left-leaning, it is believed). However, to quote the old truism, nothing is new under the sun as *Screen International* reminded us earlier this year by recalling that David O. Selznick was only 26 when he became RKO Radio's chief and Darryl F. Zanuck was running Warner in his twenties! Another interesting and important trend is the way in which production is swinging away from the major companies towards the smaller, independent outfits. Five years ago, half of all the films made in America

were coming from the several major companies like Fox, Columbia and Warner. Today that figure has dropped to 30%, which means that 70% of all production is coming from the Roger Cormans and the like.

One has, as usual, to be careful in quoting these figures. It was *Screen International* which noted that the independents have made about 300 films a year for the past few years, leaving the majors with about 70. But as the latter were generally much larger productions, made with considerably bigger budgets and sold with vast promotional campaigns, the 70 took some 85% of the total US box-office returns during 1977!

But amid all the flow of good, optimistic facts and figures and predictions there arrived a salutary (and some must have found it a pretty shocking) report about the British cinema (the bricks-and-mortar cinema) which appeared in America's *Variety* in October 1978. Compiled by Roger Watkins it began:

'What mood pervades the British Market now that attendances are up for the first time in three decades and the flow of big attractions from Hollywood seems assured for some time. Sanguine? Enthusiastic? Celebratory? Forget it.

'British theatre operators . . . are so conditioned by a climate of decline that their idea of successful operations is predicated on the somewhat paradoxical thought of keeping the overhead down against

every temptation.

'Something of the distributors' frustration is voiced by Ascanio Branca, 20th-Fox's local chieftain who has been operative [in GB] for the past twelve months having served for the company elsewhere in Europe. He says British exhibitors are facing a phenomenon they don't believe—one big hit after another creating a cinematic boom.

'"They have no faith in the business and, if they don't react now and build new theatres when things are going great, they will eventually be proven right and the business will collapse. The Americans will pack up and go home and sell their films to television," he says darkly.

'"No country in Europe is so badly served as Britain as to the condition of its theatres. Many of the multi-auditoria put up here are lousy. There are continual complaints about sound and comfort. It is pitiful," he [Ascanio Branca] moans.

'Showmen, preoccupied with the spiralling of their fixed costs, are naturally suspicious of business hiccups such as the present hike [rise] in admissions of some 40% or so. If tempted to speculate, they figure mebbe they are gonna get zapped [hit] by inflation and stagnation later.

'When the British wickets are good it is the best market in Europe by far, as witness the sparkling distribution rentals of *Jaws* (nearly £5,000,000) and *Saturday Night Fever* (around £3,000,000 so far).

'But the percentage of turkeys

Bryan Forbes, with his star Tatum O'Neal, explaining an equestrian scene in his CIC film *International Velvet*.

Famous still-photographer David Hamilton, who made his motion-picture-directing début during the year with the erotic *Bilitis*.

Michael Winner during the production of his re-make of the Raymond Chandler classic, *The Big Sleep*.

[disasters]—some of which had performed well in America and other countries—is so high that even Britain's prime entertainment conglomerate, EMI, scrammed [rejected] solo distribution and sought refuge in the bosom of the already merged Columbia-Warner distribbery [distributors].

'Market rule of thumb is some twenty films or so per annum will deliver rentals of £200,000–300,000 after launch costs of between £75,000–110,000. Those are the kind of statistics the British trade has learned to live with and to respond to. It is the five or six a year which go through the rafters which cause the intertrade furore. Perhaps they show up too many antiquated procedures or arcane methods. Or even embarrassingly illustrate what could be achieved in this market if, like the car rental company, some tried harder.'

Reinforcing these warnings came an equally strong British report, written by Chris Brown and featured in *Screen International* at around the same date.

'But what about the cinemas themselves,' asked Mr Brown, '. . . are they doing their best to ensure that the public not only enjoy the film they pay to see but also their visit to the cinema?' In a long and forthright article here are some of the more important points he raised:

'In a cinema the public pay to see the film, and if the print has been chopped about and mutilated, the patron will think Oh God, how terrible, and will think twice about going to the cinema again.

'There are less cinema seats per head of the population in the UK than in nearly any other industrialised nation.

'The profit margin of the average cinema is so small and so uncertain that running costs are cut to a minimum. This results in shabbiness or even downright dirtiness. Thus, instead of being an attractive social venue, a cinema becomes a less comfortable and less consequential place than one's own parlour.'

'One would hope,' says Chris Moore (of Rank Leisure), 'that the number of major renovations around the country, with particular regard to the technical side, can be increased. There are still a lot of improvements which can be made.

'We have not had a run like this for years. We must capitalise on this and if necessary massive changes should be made. We have to think about children's programmes in the afternoon and adult programmes in the evening, as in virtually every other country. We have to think about moving programmes round in a complex during the week, or afternoon, or evening, if necessary, to maximise the potential of the multi-auditoria.

*The cinema-owners in all cases stressed that these mini-cinemas were intended essentially as an extension of normal cinemas and not as a replacement of them. They were seen as an opportunity to site small cinemas in districts not otherwise capable of supporting normal movie-houses.

'The industry at the moment is far too complacent, and we now have probably our last chance to get people to come to the cinema and keep coming.'

Another warning note about future British film attendances came from the Henley Forecasting Centre in a report in the summer of 1978 in which—in spite of all the remarkable upsurge figures being published around that period—it was forecast that there would be a *fall* in British moviegoing to about 80 million by the year 1983 (this figure to be seen against the lowest annual attendance yet recorded (in 1976) of 108.9 millions).

In terms of cinemas the most significant new innovation has been the video cinema. EMI opened the first of these (an experimental 74-seater) at Norwich in the summer of 1978 and its success led them to open others at Woking and Purley and to plan many more.

The Star Group, after watching the successful launching of these mini-cinemas, also opened two of them in late 1978, with five more planned.

But all these facts and figures are likely to become terribly dated by the time you read them because both these chains, and other groups, appear to be making plans to open a quite considerable number of these small and easy-to-run movie houses. Indeed, had it not been for a number of technical teething troubles which cropped up, now all happily overcome, the number might have been by now much greater.*

Initially back-projection was used but it was hoped to switch quickly to normal front projection. In any case the claim was that even with rear projection the quality of the picture was already 90% that of the normal projected 35-mm film. This quality was apparently helped by the use of an 'Enhancer', an item of British equipment marketed by the Electrocraft Co, which literally enhances both the horizontal and vertical lines and so produces a sharper image.

These mini video theatres were not confined to Britain. At least a dozen were opened in Germany in 1979 and similar numbers were planned for France and Canada where, incidentally, 1978 saw the opening of what is surely the ultimate in cinema complexes. This is the Toronto Cineplex (run by showman Nat Taylor, who claims to have initiated the multi-cinema when, as far back as 1948, he 'twinned' his Elgin, Ottawa, cinema) which, costing £2 million to build, contains eighteen auditoria under the one roof, served by the one box-office. Each mini cinema seats between 50 and 120 patrons and as the walls of the cinemas can be easily moved to accommodate larger or smaller numbers, according to the success of the film showing, the permutations are almost endless. Mr Taylor's idea is that in this way he can provide a vast range of films for a wide variety of tastes, showing new films, foreign films, cult films, classics and others for which the small numbers of

people interested in seeing them would mean that they would otherwise not be likely to get a showing.*

One of the major headaches in Europe has been the increasing success of the American films shown there, a worry reflected in a major survey published in Brussels in 1978 called *The Crisis of the European Cinema* and produced for the French National Film Centre by Claude Derand.

This pointed out that the American film was increasingly dominating the screens of the Common Market countries. Between 1971 and 1977, for instance, the American share of the French market went up from 24.5% to 30.5% while the share of home-produced films during the same period dropped 9% to 47%. In Italy between 1973 and 1977 the story was much the same, with a rise in the American films shown from 26.3% to 30.4%.

In Germany between 1971 and 1976 the US proportion of films shown rose somewhat less (actually from 37.1% to 41.1%) but the proportion of German films shown in German cinemas during the same period dropped disastrously from 36.1% to 11.4%!

*In America there are now plenty of cinema-complexes with between six and eight cinemas under the one roof. *Variety* gave a figure of ninety-three cinemas with a combined total of 474 screens!

According to this survey the Italians are the most ardent film fans by a long way, with the average Italian making 8 visits to the cinema each year, as compared with 3.3 for the average Frenchman and only 2 visits each by the average Britisher and German. In Italy there is one cinema for every 2,000 citizens; in France it is one for every 3,000—and in Britain one for every 11,700! In Europe taken as a whole there is, according to the survey, one cinema for every 4,100 homes.

The survey called, as did so many other documents of a similar nature published during the past few years—alas, with little observable result—for more co-operative productions and a co-ordination of government aid right through all the Common Market countries.

Incidentally, it was revealed that, in contrast to Britain and America and other countries, attendances in France have continued to fall (in 1977 by 12%) with little evidence of any recovery during 1978-9. As a result, the French Government promised big tax concessions to the industry in 1979 to try to help it. Interestingly, it seems many in the French film industry feel that one of its basic weaknesses in production is that not enough new young talent is coming along!

Back to Britain: in his final report, Sir John Terry, the retiring Managing Director of the British National Film Finance Corporation, revealed that of the 700 films the company had helped to finance during its thirty years of existence, about one in three had shown a profit—providing you ignored the interest charges payable on Treasury Loans—and the annual loss was, on average, only about £70,000 (a bill footed by the general public, of course).

Indeed, were it not for the high interest charges the NFFC had to meet it would have made a profit of about £50,000 during the last year, with a few films like *Bugsy Malone* contributing the major proportion of this amount. Other films financially backed during the period included *The Shout, The Riddle of the Sands* and *The Sailor's Return*, all very worthwhile small-scale productions which without the NFFC support would almost certainly never have been made. But backing movies, suggested Sir John, was gambling: 'worse than gambling on the horses, with even less chance of picking a winner.'

A 40-year-old Saudi-Arabian-born, Mamoun Hassan, moved into the hot seat at the beginning of 1979, expecting to get a new government fund of £5 million to start his reign begun at a difficult period with all the industry waiting anxiously for the government's long-promised proposed restructuring of their assistance to production.

The scandal of international film piracy continued—and continues—from time to time to make newspaper headlines.*

In January 1979, former British washing-machine tycoon John Bloom was accused in New York of being involved in an alleged international pirate-film racket. Along with two Californian women he was alleged to be part of a film-piracy ring operating in California, London and the Middle East.†

About three weeks later the following story appeared in the London *Evening Standard:*

'Scotland Yard detectives, investigating what they believe to be an international racket in pirate films, found two illicit "factories" in a series of raids all over London.

'They swooped on eight addresses, mainly in North and West London, and seized video cassettes, copying machines, completed films—as well as large quantities of pornographic material.

'Detectives took away eight video recorders and large numbers of blank video-tapes ready to be used to make illegal copies of feature films on current release.

'Today they were trying to discover the last links in the chain of evidence which they hope will lead them to the men at the heart of the racket.

'These men are the source of "master films" used to make copies which are circulated among private distributors.

'Detectives believe there is an American connection. Agents of the Federal Bureau of Investigation have been carrying out a parallel inquiry over there.

'As long ago as last October they consulted Scotland Yard because it appeared London was being used as a clearing centre for the bootleg films.

'They change hands at between £40 and £100—depending on how new the pirated films are—and can make hundreds of thousands of pounds for the principal racketeers.'

In the technical field, apart from the video-cassette cinemas previously mentioned, there's again not much to report this year. Though one hardly ever sees them these days (it's years since I saw a stereoscopic film; almost as long since I saw an example of the once loudly-hailed split-screen technique, now used more-or-less exclusively and occasionally by television), 3-D films still make the trade-paper headlines from time to time with news of some innovation in stereoscopic projection. But that's about as far as it gets.

This year it was enthusiastic young actor–producer Tony Anthony who came up with a story about his

*Bloom was subsequently sentenced by a Los Angeles court, after pleading guilty to some of the charges, to a one-year suspended prison term plus a number of hours community work for a year, including washing dishes!

†According to a spokesman for one of South Africa's largest film-distribution firms, that country has the biggest pirate trade of all, being in the multi-million rand bracket. It was claimed that an organised network of some 200 'pirates' were copying and selling films and exporting them to places as far apart as Saudi Arabia and Nigeria. The business became so large and lucrative that the South African Government finally had step in and do something about it, bringing in a new Copyright Law on 1 January 1979, which may curb the pirates a little, but it is claimed, it is more likely to send the trade underground.

Alfred Hitchcock with actor Barry Foster during a break on a Covent Garden location for *Frenzy*.

The controversial Robert Altman with some of the cast of his latest film *A Wedding*.

acquisition of some 'incredible 3-D gadgets' in Taiwan leading to a system of computerised stereoscopic projection which 'literally levitates the performer into the audience'. Mr Anthony's system is centred on a camera assembled by Stanley and Lorraine Borden and, it is claimed, it is superior to the 'other five 3-D systems now in various stages of experiment'. There was even a promise of a Western from Anthony—*The Cajun Queen*—to be made in Spain with his system in 1979, but at the time of writing I've heard nothing further about this project, nor about any other 3-D system rumoured about to be announced at any moment. Incidentally, what, I wonder, has happened to 'Sensurround'? First used with 'shattering' effect in 1975 in *Earthquake*, this interesting and in some ways highly effective sound-gadget has been introduced into only two films since then, *Rollercoaster*, *The Battle of Midway* and *Battlestar Galactica*.

Two big court cases, one in America and one in Britain, of vital interest to both moviegoers and TV addicts, loomed large in 1979. Late in 1978

Writer Anthony Shaffer, star Richard Burton and director Anthony Page on the set of *Absolution*.

the BBC issued writs against both EMI and the Cinematograph Exhibitors Association alleging that the trade's five-year ban on new British films being sold to TV is unlawful. This was seemingly as a result of what has been claimed as EMI's refusal to show the Dustin Hoffman/Vanessa Redgrave starrer *Agatha*, towards the cost of production of which the BBC had made some small contribution—on the understanding, apparently, that the movie could be shown by them on the small screen after *three* years.

The American case was between Walt Disney and MCA and the Sony Corp over the legality of the owner of a video-tape cassette recorder recording a movie from the TV screen and subsequently showing it to his friends or others. Disney and MCA claimed that the practice had reduced, and would reduce, their incomes!

A shock for British moviemakers was confirmation by UK Trade Secretary John Smith of the rumour that consideration was being given to the cancellation of the British Quota System, regarded by many in the British film industry as their last line of defence against complete domination of the British screen by foreign films.*

Under the Quota Act exhibitors are required by law to show, each year, a minimum of 30% of British features and 25% of British supporting films. Introduced in 1927 with the idea of stimulating home-made movies, the Act never achieved this and for some time now it has been virtually impossible for exhibitors to fulfil their obligation. As a result of the scarcity of British productions, the Board of Trade have accepted the Act as being unworkable and taken no action against the many law-breakers. But the cancellation of this Act would undoubtedly curb still further the production of minor British movies (small-budget movies made on the assumption that even if they don't turn out to be too successful they will still get a reasonable number of bookings by exhibitors making a show of trying to some degree to fulfil their quota obligations) so making it even harder than now for young producers and young directors to get chances to prove themselves.

Finally I'm going to turn to some odd and interesting bits and pieces of news, and other stories, which help to fill in the corners of the year's overall cinematic picture.

An American statistics organisation came up with an estimate that some 330,000 feature films have been

*Another shock for Britain's film industry came in February 1979, when a High Court judge ruled that firms cannot prevent publication of film stills and that such publication does not infringe the Copyright Act 1956. The ruling came as a result of an action over the reproduction in a magazine of some still scenes from the Starsky and Hutch TV series. Judge Mervyn Davies rejected the plaintiffs' arguments that under the copyright law a photo of a single film frame from a movie was a substantial part of that movie and so infringed the law. Subsequently the plaintiffs announced that they would appeal.

made, world-wide, in the 52 years since 1915—of which the USA provided some 27,500, or about 9% of the total. Add to this the suggestion that with the addition of shorts and other films the final total would not be far short of 1,400,000! A quite separate calculation was that to date some 820,000 TV commercial filmlets have been produced.

In the summer of 1978 the American Museum of Modern Art cinema offered a series of programmes under the heading 'A Re-view of American Movies, 1975–77' which consisted of films that had 'vanished without finding an audience during this period'. I think a number of the twenty-nine films selected will give you some surprises. They include: *Assault on Precinct 13*, *The Big Bus*, *Orca*, *The Wilby Conspiracy*, *The Stepford Wives* and *Lifeguard*. All of these, I would imagine, didn't do too badly at the British box-office, though some of the other movies included were undoubtedly disasters on both sides of the Atlantic.

With the current high standard of Australian film production it is interesting to note that any Australian film costing more than, say, something between £175,000 and £200,000 has no hope of making a profit from Australian release; but a major film of international appeal costs a great deal more than that. As an indication of how inflation has hit the film industry 'down under', the successful *Sunday Too Far Away* cost only £100,000 to produce just five years ago; today it would cost at least four times as much to make. Relevant to the above, *Dr No,* the first James Bond movie, cost £500,000 to produce. The next one, *From Russia With Love,* cost double that figure. *Goldfinger* was brought in at £1½ million. And the budget for the new Bond adventure, *Moonraker*— £7½ million!

Ilya Salkind, 31-year-old producer of *Superman,* is on record as saying that it would be a disaster if his film failed to exceed the £40-million mark in the United States. In fact he thinks it should take £50 million* there!

Early in 1979 Canada discovered a celluloid treasure trove of some 500 reels of very rare films, made between 1903 and 1929, buried in the permafrost at Dawson City. Originally sent there to be shown to early 20th-century movie fans, the films were subsequently dumped in a tank outside the movie house when it closed down. This tank became buried and forgotten until recent building operations brought it to light. The films have now been taken to Ottawa for preservation and copying. They include the only surviving print of the Samuel Goldwyn silent *Polly of the Circus* (a 1917 feature starring Mae Murray) and a 1915 movie with Lionel Barrymore in the cast. As well as the features there are, it seems, quite a lot of valuable

World War I newsreels.

We all know about the harm that TV has done to the movies but there's the other side of the coin, too. For instance, during the past year or so the 1930s–1950s Bugs Bunny short cartoons have been a regular and highly popular feature of TV programmes. Now the studio that made them, Warner Bros, have invited BB's creator Chuck Jones to collect a number of these six-minute cartoons, add some twenty minutes of new, connecting footage, and then present the results as a ninety-five minute cartoon package called *The Great Bugs Bunny Roadrunner Chase.* If successful, Warners hope to do the same with some of their other old cartoons. Moreover, they have asked Jones (who made more than 300 cartoons shorts for Warners) to work on some new Daffy Duck, Porky Pig and Bugs Bunny cartoons. With reference to these, Chuck Jones has recalled that he used to make one of these short cartoons for about £15,000 but today each six-minute movie will cost something between £45,000 and £50,000!

In late March 1979 came news from Australia that the first 3-D television was to be launched there before the end of the year. Developed by two young Australians, this electronic stereoscopic system was also to be used, it was promised, on the production of a new £6 million film about Elvis Presley.

The new system does not need two lenses or two projectors but it *does* require special glasses to obtain the

3-D effect either for TV or film. It is, so far as I understand, a 'digital optics' system originally developed by BV of Amsterdam and the Ancomi Company of New York Another interesting project was that of Jacques (*Les Parapluies de Cherbourg*) Demy, who with Japanese Mataichiro Yamamoto planned to make a feature film based on the Japanese strip cartoon about the court of Louis XIV, *Lady Oscar.*

I wouldn't want anyone to imagine that in the foregoing pages I have completely covered every cinematic event of the year, significant or otherwise, even though I have scoured the news sources pretty thoroughly day by day and otherwise tried to keep pace with events. However, I trust and believe that this collection of news, opinion, facts, figures and comments does offer a reasonably comprehensive picture of the year in and around the cinema. It has certainly been a year in which my own moviegoing has yielded just about the average number of hours of delight, boredom, irritation, disgust, joy and despair which the cinema gives me every year; a year in which the occasional bright treasure has more than made up for the dullness and despair in between. And it is this kind of pattern which, even after the most diabolical movie, sends me back into the cinema a few hours later with hope and enthusiasm— something of which I earnestly trust I manage to convey in these pages year by year.

*The £50-million mark was in fact passed in March 1979!

Releases of the Year in Pictures

The films illustrated in this section are those from England, America, Canada and Australia (those from mainland Europe and other countries will be found in the following section, 'The Continental Film') which have had a general (or circuit) or floating release at any time between the beginning of July 1978 and the end of June 1979. You will find more detailed information about the films illustrated in 'The Year's Releases in Detail' in between pages 132 and 161.

Whatever difficulties there may have been during the production of the multi-million pound Ilya Salkind movie *Superman – The Movie* (for Warner release), none of them showed on the finished product, which emerged as a very smooth piece of cinema entertainment. A nicely tongue-in-cheek comedy about the famous comic-strip character from another planet who spends half his time as a shy and bumbling young reporter and the other half flying around doing marvellous and miraculous good deeds, it was a nice blend of spectacle, romance and humour. The disintegration of Superman's home planet providing the opening spectacle (i) and Christopher Reeve (shown doing one of his good deeds, preventing a train disaster—ii) making superhero a charming sort of chap, more than a match for supervillain Gene Hackman (at desk—iii).

With *Jaws* having made such a fortune-making impact at the box-office, it was hardly surprising that producers Richard D. Zanuck and David Brown returned this year with the offer of a second helping in their (CIC) film *Jaws 2*. Roy Scheider (exhausted with strain and stress, with wife, Lorraine Gary) repeated his role of the local police chief who—initially accused of needless panic when he suggests that another giant, man-eating shark has arrived on the scene at their little seaside town of Amity—finally has to face it alone in a duel to the death.

In contrast to CIC's big fish killer-thriller *Jaws 2*, United Artists came up with a more modestly made small fish killer-thriller in their *Piranha*, about a shoal of these voracious South American fish—bred as a 'secret weapon' in the United States!—who escape and start to chew their way through a summer swimming gala before Bradford Dillman bravely puts a stop to their horrid little game! With him after a finny encounter, and doing her best to bring back a smile to his flesh-torn face, is pretty little Heather Menzies as the girl who pulls the plug out and sends death down the river.

The remarkable scene in which the scientists await the landing of the spaceship from another world in Columbia's *Close Encounters of the Third Kind*, the big science-fiction spectacular which although fairly widely shown earlier did not get a general release until the summer of 1978 (which explains why it was featured in last year's annual as one of the releases of that year).

The Releases of the Year in Pictures

Soldiers-of-fortune Richard Harris, Jack Watson, Richard Burton and Roger Moore realise that they've been double-crossed by the financier-backer of their well-planned mercenary mission to release from jail, and bring out of Africa, one of the continent's more able Presidents, and now stand very little chance of getting him or themselves out alive. It all happens in a big, bloody and spectacular way in the Rank release of the Euan Lloyd film *The Wild Geese*.

Just about the most balanced and interesting of the flood of Vietnam war films to date, UA's *Go Tell the Spartans* was set in the earlier days of that struggle, when the American military presence in the country consisted of 'military advisers'. One of these, played by Burt Lancaster (with great sincerity), is a Major Barker, whose tiny force is faced with impossible odds when the enemy attack but bravely goes down fighting.

Not by a long way the biggest or the most spectacular but certainly one of the best of the year's films was Australia's *Newsfront* (a Mainline release). A perfect example of the outstandingly high standard of that country's current film production, it combined fine direction, remarkable performances and great technical skill—blending old newsreels with historical reconstruction, fact with fiction, and colour with black and white film so brilliantly that it was never obvious where one merged into the other—in the story of an ace newsreel cameraman and his coverage of most of the historically important events between 1948 and the present.

If not quite equally successful, another fine Australian film, *The Last Wave* (UA), came from Peter Weir (whose previous two films *The Cars That Ate Paris* and *Picnic at Hanging Rock* were both outstandingly original). This was about a young lawyer (Richard Chamberlain) who, defending some aborigines at their trial for murder, becomes increasingly and disturbingly involved with them and their 'magic'. Warning the lawyer about his danger is Gulpilil.

If essentially American, Fox's *An Unmarried Woman* was a fascinating and generally pretty convincing examination of the situation of any woman who, after years of happy marriage have led her to think herself secure, is suddenly told by her husband that he loves another woman and wants a divorce. Jill Clayburgh won the Best Actress award at the 1978 Cannes Film Festival for her performance as the woman who has to make a new life for herself and takes some time to face up to the situation— complicated in her case by the attitude of her daughter (Lisa Lucas) to her artist lover (Alan Bates).

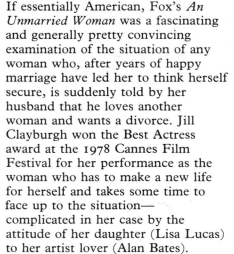

24

Though it was Vanessa Redgrave (left) who won the Oscar for the Best Supporting Actress performance as *Julia* in the Fox film of that title, it was Jane Fonda as her lifelong friend who emerged with at least equal acting honours, playing the part of authoress Lillian Hellman, with Jason Robards (*below*) as Dashiell Hammett, her author lover and literary helpmate.

The Releases of the Year in Pictures

Another of the year's best screen performances came from Glenda Jackson as the poetess *Stevie* in the Enterprise release of that title, which was based on Hugh Whitemore's completely straightforward adaptation of his own stage play—in which Miss Jackson had previously scored a big success. The film itself was quite an achievement in that it made the completely uneventful life of this surburban writer—who never ventured abroad or married but was devoted to her old aunt and enjoyed housework!—wholly absorbing. Trevor Howard played the patient friend.

Another outstandingly-acted movie was Fox's *The Turning Point*, an old-style 'woman's picture' about the conflict between marriage and career, with Shirley MacLaine (left) as the dancer who gives up a chance of ballet stardom for the sake of marriage and motherhood and Anne Bancroft as the friend who literally steps into her shoes and attains everything but satisfaction. A film of consistent good taste, with superb ballet sequences, it contained one of the best feminine confrontations, verbal and physical, in any film for a long time.

Laurence Olivier, as the motor-manufacturer tycoon, chats up the new French maid (Carol Williard) in UA's *The Betsy*, a high, wide, handsome—and certainly superficial—story of a dynasty into which are crammed lots of sex, family feuds, murder and struggling for power very much in the usual Harold Robbins manner (he wrote the book on which the film was based).

Dustin Hoffman, centre, is lined up by the cops for an identity test in Warner's *Straight Time*. The story, based on fact, centred on an unpleasant character who graduates from small-time crime to bank stick-ups and the robbery at a jewellery shop, which leads through his greed to callous murder. This was a well-made examination of a far too familiar anti-social character.

Love in a cold climate—teacher Bud Cort and girl-friend Samatha Eggar in a refreshingly simple and credible Canadian film *Why Shoot the Teacher?* from Contemporary Films. Filmed in winter in remotest Saskatchewan, it told of a young teacher's experiences at his first school in a tiny community in 1935 during the Depression.

Nothing to do with trains, Columbia's *Midnight Express* was a brutal film based on the true story of a young American caught smuggling drugs in Turkey and sent to a jail in which sadism, perversion and bestiality are the order of the day. *Below right*: the shocking scene where Billy (played by Brad Davis) is visited by his girl-friend (Irene Miracle).

Having rescued her from certain death in the snow, Keir Dullea escorts Susan Penhaligon back to his isolated Northumberland house in Enterprise Pictures's *Leopard in the Snow,* so beginning the romance between the ex-racing driver, now a hermit, and the girl he finds when he is exercising his pet leopard in the snow!

Thirty-three years after the release of *National Velvet,* the film which launched Elizabeth Taylor on her career, Bryan Forbes wrote, directed and produced for MGM/CIC release a sequel, *International Velvet,* in which Velvet Brown (now grown-up, and with a family—and played, beautifully, by Bryan's wife Nanette Newman) helps a young American girl (Tatum O'Neal) to achieve her ambition of attaining Olympic equestrian honours. Christopher Plummer (right) played Velvet's husband.

Flanked by his legal advisers, suspect union leader Johnny Kovac (played by Sylvester Stallone) testifies at a Senate Committee hearing on the subject of the rackets in which he has become involved. A long and slow-paced look at the American labour upheavals of the 1930s, *F.I.S.T* (UA) never quite measured up to its obviously serious historical pretensions.

Another film generally presumed to have had a basis in fact, CIC's *The Greek Tycoon* was the carefully-tailored story of a millionaire Greek shipowner (played by Anthony Quinn) and his romance with the widow of an American President. Jacqueline Bisset played the lady.

The serving officer's wife—and part-time hospital helper—has a happy meal with the disabled soldier patient she has invited to her home (Jane Fonda and Jon Voight) in UA's *Coming Home,* one of the many Vietnam War films which have been coming out of America since the struggle was long enough over to allow for more-or-less free critical comment. In this case, though, the story was basically a slight variation on the old eternal triangle theme, with the paraplegic veteran stealing the lady's love while hubby is away learning the horrors of conflict.

It took nine years for the early Francis Ford Coppola film *The Rain People* (Warners) to reach British cinemas, which was rather disturbing, in view of its promise of things to come from this writer–director, and the low quality of many other films which took a lot less time to make the journey. It's all about a pregnant young woman (Shirley Knight) who, feeling a failure as a wife and scared of becoming an equally hopeless mother, gets into the family car one morning and takes off, soon picking up the simple-minded ex-football player (James Caan) who teaches her the meaning of responsibility and brings her to tragedy when her initially welcomed seduction (*left*) by cop Robert Duvall goes sour.

Famous Agatha Christie sleuth Hercule Poirot (Peter Ustinov) with his aide for the occasion (David Niven) question a suspect (Jack Warden) about the murder of victim Lois Chiles in EMI's *Death on the Nile,* a very well produced and directed, scenically fascinating, and superbly acted whodunnit along familiar lines *Below*: one of the regular acid exchanges during the eventful voyage along the Nile between the bitchy Miss Bowers (Bette Davis) and her paid companion (Maggie Smith).

Private-eye Lou (Peter Falk) shuts his ears to the pleas of Betty de Boop (Eileen Brennan) and Marcel (James Coco) in Columbia's extremely amusing skit, *The Cheap Detective*, on the old Bogart-type investigators, made by the same team responsible for the previous, and similar, satire, *Murder by Death*. Neil Simon's witty screenplay included references to a number of old movies, like (*right*) the famous 'Play it again, Sam' scene from *Casablanca* (Louise Fletcher and, playing, Scatman Crothers).

More private-eye nostalgia in *The Big Sleep*, Michael Winner's remake (for ITC release) of the 1946 tough Raymond Chandler classic investigation piece. Now it is Robert Mitchum (then it was Bogart) who, as Philip Marlowe, is faced by disturbing confusion, threats and red herrings as he does his dogged best to solve what starts out as an apparent case of blackmail but is soon revealed to embrace far worse than that. *Right*: Marlowe hands back to Miss Sternwood (Sarah Miles) the revolver with which her sister has attempted to kill him! Now set in Britain instead of Los Angeles, a lot of the atmosphere if none of the wise-cracking has been lost in the re-make, an otherwise excellent piece of movie-making.

But easily the best film yet to catch the authentic atmosphere and style of the classic private-eye movies of the 1940s was Warner's *The Late Show*, an involved story of murder and detection which included a magnificent performance by Art Carney as the ageing but still active investigator Ira Wells. Equally brilliant was Lily Tomlin's Margo, whose cat's abduction is all part of the action.

The detective in EMI's *The Driver* is no private eye but a dedicated and obsessed officer in the local police force who is grimly determined to bring expert getaway-car-chauffeur Ryan O'Neal (*right*) with underworld messenger Ronee Blakely to justice. Bruce Dern (*above*) with Ryan's feminine ally Isabelle Adjani played the cop whose traps, however well planned, always fail. The duel between the two men is the basis of a compelling, if cold and oddly fleshless, film.

Detection of yet another kind, satirical, in Hemdale's *The Hound of the Baskervilles*, a singularly unsuccessful attempt to send up the famous Sherlock Holmes story in which such well-known comics as Terry-Thomas, Peter Cook, Dudley Moore and Kenneth Williams must all take their share of the blame.

Rifle v. crossbow. Lee Montague takes a shot at the killer on the roof but loses out and Katharine Ross throws herself in front of him in an effort to save him at the climax of Columbia's *The Legacy,* a highly unlikely and pretty wild, old-fashioned thriller set against a familiar background of a mysterious old dark house . . .

If as highly incredible, MGM/CIC's *Coma* was altogether a more superior thriller, a kind of whodunnit with considerable originality in the story and an unusual medical background. Geneviève Bujold played a lady medical specialist who uncovers a grisly plot by some doctors to kill off a few patients in order to sell human spare parts! And when she tracks down the head of this inhuman traffic he injects her to make her helpless and rushes her on to the operating table. . . .

Mia Farrow, as the guilt-ridden mother who blames herself for her daughter's choking to death, leaves her husband and rents a haunted house, where she starts a psychic investigation which leads to her death. And this CIC release, *Full Circle,* was a macabre little thriller.

Richard Burton (confessing to
psychiatrist Lee Remick) as the man
with the malevolent mind who, in
ITC's *The Medusa Touch*, found
as a boy he could successfully
wish anyone to death who crossed
him. Having polished off his
schoolmaster, parents and wife, he
goes on to fail an American
moonshot, destroy a cathedral and
otherwise become a major disaster
area. And even when his life support
has been torn away by enraged cop
Lino Ventura and he is pronounced
well and truly deceased, his mind
carries on with its increasingly evil
plans. A glossy, expensive and
effective thriller.

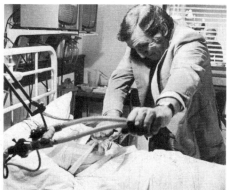

One of the nicest things about Warner's Irwin Allen thriller *The Swarm* was the inclusion among the players of some great old-timers like Ben Johnson, Olivia de Havilland, Fred MacMurray and, in the wheelchair scene, Richard Widmark and Henry Fonda, who is being pushed along by Michael Caine. And it was rather a shame that so much talent was involved in this quite minor piece about a swarm of killer bees bringing havoc and death to several small towns as they advance on Houston!

Made in America in 1974, and apparently not very successful there, Britain didn't see Bryan Forbes's *The Stepford Wives* until mid-1978, when it was brought over by Contemporary Films to be revealed as a nicely underplayed thriller about a small New York suburb in which the men, thanks to the outrageous technical expertise of a former Disney studios employee, are able to replace their wives with 'perfect' mechanical 'doubles' who answer to their every male whim without complaint. Katharine Ross (right) played the wife who suspects the worse, and Paula Prentiss (a delightful comedy performance) is one that didn't get away.

One way to break out of jail, a scene from Brent Walker's 1975 minor American thriller *The Terror of Dr Chaney*, which was all about a crazy surgeon who, when his daughter loses her sight, captures and keeps in his basement the unfortunate characters whose eyes he decides will best replace hers!

Another thriller not to be taken too seriously—even if intended to be—was Enterprise Pictures's *The Comeback*, a grisly little story about a former top pop star who comes back to Britain to fight his way up the charts but is soon fighting efforts to send him insane and murder both his former wife and present girl-friend. Lots of blood, a few horrid corpses and a reasonable performance as the persecuted singer by singer Jack Jones.

There was a lot of ingenuity, if not quite so much credibility, in the Enterprise thriller *The Silent Partner*, in which bank clerk Elliott Gould, having seen Father Christmas's aborted attempt to hold him up for the contents of his till, works out a plan to make the repeat attempt (which he suspects will take place) benefit him and nobody else. One of the best crime comedy-thrillers of the year, the movie also starred lovely Celine Lomez (*right*).

Another American film which took quite a while to reach Britain was *Three the Hard Way* (EMI), a minor 1974 thriller about a crazy scientist who invents a serum to kill anyone with a black skin and with it plans to purify the planet! But in spite of his storm-trooper-like followers he doesn't get away with *that*!

Piper Laurie as *Ruby* looks out of the window in a scene from this minor Brent Walker thriller about a lady who loves a ghost but can't convince the fellow of the depth of her feelings!

Sequels, follow-ups and the like are generally disasters and very seldom measure up to the original. But thanks largely to Peter Sellers's performances and the wit of Blake Edwards's writing and direction, the 'Pink Panther' movies are proving an exception. Certainly the latest in line, UA's *The Revenge of the Pink Panther* was quite as hilarious as any of its predecessors and one of the funniest comedy films of the year. Flanking the heavily disguised Inspector Clouseau, Burt Kwouk and Dyan Cannon *Right*: another of the inspector's disguises—and you should be able to guess who he's supposed to be in this case!

Henry Winkler, having failed to convince the world that he's the great actor he thinks he is, finds a way of keeping the wolf from the door of his family and satisfying his extrovert needs by becoming something different in the field of all-in wrestling! And though it was a comedy and generally mildly amusing, CIC's *The One and Only* could be seen as a rather pathetic story of a complete egotist.

Undoubtedly original, Miracle's Canadian release *Outrageous* starred the internationally renowned female impersonator Craig Russell and was a considerable showcase for his art, with his wicked and witty take-offs of stars like Joan Crawford, Bette Davis, Barbra Streisand and Judy Garland.

Odd-job-man David Jason makes an attempt to carry out what Graham Chapman has hired him to do—kill him! An uneven British comedy, *The Odd Job* (Columbia) veered a little unsteadily between farce, black comedy and sheer craziness as it followed Jason's ridiculous efforts to murder the man who hasn't the courage to kill himself—efforts which, to Chapman's despair, continue long after he has had a change of heart.

CIC's *Heaven Can Wait* was a straightforward reworking of the successful Harry Segall play which was the basis for the 1941 film-comedy winner *Here Comes Mr Jordan*. And though there have been changes made, such as the hero, played this time around by Warren Beatty (who was also involved with the direction, production and screenplay), being a football star—rather than a boxer as in the original—it was still great fun because through an error 'up there' he's forced into taking up residence for a while in a body not at all to his taste! And (*right*) it is only his love for Julie Christie which persuades him to accept the situation.

Another of the top comedies of the year was CIC's *House Calls,* in which Walter Matthau and Glenda Jackson both gave matching performances as the doctor who somewhat reluctantly finds himself preferring the more mature lady to the young chicks he had promised himself when his wife's death gives him the opportunity to sow the wild oats that previously have remained in their packet.

In EMI's *Convoy* Sam Peckinpah switched from men to machines for his scenes of destruction, but hardly to anyone's advantage. The main motivation was the long-standing—indeed, long running—personal feud between Arizona County cop chief Ernest Borgnine and trucker leader 'Rubber Duck' Kris Kristofferson, a battle of brains and brawn which leads to the sort of pile-ups illustrated.

A more romantic than real—one
suspects—look at the Hollywood
stuntman was given in Warner's
Hooper, with Burt Reynolds as a
high-spirited daredevil always out to
create some new record while
sometimes uncomfortably aware of
the youngsters anxious to snatch his
crown. Entertaining hokum, well
played by Reynolds and Sally Field,
as his girl-friend. *Below right*: one of
the many stunts which added the
thrills to the fun.

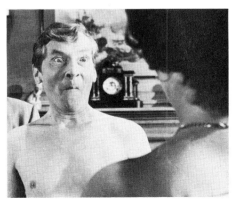

Regretfully, comedy hasn't been the
strong point of British film
production recently and of those that
have been made one can hardly
credit any of them as being
memorable movies. A case in point
was the 30th 'Carry On' film, *Carry
On Emmannuelle* (Hemdale), which
featured many of the old familiar
faces in the cast including Kenneth
Williams (*left*) as well as glamorous
newcomer Suzanne Danielle, but
lacked a lot of the old comic
inspiration.

Essential's *Between the Lines* was an interesting youth-orientated American film about an underground newspaper which is taken over by a press tycoon and the effect this has on the lives of various members of the staff. The director was Joan Micklin Silver whose previous, and very different, movie *Hester Street* was so memorable.

On the edge of violence, one of the incidents in The Other Cinema's feature documentary, *Harlan County USA*, an account of the Kentucky coal miners' strike of 1972–3 and its place in the context of the American labour scene.

Steve McQueen, in hirsute disguise, in his own production based on the Arthur Miller adaptation of the Henrik Ibsen play *An Enemy of the People* which, in its arguments about political expediency and democracy, is as pertinent today as the year it was written. An Enterprise release, it also included a very fine performance by Charles Durning (centre).

Beauty Trish van Devere and beast George C. Scott in a very odd little movie based on the famous tale of *Beauty and the Beast* (Hemdale). But it was at least a nicely gentle contrast to Walerian Borowczyk's flashily erotic version (*The Beast*) of the same story also shown during the year.

After the flood of pornographic films of just a year or so ago the current comparative scarcity of such films may or may not be a reflection of public taste. One of few genuinely erotic movies of the period was New Realm's *Bilitis*—well known still-photographer David Hamilton's first movie—and a quite charming, leisurely-paced example of the genre, set in the south of France and starring a newcomer of real star potential in Patti d'Arbanville.

Hero Jeff Cooper finds the girl (Erica Creer) who has given him a night of love crucified in the morning—one of the many strange scenes in the Rank release of *The Silent Flute*, a film which mixed poetic images with kung-fu-type fights (*left*, Cooper has an unarmed combat with a very able blind man) and embroidered both with some pretty high-flown dialogue.

Cute little cabin-boy Ashley Knight explains to *Onedin Line* captain Peter Gilmore and inventor Doug McClure what villainous crew-members Hal Galili and John Ratzenberger are up to in EMI's delightful piece of Hollywood hokum, *Warlords of Atlantis*, in which the spectacles included the horrid sea beast (*below right*).

Along the same lines, Warner's *The Amazing Captain Nemo* was about two US Navy divers who come across the *Nautilus* trapped under the sea and—inside it, in suspended animation—Captain Nemo, who then invites them to accompany him on a new Jules Verne-type under-sea journey to find the lost continent of Atlantis. At the controls: Lynda Day George and Jose Ferrer (Captain Nemo).

The hectic dance contest in Warner's *Thank God It's Friday* which—as one of the first of the so-named 'disco' musicals happened also to be one of the best—made its visual and aural assault with a good deal of humour and not a little youthful charm.

UA's *The Last Waltz* was in fact Martin Scorsese's two-hour record of the final concert, before break-up (after twenty years together), of The Band, led by Robbie Robertson (2nd from left); others, Rick Danko (left) and Garth Hudson with guest star performers Bob Dylan. Lots of rock music, lots of guest stars, and the delightful, contrasting theme tune.

Olivia Newton-John and John Travolta were the stars of CIC's big modern musical *Grease*, which, based on the successful Broadway show, hammered over a series of very loud chart-climbing numbers of great appeal to the younger generation, even if the acting honours were 'lifted' rather easily by Sid Caesar and Eve Arden (*below*).

Distressed Nancy Allen tries to explain her woes to a kindly security officer in CIC's *I Wanna Hold Your Hand*, which, set in New Jersey in 1964 at the height of The Beatles' success, was all about the struggle of some of their fans to gate-crash an Ed Sullivan show on which the quartet were due to appear.

Tim McIntire played American disc-jockey Alan Freed in CIC's *American Hot Wax,* the story of this DJ's championing of the then (1959) new rock-and-roll music which led to his suspension, and battles between the cops and the kids.

Sara Dylan in *Renaldo and Clara* (Artificial Eye release), Bob Dylan's production (he wrote the script and directed) of his own story.

The Disney studios continued with their successful 'family fare' output including a satire on the space cycle of movies, *The Cat from Outer Space.* Called Jake (*below*), the talking feline arrives in a space capsule with a power source which puzzles (*l to r*) Hans Conried, Ken Barry and Harry Morgan. And it was all rather jolly.

Very Disneyesque in atmosphere was the Raffill–Warner film *Shipwreck*, about an adventurous dad (Robert Logan) who sets off with his two daughters, and a young girl (plus a little black stowaway) to sail around the world but is shipwrecked on a remote island in Alaska, where they are faced with a battle for survival. And it was all done with a charming simplicity.

Even the Disney studios have never previously so perfectly combined cartoon with live action as they achieved in their delightful *Pete's Dragon*, the story of a little boy with an endearing and unusual pet! Sean Marshall played the little lad, Charlie Callas provided the dragon's voice and the arch-villains were 'magician' Jim Dale and the lad's self-appointed guardian, Shelley Winters. On extreme left (*below*) you'll see a bowler-hatted Red Buttons.

Some of the creator/artists who worked on Martin Rosen's CIC-released animated feature *Watership Down* once did the same kind of thing for Disney studios and this Disney-type charm was at times reflected in this story of some rabbits' adventures as they forsake their old burrow when it is about to be bulldozed for the foundations of a new housing estate and make their eventful journey in search of a more suitable new home.

Kathleen Lloyd helps distraught Frederic Forrest pull the trigger to kill the murderous mutant baby in Warner's follow-up—*It Lives Again*—to their previous thriller about a child which crawls out of its cot to go off on a murder rampage (*It's Alive*).

Coming some sixteen years after Carl Foreman's big success with *The Guns of Navarone*, Colombia's 1978 release of *Force Ten from Navarone* was something of a sequel in that it used the same characters—now played by different players—and had a story along vaguely the same lines: a desperate mission into enemy territory in World War II. This time it was to kill an enemy agent infiltrated into the Yugoslav partisans and to blow up an all-important bridge. The mission was led by Robert Shaw (one of his last screen performances), shown here snapping into action, aided by quiet explosives-expert Edward Fox (extreme left), during their break-out from their block-house prison. And it was all simple, spectacular and jolly good thriller stuff. *Above right*: Barbara Bach as the very active lady involved, taking a bath before getting down to work!

More bathing and more Nazis in the Tedderwick release *Just a Gigolo*, the bather being star David Bowie, the audience Curt Jurgens. A very odd film; the good parts of which never quite jelled into a good whole, though it never failed to be fascinating as it told the story of a young German (Bowie) who, too late to become the wartime officer hero he dreamed of, drifts along in the unhappy Germany of the 1920s and 30s, eventually becoming the paid partner of the title. Some of the good things in the movie included some black humour, fine photography, magic from Marlene Dietrich and good old-time Hollywood glamour from Kim Novak (*right* with Bowie).

Confrontation between the dedicated Nazi medical scientist (Gregory Peck, left) and the equally dedicated Jewish Nazi-hunter (Laurence Olivier, right) in ITC's *The Boys from Brazil*. Highly incredible, but very well made, and quite outstandingly acted by a truly all-star cast, the movie was about the scientist's plan to revive the old swastika-draped dream of German world domination with the help of dozens of identical, authentic little Hitlers—the boy in the foreground, Jeremy Black, being one of them.

This year the Australian film again kept up its remarkably high and consistent standard with, among other productions, Fox's *The Chant of Jimmie Blacksmith*, written and directed by Fred Schepisi. Based on a shocking multi-murder case at the turn of the century, when an aboriginal boy brought up by a white clergyman suddenly and violently rebelled against his treatment by his white bosses and killed a whole farming family before going on the run, totting up seven killings in seven months before being caught, condemned and hanged. And the film was both an accusation and a warning. A remarkably good performance by Tommy Lewis as Jimmie (and a very good one, too, by Ray Barrett as the drunken, sadistic cop for whom he works for a while).

The new and exciting climax to the Rank release of the third film version of John Buchan's famous spy thriller *The Thirty-nine Steps*, with Robert Powell now the young man who becomes, not very willingly, involved in some nasty international espionage and ends up at the Palace of Westminster clinging to the always moving hand of the clock, painfully aware that the killers are waiting for him if he tries to climb back into the clock-tower to safety! *Left*: John Mills as the British MI5 agent who persuades Powell to help him.

The elegant gentleman talking out of the side of his mouth to equally elegant Donald Sutherland is Sean Connery, who played a Raffles-type thief in UA's *The First Great Train Robbery*, in which the plan was to lift some £25,000 (quite a fortune in those days!) in gold bullion from a train during its journey from London to Dover. And it was noteworthy for its very impressive reconstruction of the England of the period. *Below right*: Connery with the girl who helps the gang, lovely Lesley-Anne Down, who contributed a very impressive and amusing performance to the proceedings.

The Star line-up in CIC's *Sergeant Pepper's Lonely Hearts Club Band*: The Bee Gees, Peter Frampton (second from left) and veteran comic George Burns (centre). With a background of Beatle hits, it was a fantasy about the group's rise to fame and fortune in New York; and final return to their threatened home-town (threatened by villainous real-estate representative Frankie Howerd) magically to put everyone and everything happily right.

56

The (terrified) *Eyes of Laura Mars* (Faye Dunaway) expecting to see the killer chasing her in the Columbia release of that title, a somewhat contrived whodunnit about a famous fashion photographer who starts to get horrible visions of the murders which actually occur later, falls in love with the cop put in charge of the case, and then has a shock when the killer's identity is revealed.

Business tycoon William Holden realises that his over ambitious assistant, Robert Foxworth, would like to take over his chair in Fox's thriller *Damien Omen 11*, a follow-up to the original *Omen* film and continuing the story of the little devil who after killing his dad (Gregory Peck) at the end of the first *Omen* doesn't do any good to uncle Holden, who has adopted him. And it was interesting to see veteran Sylvia Sidney (*above*) in the cast. The boy, her nephew, and the tycoon's real son, shown with her, was played by Lucas Donat.

Claude Chabrol's first all-American film was hardly a happy excursion for him for although this Rank release, *Blood Relatives,* started out with all the usual Chabrol polish and perfection it all too quickly drifted down, losing nearly all its credibility as it went. Donald Sutherland played the gloomy cop trying to find out who killed the young victim, here questioning the girl most closely involved in the attack (Aude Landry).

Goldie Hawn is so absorbed in the action on the screen that she's totally unaware of the murder being committed in the next seat in CIC's amusing comedy–thriller *Foul Play*, in which she takes the role of a girl who becomes entirely innocently involved in the plans of a fanatical religious sect to murder the Pope, and whose name is added to the list of people who must be murdered along the way. *Far right*: the comic confrontation between kung-fu fighters Burgess Meredith and Rachel Roberts.

Kirk Douglas comes to the aid of a distraught Amy Irving in' Fox's *The Fury*, a somewhat unlikely tale about a young man with strange powers (Mr Douglas's son) who is abducted by a very, *very* hush-hush US Government Agency who plan to experiment with him with a view to using him as a sort of secret weapon!

Pretty silly, too, if you started to analyse it closely, Fox's *Damnation Alley* won admiration for the spectacular way in which it whipped across the story of a few survivors of an atomic holocaust who set off in their strange 'land machine' to see if anyone else has managed to live through the explosions and the radiation that followed. In the driving seat (General) George Peppard; sharing the action, happy assistant Jan-Michael Vincent.

Getting ready for the rocket-launch at Mission Control, Houston, in ITC's *Capricorn One*, an increasingly tense thriller about a gigantic space spoof initially suspected by newsman Elliott Gould (with female newshound Karen Black, *far right*). And the climax comes when the surviving astronaut persuades crop-dusting pilot Telly Savalas to help him escape his murder-minded pursuers, leading to a brilliantly staged duel between the old biplane and the killers' helicopter.

Jose Ferrer at the controls of the underwater marvel *Nautilus* (created by Jules Verne), along with assistant Lynda Day George. In Warner's *The Amazing Captain Nemo,* the Captain, after having been in suspended animation for a century, returns to some intense activity by preventing villain Burgess Meredith (*right*) from blowing up Washington DC, from his atomic-armed submarine after which the Captain goes on to stop a sea-bed radiation leak and discover Atlantis! Simple, comic-strip stuff with lots of laughs and surprisingly serious and excellent performances by both Ferrer and Meredith.

Donald Pleasence hopes that the tapes will lead him to the truth about the suspect Narriman Company in *Power Play,* a Rank release about a police state which in getting rid of one dictatorship seems likely to be exchanging it for another. The cast included Peter O'Toole and David Hemmings.

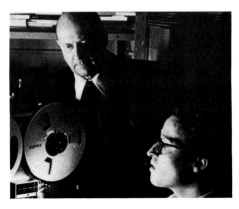

Sombre, threatening shadows, fear and a zombie on the stairs in the Brent Walker horror thriller *Revenge of the Dead*.

One of the oddest film titles of the year was that hung on the Warner comedy *Every Which Way But Loose*, in which Clint Eastwood played a truck driver who enjoys the occasional brawl and has an orang-utan, won in a wager, as a mate (*left*).

The girls strip for action, not knowing that a male student is watching them from the window in CIC's *National Lampoon's Animal House* (another of the year's odder titles!) which turned out to be a wild, bitterly satirical and in some ways terrifying comedy about life in an American college where the students wilfully destroy property, get violently drunk, fornicate and assault the local citizens.

Still with the odd titles, how about *FM* for a candidate? In fact the letters represent the call sign for a small independent Los Angeles radio station where the managing disc jockey takes the staff out on strike when he is aked to put over some corny US Army recruiting ads.

Robert Altman's Fox film *A Wedding* was just that: an ironically observed and recorded top people's celebration of a marriage, which at the subsequent reception explodes when the bride's sister is revealed to be pregnant by the groom, the bride's mother decides to go off for an illicit weekend and there's a death upstairs which the drunken doctor—busy giving the groom's mother her fixes in the bathroom—tries to keep secret. Witty lines delivered with fine timing, a good pace and a general excellence which even the outrageous lurch to drama along the way couldn't quite cancel out. Included in a very long and excellent cast: Carol Burnett and Diana Merrill, and (*far right*) Lauren Hutton.

Robert Morley as gourmet publisher Vandervere gave GTO's *Too Many Chefs* its brightest and best moments. With him Madge Ryan, as the secretary whose determination to save him from his greedy self leads to some pretty drastic deeds. . . . The story was a whodunnit, concerning who is killing off the great chefs of Europe—among whom are Philippe Noiret and Jacqueline Bisset (*far left*).

Though it had a pretty preposterous plot, CIC's *Same Time Next Year* proved to be a delightfully entertaining comedy with grand performances by Ellen Burstyn and Alan Alda as the couple who, both happily married, meet in a hotel dining-room, end up in bed and vow to repeat the adventure every year from then on, which they do. And playwright Bernard Slade produced some hilarious situations and sparkling lines in his own adaptation of his stage-play to the screen. *Below*: two of the changes wrought in Miss Burstyn during the years.

Geraldine Chaplin as Anthony Perkins's first wife who comes out of the past to haunt his second marriage in Columbia's *Remember My Name*, produced by Robert Altman and directed by his protégé, Alan Rudolph, and with plenty of the Altman Trademarks about it.

Sylvester Stallone's third movie, CIC's *Paradise Alley* did little to enhance his reputation as writer–director with its loosely constructed and routine story of three brothers living in the 'Hell's Kitchen' district of New York in the late 1940s and the reactions between them when one becomes a gentle giant of a wrestler. The trio were played by Armand Assante, Stallone and Le Canalito.

Rudely awakened, Sarah Douglas faces another brutal attack from her sadistic husband, Julian Glover, in the British film about the social problem of wife-battering in the Rank, British, release *The Brute*.

John Galdes and the dog, Champion Ra of Attard, in Rodney Holland's visually delightful half-hour interest film, *The Detour* (GTO), made on location in Malta and based on the local legends about the (tenuous) connection between the island's hunting dogs and the ancient Egyptian god, Anubis.

Marilyn Jones and Randy Danson as the sisters who share a dreary and uncommunicative lover (Kevin Wade) in Mark Rappaport's *The Scenic Route* (Scala) which boasted the rather grand intention of saying something about 'the difference between what we say and what we feel, and what we say and what we mean'.

One of the more interesting off-beat productions of the period was Claudia Weill's *Girl Friends*, which started life as a 30-minute short but was gradually expanded to full feature length (87 minutes) during the three years it was in production. A lively effort to show women struggling to find a place of their own in a man's world; and something, too, of true feminine friendship. A nice leading performance by Melanie Mayron (right).

One of the few all-cartoon features released during the year was CIC's *Race For Your Life, Charlie Brown*, a further segment in the adventures of comic-strip hero Charlie and his dog, Snoopy.

A scene from Ron Peck and Paul Hallam's Cinegate release *Nighthawks*, a story about a rather unhappy homosexual schoolteacher, which gave a vivid impression of the shadowy world of male pick-ups.

Understandably more appreciated in America than in Britain in view of its subject, EMI's 1979 Oscar-winning (for Best Film) *The Deer Hunter* was an admirably sincere and intermittently impressive effort to show the impact that the Vietnam War had on so many American families and, more particularly, on the young men who went off, many with cheerful patriotism, to fight and came back maimed in body and mind. Also the film was something of a tribute to the loyalty and love hidden beneath the rough horse-play of many male friendships. Robert de Niro (playing the leading role) is shown trying to rescue a badly injured friend and comrade, John Savage. *Above left*: the marriage of the latter to Rutanya Alda, which took up the best part of the first of the film's three hours.

The tough Basque shepherd–guide Anthony Quinn deals effectively with one of the SS villains trying to stop him leading the professor, James Mason, and wife, Patricia Neal, across the mountains from Occupied France to safety in Hemdale's *The Passage*— a film notable for some very nasty scenes of Nazi brutality and an unrestrained performance by Malcolm McDowell (*below*) as the sadistic and unrelenting pursuer.

If *The Deer Hunter* was always— literally—deadly serious, Michael Winner's cheerfully confusing Bond- like thriller, ITC's *Firepower* certainly was not! The story of the efforts of (unofficial) US agent James Coburn and black aide O. J. Simpson to kidnap and take back to the States a 'wanted' millionaire–criminal living a life of luxury in a Caribbean hideout, where he is surrounded by a small army of thugs, the cast included Sophia Loren, whose husband's death at the hands of the crook's henchmen starts the whole thing off—though subsequently it was often pretty difficult to fathom which side of the net she is playing her game.

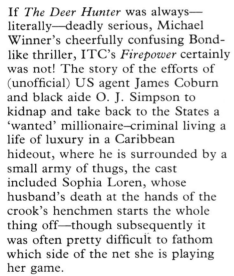

Death on the film set in the Heroux–Subotsky, Rank-released thriller *The Uncanny*, with nasty villain Peter Cushing about to let go the rope which will send the guillotine blade (the steel one he has substituted for the harmless rubber one provided by Props) crashing down on the neck of his unsuspecting wife Catherine Bégin—one way to achieve instant divorce!

65

Professional 'hit man' Max Von Sydow takes aim at General Patton (George Kennedy) in MGM–CIC's *Brass Target*, a somewhat fanciful thriller based on the hypothesis that instead of his being killed in a car crash, as formerly accepted, the General was in fact murdered by some of his own staff-officers when they feared he would uncover their successful plot to steal a pot—a very large pot—of Nazi gold while on its way by train to the bank. *Far right*: Investigating the case, John Cassavetes meets an old friend, and former mistress, Sophia Loren.

Fugitives Nick Nolte and Tuesday Weld watch and wait for the inevitable moment when their pursuers will find their mountain-top hideout in UA's oddly titled *Dog Soldiers,* which had nothing to do with dogs and only a little to do with soldiers in its story about a war correspondent who decides he'll take advantage of his position to make a fortune out of dope when he finishes his job in Vietnam. It was a hard, rough and brutal, but well-made, drama.

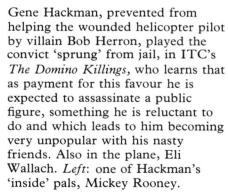

Gene Hackman, prevented from helping the wounded helicopter pilot by villain Bob Herron, played the convict 'sprung' from jail, in ITC's *The Domino Killings*, who learns that as payment for this favour he is expected to assassinate a public figure, something he is reluctant to do and which leads to him becoming very unpopular with his nasty friends. Also in the plane, Eli Wallach. *Left*: one of Hackman's 'inside' pals, Mickey Rooney.

While extreme pornographic violence has been considerably less obvious on the screen this period, there have been some pretty nasty and needlessly sadistic films around. Not exactly a pretty sight at times was Wes Craven's New Realm release *The Hills Have Eyes,* about a family stranded in the (American) desert who become the victims of some cannibalistic freaks whose idea of a culinary treat is the besieged family's baby! All rather sad, too, in that director–writer Craven showed some very real talent when not concerned with overdoing the brutality.

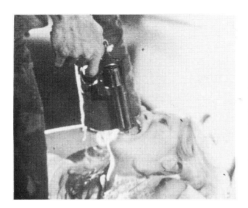

Easily one of the most effective thrillers of the year was that of the brilliant young director John Carpenter (whose credits include *Dark Star* and *Assault on Precinct 13*) whose Miracle release, *Halloween,* was a skin-pricking affair about an escaped homicidal maniac who returns to the scene of his former crime with the idea of adding to his personal death-list. And Carpenter's achievement here was to give an atmosphere of brooding menace to familiar objects and everyday scenes. Possibly, and sadly, the most critically under-rated thriller of the year.

Bigger is not necessarily better, as the screen has so often proved, and the Solo/Kaufman–UA remake of the classic little mid-fifties thriller *Invasion of the Body Snatchers* added weight to the lesson. The new version, though done well enough, hardly benefited from the change of locale (to San Francisco), extra length and bigger budget, even if the story of an invasion of pods from outer space, which develop into soulless replicas of the humans they engulf, was still pretty good sci-fi entertainment. Donald Sutherland, one of the first to realise what is happening, tries to escape with girlfriend Brooke Adams and spends most of the film trying to stay one step ahead of the pursuing pods!

The ventriloquist, Anthony Hopkins, with the devilish dummy who murders their manager, Burgess Meredith, in the Fox thriller *Magic*. *Below right*: Ed Lauter and Hopkins find another victim of the doll. Though not always convincing, the film did have both power and a certain subtlety.

Well, you'd have to sort through a lot of movies to find one with such an old-fashioned, unabashedly melodramatic and unconvincing story as that which provided the script for Columbia's *Ashanti*, in which Peter Ustinov played a dastardly slave trader who kidnaps white doctor Michael Caine's lovely black doctor wife, Beverly Johnson, and offers to sell her to a handsome Arab prince, Omar Sharif.

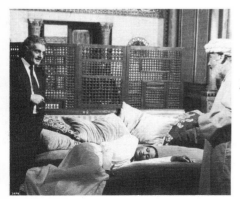

In similar garb, but a highly contrasting role, Peter Ustinov played the Caliph in the same company's (Columbia) jolly little Arabian Nights entertainment, *The Thief of Baghdad*. *Right*: Pavla Ustinov, Peter's own daughter, as the Princess being hushed into silence as he decides which of her many suitors she must marry, after she has turned down so many.

A possible pointer to cinematic
things to come, and a good example
of the curiously ambivalent
relationship between TV and the
cinema, CIC's sci-fi feature about
interplanetary wars *Battlestar
Galactica* was a two-hour compilation
of a number of episodes from the
highly successful American TV series
given the added dimension of
cinema-shaking Sensurround.
Captives of the 'Thing' are Richard
Hatch (right), Jane Seymour and
Tony Swartz.

One of the most original and
delightful family-fun films of the year
came from the shrewd directing hand
of Lionel Jeffries (*The Railway
Children,* etc) whose adaptation of
the Charles Kingsley classic story
The Water Babies (released in Britain
by Pethurst International) was a
highly original sandwiching of a
charming animation sequence (*far
right*)—made in Poland and with all
the charm, humour and melody of the
early Disney films—between two live-
action sequences in which sweep's
boy Tom (Tommy Pender) meets
Ellie (Samantha Gates) and her
mother (Joan Greenwood) and goes
down milord's chimney, and up in
the world! Inset, the line-up of
gamekeeper Paul Luty, villain James
Mason, milord David Tomlinson and
Mason's partner, Bernard Cribbins.

Those two children with strange powers of levitation, first seen in the sequel to *Witch Mountain movie,* returned to the screen in Disney's *Return from Witch Mountain.* This time Tony (*far right:* demonstrating one of his achievements) becomes the victim of some nasty scientific experimenters who plan to gain power by means of their mind-control machine. Rising, Ike Eisenmann as Tony; audience, Denver Pyle and Kim Richards. *Above right:* experimenters (l. to r.), Anthony James, Bette Davis and Christopher Lee; victim, Ike Eisenmann.

Patient (Kathleen Quinlan) and doctor (Bibi Andersson) discuss a problem in the Roger Corman–New World release *I Never Promised You a Rose Garden,* a most commendably restrained and therefore all the more moving picture of life within a women's mental institution, seen largely through the eyes of a young problem girl, who during three years as a patient is helped back to, hopefully, a normal adult life by the patience, understanding and sympathy of the doctor; beautiful performances by both these players.

Though in many ways original and with impact, Universal–CIC's *Blue Collar*—with its story about three car-assembly-plant-workers (Richard Pryor, Harvey Keitel and Yaphet Kotto) whose own small-time law-breaking leads to their discovery of big-time crime in their trade-union leadership—was somewhat unpleasantly noteworthy for the constant foul language and gutter expressions used by the characters involved, and raised the whole question of the inclusion of this needless kind of verbal unpleasantness in movies.

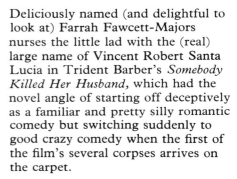

Deliciously named (and delightful to look at) Farrah Fawcett-Majors nurses the little lad with the (real) large name of Vincent Robert Santa Lucia in Trident Barber's *Somebody Killed Her Husband*, which had the novel angle of starting off deceptively as a familiar and pretty silly romantic comedy but switching suddenly to good crazy comedy when the first of the film's several corpses arrives on the carpet.

Tough cop Charles Bronson goes into action in Lew Grade/ITC's *Love and Bullets*, a run-of-the-mill cops-and-robbers piece in which he finally brings—*very*—rough justice to the crooks when they kill the girl with whom he has fallen in love and who is murdered because she knows, and has seen, too much for the gang's good.

Burt Reynolds is on record as saying that he has a large loyal audience—no matter what the critics say (of his work)—but he seemed to be trying to stretch that loyalty to something like breaking point with his UA release *The End*, described as a black comedy about death but mixing with the authentic darkly humorous thread some examples of bad taste, vulgarity and a modicum of wit as it told the story of a man (Reynolds) who discovers he has only a little while to live and who tries, half-heartedly, to cheat death by taking his own life. Compensations included the appearance of grand old-timers Myrna Loy and Pat O'Brien.

Some of the guests at *Don's Party*, a very rough and drunken get-together on the night of the 1969 Australian elections; a party in which drink reveals the sexual appetites, the marital unhappiness and the crude behaviour of everyone present. But, as with so many modern Australian films, it is all tremendously powerful and horribly convincing. An Australian Film Commission production released in Britain by Miracle.

Hugh Corcoran, Stella Stevens, Tony Curtis and Ann Sothern join hand and hope for manifestations in Avco Embassy's *The Manitou*, but they hardly expect the horrifying head which suddenly rears up in mid table to terrorise them in this macabre thriller about the reincarnation of a 400-year-dead Indian medicine man.

Gary Busey played the title role in *The Buddy Holly Story*, relating the life of the famous rock 'n' roll star, who died in 1959 at the peak of his success in an airplane crash.

The American street gang The Warriors make their hazardous journey homewards—ambushed and waylaid by other gangs along the way—to the comparative safety of their own Coney Island 'territory'. This is Paramount/CIC's release of the Lawrence Gordon production *The Warriors*, a sensation in America, where it caused such trouble when it was shown that the distributors offered to reimburse the cinemas for extra policing staff needed to keep the peace.

Yet another brilliant film to add to the Australian tally was the Bruce Beresford-directed Tedderwick release *The Getting of Wisdom*, a warm, funny and wholly convincing story of a girl from the outback who goes to school at Melbourne at the turn of the century where she comes to terms with the big-city environment and more sophisticated fellow-pupils and finally triumphs (with a musical scholarship) without ever losing her strong individuality.

The Continental Film Releases in Pictures

Crippled writer Jean-Pierre Cassell explains to bank clerk Jean-Louis Trintignant what he wants him to do in order to advance the latter's career by way of various female conquests, and so provide the various pleasure of the power he craves but cannot personally achieve, in Watchgrove Films' *The French Way*—an amusing if never quite successful effort.to blend satire and black comedy. *Far right*: one of the prettiest of the ladies involved, Jane Birkin.

There was the haunting theme melody running through Claude Lelouch's *Second Chance—Si C'Etait à Refaire*, which has become something of a trade-mark of this director. A story of a woman (Catherine Deneuve) who comes out of prison after fifteen years, spent there for assisting in her lover's unpremeditated murder of her rapist–boss, it related her efforts to face up to the problems of making a new life for herself and her young son (Jean-Jacques Briot) who at first is not aware of their relationship and later, to her initial dismay, becomes the lover of her best friend (Anouk Aimée, *above centre right*). A UA release.

Thanks to the sparkling script and brilliant playing of Annie Girardot— as Paris's first lady police inspector, trying to solve a triple murder while dallying with Sorbonne professor, and lover, Philippe Noiret— Entertainment Films' release of Philippe de Broca's *Dear Inspector* added up to not only one of the best French comedies of the year but the most entertaining from any source.

And taken in the right (or wrong?) spirit there was quite a lot of fun to be had from Walerian Borowczyk's seriously-intended New Realm film *The Beast*, yet another variation on the old Beauty and Beast legend and this one the excuse for one of the director's heavily erotic if highly decorative celluloid excursions.

The only real sufferers in the *circa* 1915 war between isolated and previously neighbourly French and German settlements in Africa: the unfortunate local natives, press-ganged into battle by both sides in UA's *Black and White in Colour*, a modest little French satire exposing to the full the follies, futility and farce of impersonal war. The film won the 1977 Oscar for the 'Best Foreign Film' of that year.

After a very successful, hilarious and cruel look at the British-seaside-resort hosts of a group of French youngsters in his previous film, *A Nous Les Petites Anglaises*, Michel Lang turned his attention to his own countrymen on holiday in Brittany in the Gala release *L'Hôtel de la Plage*. But, amusing as it was, it—perhaps understandably—lacked some of the bite of the previous film. The picnicking youngsters are Bruno du Louvat, Jean-Paul Muel, Phillipe Ruggier and Bernard Soufflet—the last complicating the group's holiday by developing a violent passion for their hotel owner's attractive wife (Martine Sarcey, *far right*).

78

Called 'Visconti's lost masterpiece' in that it has taken so many years to get a showing in Britain, MGM-Premier's *Ludwig* was a slow but beautifully ornate film about the last, mad, King of Bavaria (Helmut Berger, *far right*) who spent the country's money on a series of architectural follies.

Rainer Werner Fassbinder's major contribution to the year's German films (imported into Britain) was his elaborate and internationally-slanted *Despair* (Gala release), based on a novel by Vladimir Nabokov, with a Tom Stoppard screenplay and Dirk Bogarde heading the English-speaking cast as the Berlin chocolate-manufacturer who in the depths of existentialist despair murders a tramp in order to steal his name. A heavily Germanic movie of considerable interest in its attempt to combine black comedy with a psychological-thriller content.

Reflecting the renewed German, and indeed, international interest in Hitler and his regime, GTO Films' feature–documentary *Hitler—A Career* was a combination of newsreel and other—some private home-movie—clips which illustrated the story of the German dictator from obscure Austrian beginnings to his complete capture of the German people with his rousing oratory.

Scala's Fassbinder film *Germany in Autumn* was a collection of filmlets by other young German directors plus his own considerable, amusing, contribution, which added up to a political statement about Germany in the autumn of 1977, under the threat of terrorism and official reaction to that threat. The lady onlooker is Angela Winkler.

One of Ingmar Bergman's favourite actresses, Gunnel Lindblom, directed *Summer Paradise* (Contemporary Films), and Bergman in fact produced this 'message' film about the summer vacation of a lady doctor and her family which ends in suicide and disaster, and which offered a warning about the Swedish State's increasing tendency to take over the individual's responsibility and the consequent production of a cold and materialistic society. Cast included Agheta Ekmanner, Holger Löwenadler, Maria Blomqvist, Anna Borg and Göran Stangertz.

Sven Klang's Combo, the small dance band of the 1950s which gives this brilliant little Swedish film its title. On the extreme left, the wholly professional saxophonist whose advent and musical ambitions bring about the break-up of the former happy-go-lucky group. An Essential Films release.

With the one-time flow of movies about kung fu and allied martial arts now almost entirely ceased, just two or three rather indifferent examples trickled on to the British screen during the year, one of which was EMI's *Game of Death*. While making the film Bruce Lee died and, five years later, the film was modelled around the one fight scene which Lee had already completed.

From a brief examination of the annual output, it rather appears that the Japanese turn out more animated features than any other country in the world. One of the few examples to be shown in Britain, Enterprise Pictures' *Space Cruiser*, was an imaginative space epic set '200 years beyond 2001', showing plenty of imagination and good draughtmanship.

Considering the vast size of Japanese film production it is rather surprising that only one or two examples reach Britain in a normal year. Most of those that do arrive are of a high standard, however, such as this year's World Wide Film release, *The Boxer*, with its highly original and stylish treatment of the conventional story about the apparently beaten pugilist who makes a miraculous recovery and swings the last, winning, punch.

Pretty beastly fun at the depraved party in Gala's release of the German/Yugoslav film *Don't Cry For Me Little Mother*, with Elga Sorbas the victim. The film, with its story of the small-part actress (*left*) who uses her physical attraction to climb from the slums into the president's bed and thence on to the throne of a South American republic from where she is soon virtually running the country, was very close to certain famous historical facts.

A collector's piece and a remarkably successful example of hybridisation was the Russian-made, Japanese-directed and Siberian-set Curzon release *Derzu Uzala*. The story of a trio of expeditions into remotest eastern Siberia at the turn of the century led by a Russian military explorer and the local guide who saves his life and becomes his friend, the film was directed by Akira Kurosawa (of *Rashomon* fame), beautifully acted by Yuri Solomin and Maxim Minsuk, and a well-deserved winner of the 1975 'Oscar' for the Best Foreign Language Film of the year.

On the basis of Zanussi's *Camouflage* (Contemporary) it is valid to wonder if the Polish Film might regain the high place it held in European production some years back. For this literate, verbally developed film had the sharp satirical wit we once associated with that country's movies. The story of a largely argumentative—but finally physical—confrontation between two professors, one middle-aged and disillusioned, the other young and idealistic, the film contained a number of sly comments on political interference with education and intellectual honesty.

The Story of the Film Magazine

by Anthony Slide

Film magazines have come and gone with surprising regularity since the beginnings of the cinema. Many, such as *Variety, Sight and Sound, Photoplay* and *The Monthly Film Bulletin*, have survived to become institutions, known, although not always respected, throughout the world. More than a few have blossomed and faded as quickly as have cinema fads such as 3-D and Cinerama. There is no accurate count of the number of film periodicals published during the past eighty years; their number is certainly well over 1,000, and the library of the British Film Institute boasts holdings of more than 800 film magazines, from Algeria's *Filmafric* through *Bulgarian Film Review* and *Indian Film Culture* to Peru's *Hablemos de Cine* and New Zealand's *Screen Parade*.

There are basically five categories into which film magazines fall: the fan magazine; the 'highbrow' or would-be intellectual journal; the trade paper; the house organ; and the informational publication issued by the film organisations of individual countries. The last-mentioned are perhaps the least interesting group, and include *Bulgarian Films, Czechoslovak Film, Unifrance Film, Unijapan Film Quarterly* and *Soviet Film;* they are generally available at a nominal charge to provide distributors and others with information on current productions. Not unsurprisingly the country which provides the largest number, and the most popular, of films—the United States—has no need of such a publication.

The most famous, not to mention the most enduring of fan magazines, is *Photoplay*, which is now published in both American and British editions. Subtitled 'The National Movie Magazine', *Photoplay* began publication in 1911, and in the first years its content was almost exclusively lengthy stories based on the current film releases. By the mid 1910s it was selling for fifteen cents and featured articles such as 'Growing Up with the Movies' by Florence Lawrence in collaboration with Monte M. Katterjohn, 'Training Recruits with Motion Pictures', 'The Pro and Con of Police Censorship', and 'Hints on Photoplay Writing'. Today it retails for ninety-five cents, and the articles have titles such as 'Kris Kristofferson: The Sex Symbol Who Hides from Women', 'Sally Fields Tells Why I Don't Have To Marry Burt To Love Him', and 'Perry King: My Wife Was a Novice Nun'. Tempus fugit—or perhaps I should say how have the mighty fallen!

The two men most responsible for *Photoplay*'s quality in the early years were Julian Johnson and James R. Quirk. Johnson was the first important editor of the magazine, and it was he who introduced its column of critical reviews, under the title of 'The Department of Comment and Criticism of Current Photoplays', in the issue for November 1915. His reviews and those of his successors as the

JUDITH ALLEN

The cover of *Picturegoer*, issue dated 11 November 1933.

magazine's lead critics, Randolph Bartlett and Burns Mantle, later published under the standard heading of 'The Shadow Stage', went a long way towards establishing serious film criticism in the United States. From 1932 until the end of 1957 Julian Johnson was the head of the Story Department at 20th Century-Fox, and he died, at the age of seventy-nine, on 12 November 1965.

James R. Quirk, whose name first appears in *Photoplay* in its January 1915 issue as its Vice-President, was the colourful owner of the magazine. Long-time *Photoplay* writer and its

editor during much of the 1930s, Ruth Waterbury recalled for me, 'He was a very amazing man; he was a very colourful man. He was a kind man, and witty, and so sophisticated, which, heaven knows, his correspondent [Miss Waterbury] was not. But he was forever firing people. He did have an impulse to fire people. I can't tell you the number of days I would come into the office in the morning and everybody would have been let out, the telephone girls, the file clerks, everybody.' In 1920 Quirk introduced the *Photoplay* Gold Medal Awards, reintroduced in the 1950s by its then editor Adele Whitely Fletcher, and still presented, and televised, to this day. Silent star May Allison became Quirk's wife in 1926, the same year in which he gained complete control of the magazine. James Quirk died on 1 August 1932, at the age of forty-seven.

Ruth Waterbury believes it was World War II which altered *Photoplay*'s outlook and content, and which perhaps changed the film industry. For as the industry changed, as the star system disappeared, and, most importantly, as the cinema lost its audience, *Photoplay* had no choice but to change also. It was obvious that it had to embrace television, where most of the new stars originated, and it had to offer the fans light gossip and vague scandal if it was to continue publication.

Miss Waterbury was one of the pioneers among fan-magazine

writers, and she remained active in the field almost to the present. Other pioneering ladies include Gladys Hall, who died on 18 September 1977 at the age of eighty-six, and who published a syndicated column, 'Diary of a Professional Movie Fan', in the 1920s, and was co-author with another pioneer, Adele Whitely Fletcher, of the popular 'We Interview' series in *Motion Picture Magazine* in the early 1920s, and Adela Rogers St Johns. Born on 24 May, 1894, Adela Rogers St Johns wrote a series of intimate, personal portraits of major stars of the 1920s in *Photoplay*, calling herself the 'Mother Confessor of Hollywood'. She is still active today, and in recent years has published two books, *Some Are Born Great* (1974) and *Love, Laughter and Tears* (1978), dealing, in whole or part, with Hollywood. Adele Whitely Fletcher began writing for fan magazines in 1916, while on the staff of the publicity department of the Vitagraph Company; she ghosted Anita Stewart's articles, 'Talks to Girls', and contributed to *Photo-Play Journal*, a high-quality, glossy fan magazine which also published some of the first writings of film and literary scholar Edward Wagenknecht. She edited *Movie Weekly* and *Photoplay*, but her first editorship was of *Motion Picture Magazine*, which she took over with its issue of February 1920. It had previously been edited by the young and immensely talented writer, Frederick James Smith.

The cover of *Film Weekly*, issue dated 2 January 1932.

Motion Picture Magazine was founded in February 1911 by Eugene V. Brewster and J. Stuart Blackton as *Motion Picture Story Magazine;* its name was changed in March 1914. Like *Photoplay*, initially it published only lengthy stories based on current releases, and it has always amazed me how its writers could take a ten-minute short and from it produce a story which would take thirty minutes to read. Eugene V. Brewster, like his competitor James R. Quirk, was a colourful man, who also launched *Motion Picture Classic, Shadowland* and *Movie Weekly*. He died on 1 January, 1939, after unsuccessfully attempting to promote his third wife, Corliss Palmer, as a film star.

Competing with the American fan magazines on a very much lesser scale in England were *Pictures and the Picturegoer, Picture Show, Boys Cinema, Girls Cinema* and *Film Weekly*. The last-mentioned was the most intellectual of British fan magazines, including Paul Rotha among its contributors. It began publication in 1928, but the wartime paper shortage forced it to combine with *Picturegoer* in 1939, and after the war there was no chance of it ever being revived as a separate entity.

So far as I am concerned, the most famous name in the field of writing for British fan magazines is Edith Nepean, who published a column in *Picture Show* from the issue of 20 November, 1920 until the magazine's demise in 1960. When I edited and published *The Silent Picture*, I was delighted to revive the Edith Nepean column, with myself writing the column as a poor substitute for that grand lady. The best known and most respected of *Picturegoer*'s writers was probably Margaret Hinxman, who was with the magazine during its final days—like *Picture Show*, *Picturegoer* ceased publication in 1960, and somehow managed to be merged with a record magazine— and it is pleasing to note that Miss Hinxman dedicated her fine book on *The Films of Dirk Bogarde* to the memory of *Picturegoer*.

Before turning away from fan magazines, I would be remiss not to mention *ABC Film Review*, which was published monthly for twenty years between 1952 and 1972, and which to me was as important a part of going to an ABC cinema as the film itself. *ABC Film Review* was six (old) pence well spent, and I have fond memories of a questions-and-answers column, run, I believe, by Peter Noble; if you were lucky enough to have your question published, you received a free pass for one month at your local cinema. I was never that lucky but my teenage cinemagoing companion, Jeffrey Richards, was, much to my annoyance, with a question as to what had happened to RKO.

Sam Rubin's tabloid, *Classic Film Collector*, now in its thirteenth year, is the fan magazine for film collectors. It mixes articles on stars of the past, many of them fairly obscure, with news of films currently for sale to collectors, reprints of obituaries from the *New York Times*, press-releases from film institutions, and a column titled 'Dani's Donuts', which features Sam's granddaughter in a variety of film-collector-orientated adventures. *Classic Film Collector* is in the tradition of the British *Amateur Cine World*, which was published from the mid 1930s until the mid 1960s, and which one read not out of an interest in amateur cinematography but for Kevin Brownlow's column on film collecting.

Intellectual is perhaps too broad a heading under which to discuss

The cover of *Film Weekly*, issue dated 21 March 1931.

publications as diverse as *Sight and Sound* and *Films in Review* or *Sequence* and *Focus on Film,* and yet, diverse as their readership may be or may have been, each has the right to claim such a description. Some, such as *Films Illustrated,* border on being fan magazines and, in a way, have replaced the older fan magazines, in acknowledging that there is an audience which wants neither articles on obscure aspects of film history, semiology and the aesthetics of film nor on Burt Reynolds's sex life and the rise to fame of the latest television star.

Any commentary on intellectual film magazines must begin with *Sight and Sound* which, for sheer longevity alone, has to be regarded as the most famous serious film quarterly in the history of the cinema. However, its beginnings were not in the area of serious film criticism but rather as a journal devoted to audio-visual aids and the use of film in education. It was subtitled 'A review of modern aids to learning', and began publication in spring 1932 under the sponsorship of the British Institute of Adult Education. Interestingly, that first issue contains an article, by A. C. Cameron, on 'The Case for a National Film Institute', along with a column on 'Films You Ought To See' by C. A. Lejeune plus a piece by J. Russell Orr on 'The Cinema and The Empire'.

The British Film Institute adopted *Sight and Sound* with its winter 1934 issue. An editorial in the magazine commented, '*Sight and Sound* now becomes the official magazine of the latter [The British Film Institute] and takes up, with renewed vigour, the task of spreading information and affording a forum for discussion concerning the educational and cultural uses of the film and kindred scientific inventions.' C. A. Lejeune disappeared, and was replaced by Paul Rotha. It was not until the mid 1940s that the publication moved away from the audio-visual field and into serious film discussion, with articles by such film heavyweights as Herman Weinberg, Ivor Montagu, Seymour Stern, Georges Sadoul and Roger Manvell. It published articles

by John Betjeman and Peter Ustinov, and in its spring 1946 issue, Sergei Eisenstein commenced a series of exclusive articles on Chaplin.

Gavin Lambert's appointment to the magazine's editorship with the December 1949 issue heralded a new era for *Sight and Sound,* and I do not believe it is untrue to claim that the publication was at its best under his editorship, which lasted until spring 1956 issue. Penelope Houston took over the editorship that year and has continued as its editor to this day. One of the magazine's problems seems to be that it is uncertain as to exactly what role it should be playing in the world of film magazines. Articles on obscure aspects of film history such as pioneer Yorkshire film-makers and the 1913 white-slave film, *Traffic in Souls,* uneasily rub shoulders with dull articles on regional television in England and major pieces on current American film-makers. One very valid criticism is that *Sight and Sound* does not devote enough space to past or present British cinema. As a sponsored publication of the British Film Institute it should be providing historical pieces on the likes of Maurice Elvey or Graham Cutts and not worrying about the latest Italian director who will be out of vogue before the article on him reaches the news-stands.

Sight and Sound's sister publication, *The Monthly Film Bulletin,* with its detailed credits, synopses and commentaries on current films, is an invaluable research tool which the

ALL ABOUT THIS WEEK'S PICTURES

Picture Show

The cover of *Picture Show,* issue dated 24 December 1932.

American publication, *Filmfacts,* now published by the University of Southern California, has tried to emulate without any great success. However, *The Monthly Film Bulletin* was not always so valuable. Beginning publication in February 1934, its early issues were devoted almost exclusively to documentary films, and it was not until the late 1940s that it began publishing detailed credits. Today, along with *Film Dope,* which is more of an encyclopedic biographical dictionary of the cinema than a magazine, it stands as the single most important reference periodical in the film field.

Because of the involvement of Gavin Lambert and Penelope Houston, *Sequence* is closely allied to *Sight and Sound.* It began life in summer 1947 as a publication of the Oxford University Film Society, under the editorship of Lindsay Anderson, Penelope Houston and Peter Ericsson. By the third issue it had moved to London, and in an editorial thanked its critics and well-wishers 'who have made us feel that *Sequence* is supplying a want, and encouraged us to continue in the struggle for survival'. The struggle for survival lasted fourteen issues, and during that time *Sequence* published many first-rate, serious pieces, among which were 'The Films of Mark Donskoi' by Catherine de la Roche, 'Shooting Caesar' by David Bradley, 'The Films of Preston Sturges' by Peter Ericsson, 'The Films of Alfred Hitchcock' by Lindsay Anderson and '*They Were Expendable* and John Ford' by Lindsay Anderson.

Sequence was the natural descendent of *Close Up,* whose existence from July 1927 until December 1933 makes it the world's first serious film journal. *Close Up* was terribly intellectual and terribly superior. Its editors, Kenneth MacPherson and Bryher, were wealthy and produced the magazine out of a château in Switzerland. For all its pretension, *Close Up*'s articles are generally slight, but there are surprises, such as a piece on screenwriting for the American Flying A Company in the 1910s and an occasional put-down of a classic, such as Murnau's *Sunrise,* in

favour of a popular feature, such as Mary Pickford's *My Best Girl.* Britain's *Cinema Quarterly* (1932–5) and the United States' *Hollywood Quarterly* (which began publication in 1945 and is now published by the University of California as *Film Quarterly*) also owe much to *Close Up.* (It must be admitted, however, that *Film Quarterly*'s endless, convoluted articles could never be described as 'slight', no matter how else they may be described.)

In the United States *Film Comment* and *Film Culture* are the most important of the intellectual film magazines, but *Film Culture,* with its occasional publication and its quite definitely non-popular approach to film, lags behind the influential and widely-read monthly, *Film Comment.* Under Richard Corliss's editorship, *Film Comment* has come a long way from the publication which Gordon Hitchens first edited and published in the early 1960s under the title of *Vision.* In October 1975 the American Film Institute began publication of *American Film,* a glossy, superficial monthly, which has now the largest circulation of any film magazine in the USA. All other US film magazines have the right to be envious of the large grant from the National Endowment for the Arts which enabled the publication to come into existence.

Where would film history be without *Films in Review*? Sponsored by the National Board of Review, which in years past has published *Exceptional Photoplays* and the delightfully-titled

The cover of *Film Pictorial*, issue dated 25 March 1939.

A Garden of American Motion Pictures, the magazine commenced publication in February 1950 under the editorship of Henry Hart. With its first issue it established a policy of publishing career articles on film celebrities, although the accompanying filmographies did not appear on a regular basis until a few years later, and the early contributors to *Films in Review* included Siegfried Kracauer, Gilbert Seldes, Theodore Huff and Richard Griffith. In 1952 Herman Weinberg commenced his column of intellectual gossip, 'Coffee, Brandy and Cigars', in *Films in Review*, later taking it to *Film Culture*

and *Take One*, but returning to its birthplace in October 1978 and renaming the column, 'The Weinberg Touch'. Aside from its career articles, *Films in Review* was notorious for its outrageous film reviews, whose writers were ever watchful for signs of communism or sexual perversion, and which reviews were often signed by ladies such as Elaine Rothschild, Eunice Sinkler, Gweneth Britt and Flavia Wharton, which everyone was sure were pseudonyms. I always recall a review by Henry Hart of *Isadora*, which began, 'Vanessa Redgrave resembles Isadora Duncan only in her insistence on having children out of wedlock'. Under Henry Hart's editorship one also looked forward to Miss N. C. Chambers's reviews of the annual Academy Awards, which would contain such venomous comments as, 'Walter Matthau, still ridiculous in his overcompensating-for-insecurity garb' or 'Barbra Streisand accepted her Oscar with the vulgarity that's her stock-in-trade'. Henry Hart retired in February 1972, twenty-two years to the month of his founding *Films in Review*, and was replaced by Charles Phillips Reilly who has done much to raise the level of scholarship in the articles in *Films in Review* but also—sadly, so far as I am concerned—has toned down the reviews. Today the magazine boasts writers of the calibre of William K. Everson and DeWitt Bodeen, plus regular columns on Film Music by Page Cook, Television by Alvin H. Marill and

Film Collecting by this writer. Alan G. Barbour's *Screen Facts*, which ran for some twenty-four issues, was similar in some respects to *Films in Review*, providing career articles on celebrities such as Pola Negri, Deanna Durbin, Rudolph Valentino, Geraldine Farrar and Bette Davis. Its demise was unfortunate and it is sadly missed. Also sadly missed is Leonard Maltin's *Film Fan Monthly*, which demonstrated quite appropriate affection for the likes of Thelma Todd and Robert Youngson. Since the magazine's passing, Maltin has anthologised many of the articles in paperback books such as *Hollywood: The Dream Factory*.

Films in Review's only major competitor is the British *Focus on Film*, published by the Tantivy Press, which commenced publication in January 1970 under the editorship of Allen Eyles. It has published valuable career articles on Edward Everett Horton, Lon Chaney, 'Ronald Colman and the Cinema of Empire' and others. Its spring 1971 issue was devoted to John Ford and included important articles by William K. Everson and Jeffrey Richards. If one has any complaint about *Focus on Film* it is its awkward, cinemascopic size.

Mention should also be made of the quarterly journal of George Eastman House, *Image*, which has been published on and off for many years, and thankfully is currently on, under the editorship of George Pratt. As befits a publication from a

The cover of *Picturegoer*, issue dated 16 May 1959.

photographic museum, it is beautifully produced on expensive art paper, with gorgeous photographic reproductions. It is not exclusively devoted to film, but each issue contains at least one film article, and recently *Image* has published some of George Pratt's interviews with silent celebrities such as Harold Lloyd, Cecil B. DeMille, Alice Terry and Buster Keaton.

In November 1968 this writer, with Paul O'Dell, founded *The Silent Picture*, the only serious quarterly devoted to the art and history of the silent film, which continued in existence until the end of 1974. The best description—and one of the finest—of the magazine that I have read is by William K. Everson in his new book, *American Silent Film:* 'An admirable little magazine, never very large or ambitious, but full of useful research and interview material'. As its editor I am proud of the publication's pieces on D. W. Griffith and its rediscovery of George Pearson.

Everson also speaks kindly of *The Velvet Light Trap*, which Russell Campbell founded while he was a student at the University of Wisconsin, Madison. Nowadays issues are fewer and farther between and its days are probably numbered, but it was an excellent source of serious articles on American cinema of the 1930s until the 1950s, with particular emphasis on Warner Bros. It stands, or should I say stood, on a par with other serious US film magazines such as *Film Literature*, *Film Library Quarterly*, and the journals of the Society for Cinema Studies, *Cinema Journal*, and of the University Film Association.

In discussing non-American and non-British film journals, I might mention *Cahiers du Cinema* (an English-language version of which, under the editorship of Andrew Sarris, was published during 1966 and 1967), or *Image et Son*, or *Bianco e Nero*, or *Chaplin* or *Film Kurier*. Instead, I would select one magazine from Canada and one from Australia. Peter Lebensold's *Take One* is not only Canada's best film magazine; it is one of the best film publications in the world, with good reviews, intelligent articles and a group of regular contributors who represent both old and new cinema. It has every right to the title of 'The Magazine of the Movies'. From Australia comes *Cinema Papers*, a large-format publication which began life in 1967. The emphasis here is on Australian cinema, but there is good coverage also of world cinema, present and past. *Cinema Papers* has also been publishing a superb historical survey of film periodicals, written by Basil Gilbert.

Before moving on to trade papers, a quick comment should be made on five British periodicals. *Films and Filming* and *Film* (the journal of the British Federation of Film Societies) both began publication in 1954. *Film* no longer has Kevin Brownlow writing the pieces which were to be the basis for his *The Parade's Gone By*, but it is still a worthwhile publication. The same cannot honestly be said of *Films and Filming*, which in its early years, under the editorship of Peter Brinson, was one of the best film magazines in the world. Its first issue, in October 1954, included contributions by Catherine de la Roche, Roger Manvell, John Minchinton and John Grierson. Today it has shrunk considerably in size and seems to rely too heavily on a photographic content which is seemingly intended for a gay audience. Despite its photographic content—quite definitely heterosexual in nature—*Continental Film Review* is

The cover from *Picture Show*, issue dated 21 November 1953.

a surprisingly intelligent magazine with a good coverage of foreign-language productions. Ian Cameron's *Movie* was in vogue for a while but the magazine's critical style has become less popular, and too many American journals, such as *Film Comment* to a greater degree and *Movietone News* and *Bright Lights* to a lesser degree, offer similar in-depth critical evaluations. Who remembers *Cinema Studies,* the tiny little journal of the Society for Film History Research? I do, because *Cinema Studies* published the first piece that I ever wrote on film history back in January 1963, and for several years I

was the Honorary Secretary of the Society. Its articles on such minor subjects as 'The Development of Sound Films in Leicester', 'The Outlook of C. A. Lejeune' and 'The Cinematograph in the London Music Hall' still have value, and it is surprising that so few of its pieces have been reprinted in book form. Trade papers, the film industry's news magazines, which are the primary source for research into the history of the cinema, tend to have had longer lives than other types of film magazine. That does not mean, however, that there were not and are not so many of them. In an essay such as this it is not possible to consider them all, and one can only salute in passing *Billboard, Box Office, Motography, Exhibitors Trade Review, Film Daily, Daily Cinema, Greater Amusements, The Cinema, Daily Film Renter, The Era* and *Movie TV Marketing.*

Today, Britain's film interests are represented by *Screen International,* a weekly trade journal, glossy in look and glossy in content, which features Peter Noble's 'In Confidence' column and 'Inside Hollywood' by John Austin. Its origins go back to the beginnings of the cinema, through *Daily Cinema,* to *The Kinematograph Weekly,* which was founded on 15 June 1889 as *The Optical Magic Lantern Journal and Photographic Enlarger.* In May 1907 it adopted the slightly more catchy title of *The Kinematograph and Lantern Weekly,* affectionately known for more than sixty years as *The Kine*

or *Kine Weekly.* On 25 September, 1971 it was merged with *Today's Cinema* which had begun life in 1912 as *The Cinema News and Property Gazette.* The *Kinematograph Weekly*'s one competitor was *The Bioscope,* which commenced publication on 18 September 1908 and ceased on 4 May 1932. Of the two, *The Bioscope* is probably the more worthwhile from a research point of view.

Not the first, but the best known, of early American trade periodicals was *The Moving Picture World,* founded by James P. Chalmers Jr, which began publication on 9 March, 1907 as *The Moving Picture World and View Photographer.* It described itself as 'the only independent weekly journal published in the interests of manufacturers and operators of animated photograph and cinematograph projection, illustrated songs and lantern lectures and lantern slide makers'. *The World*'s most important early contributors were George Blaisdell, who joined in 1912, Edward Weitzel, who joined in 1915, and Lynde Denig, who also joined in 1915, but left the following year to become editor of the *New York Dramatic Mirror.* (It was *The Mirror* and its photoplay editor, Frank E. Woods, who introduced serious film reviewing to trade papers.) *The Moving Picture World* was published weekly until 7 January, 1928 when it merged with *Exhibitors Herald.* In time the publication became *Motion Picture Herald* and eventually *QP Herald,* under which title it folded on 4 May,

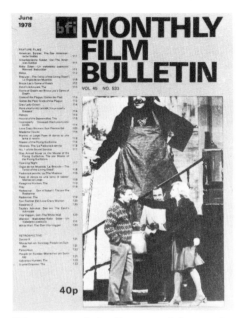

The cover of the June 1978 issue of the BFI's *Monthly Film Bulletin*.

1973. *QP Herald*'s passing marked the end of the Quigley Publications empire, founded in 1915 by Martin Quigley (who died in 1964), the most famous publication of which was the annual *Motion Picture Almanac*. In competition with *The Moving Picture World* was *Motion Picture News*, which commenced publication in 1908 as *The Motion Picture World*. In time, it also became part of the Quigley empire, merging with *Exhibitors Herald and Moving Picture World* on 3 January, 1931. The most famous and the most important of trade papers is, of course, *Variety*—not that it is solely devoted to the cinema, embracing, as it does, theatre, music, television, radio and the recording industry. When it first appeared on 16 December, 1905, its chief interests were the legitimate stage and vaudeville. As Douglas Gilbert writes in his definitive volume, *American Vaudeville*, 'It hit Broadway like a thousand of brick: an honest publication whose summaries of acts and plays were fearless and uncompromising, one that flayed an act with a left-hook critique, often printed in the same issue containing the act's paid advertisement'. Its founder and first editor, Sime Silverman established a reputation for honesty and integrity in reviewing which *Variety* has never lost.

Famous for its abuse of the English language, with headlines such as 'Stix Nix Hix Pix' (meaning films about rural Americans were not popular in rural America), *Variety*, surprisingly, did not begin exhaustive coverage of film until around 1914, but when it did its coverage was the best available. In 1933 the New-York-based weekly *Variety* spawned a daily Hollywood *Variety*, the first issue of which was published on 6 September under the editorship of Arthur Ungar. *Daily Variety* was in answer to *The Hollywood Reporter*, which W. R. 'Billy' Wilkerson had first published on 3 September, 1930. Both trade papers are published to this day and both, despite individual circulations of less than fifteen thousand, have tremendous influence. *Daily Variety* boasts columnist Army Archerd, who is known to millions of television viewers for his coverage of stars arriving for the Academy Awards, while *The Hollywood Reporter* has Hank Grant, Radie Harris with Broadway gossip, Robert Osborne on location and Richard Hack on television. Radie Harris is probably the best known, best liked and longest lasting of trade paper columnists, having previously worked for *Photoplay*.

House organs, published by individual producers and distributors, are as old as the cinema itself. Among the first house journals were *The Edison Kinetogram*, *Vitagraph Life Portrayals*, *Essanay News*, *Essanay Guide*, *Kalem Kalendar*, *Lubin Bulletin*, *The Triangle*, *The Triangle News* and *The Universal Weekly*. In Britain there were *Pathe Cinema Journal*, *Stoll Herald* and *Walturdaw Weekly Budget*. It seemed as though every company had a house organ—the Christie Comedy Company published *Film Follies*; Mutual published *Reel Life*; Selig published *Paste-Pot and Shears*, and the Imp Company published *The Implet*.

With the coming of sound the house organs were still the most popular means of getting word out to the exhibitors concerning new films; they were far more reliable and, obviously, more controllable than trade papers. In England there was *Gaumont British News*, suitably gentlemanly in style, while in America the leading house organs were *Columbia Mirror*, MGM's *The*

The cover of the Spring 1978 issue of the BFI's quarterly *Sight and Sound*.

Distributor and RKO's *The Radio Flash*. The *Distributor*, published weekly by MGM's sales department in New York, tends to be of minor interest, devoting space to only a couple of films per issue but, because of the product it was selling, it must stand supreme. In 1935 *The Distributor* announced, 'Only one company can be the first. The answer has been the same for 11 years.' It was not necessary for *The Distributor* to name the company concerned. Each issue of *Columbia Mirror* was

usually devoted to a single film, making it more a campaign book or press sheet than a house journal. *The Radio Flash* was chock-full of RKO gossip, with an editorial entitled 'Heart to Heart' by Jules Levy, which usually began with Levy's noting that it was no longer conjecture that such and such RKO feature was a box-office hit or in the top grossing class. Levy resigned in October 1939 and his editorial was replaced by 'Personal Talks' with Ned E. Depinet.

The least known—because they were originally intended for a specific audience which excluded the general public—and consequently the least used and, in many cases, the least available in libraries, house organs are one of the most important research tools for film historians and students, for beneath all that puffery are a lot of hard facts.

Finally I must apologise for all the film magazines that I have not been able to cover. Should I really have ignored *American Cinematographer, Picture Play, Views and Reviews, Action, Cineaste, Film Heritage, Funnyworld, Filmmakers Newsletter* or *Screen Romances*? Of course not. *Rob Wagner's Script*, which was once to Los Angeles what *Time Out* and *What's On* are to London, deserves space because of the completely unknown, yet superb, film reviews and cover stories by Herb Sterne. Or what about *Screen,* which once served a purpose as a forum for film education? No, I think enough has been written.

As a footnote to Anthony Slide's feature, below is appended a list of some international film-periodicals, with the publishers' addresses. This information is taken from the far more extensive list and more detailed information carried each year in the 'Film Magazines' section of *International Film Guide,* edited by Peter Cowie and published by the Tantivy Press, Magdalen House, 136–148 Tooley Street, London SE1.

Action. Directors Guild of America magazine. 7950 Sunset Boulevard, California 90046, USA.

L'Avant-Scène Cinéma. Monthly screenplays of new and classic films, etc. 27 Rue Saint-André des Arts, 75006 Paris, France (or from the Tantivy Press who are the British agents).

American Film. The American Film Institute magazine, ten issues a year. P.O. Box 1571, Washington DC 20013, USA.

Cahiers du Cinéma. Paris-published monthly. 9 Passage de la Boule-Blanche, 75012 Paris, France.

Celuloide. Portugese monthly. Rua David Manuel da Fonseca 88, Rio Maior, Portugal.

Chaplin. Swedish bi-monthly with reviews, features, etc. Svenska Filminstitut, Box 27 126, S-102 52 Stockholm, Sweden.

Cine al Dia. Venezuelan monthly. Apartado 50, 446 Sabana Grande, Caracas, Venezuela.

Cineaste. 333 Sixth Avenue, New York, NY 10014, USA.

FOCUS ON FILM

Price 70p ($2.00)
20TH CENTURY-FOX & CINEMASCOPE
EAGLE-LION: THE VIOLENT YEARS
Career of NANCY COLEMAN
Interview with JOHN SCHLESINGER

31

☐ VANESSA REDGRAVE, RICHARD GERE AND CHICK VENNERA IN *YANKS*

The cover of No 31 of *Focus on Film*.

Cine Cubano. Coverage of all Latin American cinema—in Spanish. Calle 23 no 1155, Havana, Cuba.

Ciné Dossiers. Belgian review. L'Action Cinématographique, 30 Rue de l'Etuve, 1000 Brussels, Belgium.

Cinema. Good Swiss coverage in French and German. Postfach 1049, CH 8022, Zurich, Switzerland.

Cinema. South African glossy full of features. P.O. Box 1574, Johannesburg, South Africa.

Cinema Canada. Bi-monthly championing Canadian production. 6 Washington Avenue, No 3, Toronto, Canada.

Cinema 2002. Excellent Spanish monthly. Ardemans 64, Madrid 28, Spain.

Cinéma 79. The French Federation of Film Societies' official publication. 6 Rue Ordener, 75018 Paris, France.

Cinema Papers. Large and impressive Australian quarterly. 143 Therry Street, Melbourne, Australia.

Cinéma Québec. French-Canadian magazine published ten times a year. CP 309, Station Outremont, Montreal, Canada.

Continental Film Review. Long established monthly coverage of foreign films shown in GB. Roding

Trading Estate, London Road, Barking, Essex.

Eigashi Kenkyu. Japanese quarterly in Japanese and English. c/o Tadao Sato, 5–10–4 Matsubara, Setagaya-ku, Tokyo, Japan.

Ecran '79. Picture-packed French monthly. Editions de L'Atalante, 60 Avenue Simon Bolivar, 75019 Paris, France.

Ekran. Slovenian magazine with reviews, features, etc. Dalatinova 44/11, Soba 9, 61000 Ljubljana, Yugoslavia.

Film. Monthly journal of the British Federation of Film Societies. 81 Dean Street, London W1.

Film. Polish film weekly. Pulawska 61, 02-595 Warsaw, Poland.

Film. Turkish film monthly; official publication of the Sinematek Dernegi. P.K.307, Beyoglu, Istanbul, Turkey.

Film a Doba. The main Czech film periodical; monthly. Vaclavske nam 43, Praha 1, Czechoslovakia.

Film Dope. British quarterly. 5 Norman Court, Little Heath, Potters Bar, Herts.

Filmfacts. Fortnightly check-list of all US releases. P.O. Box 213, Village Station, New York, NY 10014, USA.

Film Guia. Internationally-slanted Spanish bi-monthly. Marquesa Caldas de Montbuy 27–29, Barcelona 16m, Spain.

Film Kultura. The leading Hungarian film publication. Nepstadion ut, 97 Budapest XIV, Hungary.

Filmkunst. Old established Austrian film periodical. Rauhensteingasse 5,

1010 Vienna, Austria.

Films and Filming. Well established British monthly, Hansom Books, 2 Old Pye Street, London SW1.

Films Illustrated. Good British monthly film magazine. 44a High Street, Ryde, Isle of Wight.

Film Review. British monthly with reviews of the new movies. The Old Court House, Old Court Palace, 42–70 Kensington High Street, London W8.

Filmrutan. Swedish Federation of Film Societies publication. Ringavagen 54, S-L81 34 Lidingo, Sweden.

Film World. Indian glossy monthly. 8 Horniman Circle, Botawala Building, Bombay 400023, India.

Focus on Film. Extremely interesting and collectable British film quarterly. The Tantivy Press, Magdalen House, 136–148 Tooley Street, London SE1.

Guia de Filmes. Bi-monthly Brazilian equivalent to Britain's *Monthly Film Bulletin*. Rua Mayrink 28-5 andar, Rio de Janeiro, Guanabara, Brazil.

Iskusstvo Kino. The long established, leading Russian film magazine. 9 ulitsa Usiyevicha, 125319, Moscow, USSR.

Journal of the Society of Film and Television Arts. Long-running film quarterly published for the British Film Industry. 80 Great Portland Street, London W1.

Kino. Very good Polish film monthly. Ulica Pulawska 61, 02-595, Warsaw, Poland.

Kosmorama. Denmark's leading film publication; quarterly. Det Danske Filmmuseum, Store Sondervolstraede, 1419 Copenhagen, Denmark.

Montage. Duplicated but interesting and well-packed quarterly published by the London Regional Group of Film Societies. 2 Colnbrook Street, London SE1.

Monthly Film Bulletin. The British Film Institute's full reviews, with extended credits, of all films released in Britain. 81 Dean Street, London W1.

Movie. British quarterly. 25 Lloyd Baker Street, London WC1.

Photoplay. Really the last of the surviving English fan periodicals. Glossy. 12–18 Paul Street, London EC2.

La Revue du Cinéma. Well known French monthly. 3 Rue Recamier, Paris 7, France.

Positif. High-level French film monthly. 39 Rue d'Amsterdam, 75008 Paris, France.

Sequence. Quarterly in English. Vintage Publications, 152 Azimpur Road, Dacca 283463, Bangladesh.

Sequences. French-Canadian quarterly. 1474 Rue Alexandre-Deseve, Montreal 133, Canada.

Sight & Sound. High-brow, solid and very serious quarterly published by the British Film Institute, 81 Dean Street, London W1.

Skoop. Lavish Dutch movie magazine. Boekencentrum NV, Scheveningseweg 72, The Hague, Holland.

Sovyetski Ekran. Long established Soviet fortnightly film-news periodical. ul Chasovaga 5B, Moscow, USSR.

Stars et Cinéma. Glossy Belgian monthly with international outlook. 7 Place Georges Brugmann, 1060 Brussels, Belgium.

Take One. Large, lavish and interesting Canadian monthly. Unicorn Publishing, P.O. Box 1778, Station B, Montreal, Canada.

What's On In London. Oldest established (1935) of the London entertainments magazine with full coverage of cinema and club programmes, reviews (by F. Maurice Speed), interviews, etc. 79 Temple Chambers, London EC4.

Note: This list is in no way complete and excludes various trade, technical and national publications of which there are some twenty or so listed in *International Film Guide*.

The Influence of German Expressionism on American Cinema

by William K. Everson

With the recent spectacular resurgence of the German cinema, and with some of that country's top new directors—Werner Herzog and Wim Wenders among them—seeing the United States as at least a partial base of operations, perhaps now is a good time to look back and remind ourselves just how dynamic and long lasting has been Germany's influence on English-speaking cinema.

I have limited myself to expressionism since Germany was the only country to develop a whole school of expressionist cinema in the 1920s, and since a *visual* style (which could apply to acting almost as much as to set-design and camerawork) was far more important to the Germans than editing or writing styles, its influences are more readily recognisable.

The word 'influence' is important. Neither Hollywood nor British studios were ever ready to import a total commitment to expressionism, and such *wholly* expressionist films as *The Cabinet of Dr Caligari*, *Raskolnikov*, *Genuine* and *Destiny* remained a German speciality. But the best of expressionist style was certainly adopted, mixed with borrowed camera- and lighting-styles, and romanticist narratives, to ensure a strong German input into American (and British) films from 1920 on, which reached its zenith in the late 1920s and early 1930s.

Of course, expressionism was never as fashionable nor as easy to assimilate as Russian montage. Hollywood never really understood what montage was all about, but they did know that it made for effective razzle-dazzle sequences involving time-transitions, dreams or such bravura episodes as the opening of the Hecht–MacArthur *Crime Without Passion*, or the clearly Eisenstein-influenced beginning of the earthquake in *San Francisco*. MGM even established an official Montage Department, and had they known how to exploit Garbo or Gable via expressionism, they would probably have set up an Expressionist Department as well!

But while it is relatively easy to construct a script to incorporate elements of montage, it is much more complicated (and not even especially desirable) to set out to write an 'expressionist' script. In most Hollywood films, expressionism was present effectively only if the director—a Paul Leni or a Robert Florey—was involved in the design concept of a film from the very beginning. Otherwise, its use was fragmented and isolated, limited perhaps to sets that somehow lent themselves to a stylised design. In many cases, too, expressionism was *imposed* on a film, over and above its design, by purely technical means. A case in point is William K. Howard's 1927 classic, *White Gold*, taking place in the confined and basically realistic sets of a Western ranch, barn and bunkhouse. However, in the sequence wherein drifter George Bancroft debates with himself whether or not to attempt the seduction of his boss's wife, we are treated to stylised superimpositions of ticking clocks and swinging pendulums (a favourite visual trick of Howard's) and triple images of Bancroft as he listens to the urgings of both his good and evil personalities.

The influence of German technique was of course by no means limited to Hollywood, and indeed it was perhaps seen in its most undistilled form in the British cinema of the 1920s. In *Trapped by the Mormons*, one of those peculiar films in which the British somehow—and here, literally—equated Mormonism with white slavery, the head Mormon is presented as a Caligari figure who impresses his would-be converts with a fake miracle performed in a caravan with an interior suspiciously like that of the ubiquitous Dr C. Later in the 1920s, British–German collaboration and co-production was so close that many films give no clues at all as to their national origin. *Moulin Rouge* and *The Informer*, directed by E. A. Dupont and Arthur Robison respectively, with their European casts and cameramen, and non-British locales, would pass for unadulterated UFA anyday. They are still stunning productions. Many German technicians such as cameramen and designers stayed in Britain, so it's not at all surprising that a German 'look' stayed along with them, especially in films made by directors (like Michael Powell) who had always admired German technique. Powell's little gem, *The Spy in Black,* made in 1939,

frequently reminds one of the old German *Nosferatu*, a reminder helped along by the sinister presence of Conrad Veidt as the titular spy. When Hollywood directors came to Britain, they frequently tried to beef up rather staid scripts by injecting expressionist elements into realistic surroundings. William K. Howard's *The Squeaker* was based on a fairly straightforward Edgar Wallace thriller, but, for its climax, Howard's stylised treatment of the killer's downfall—he is apparently confronted by the shades of his former victims as he is escorted through Scotland Yard—sends one's mind scurrying back to Fritz Lang and Dr Mabuse's two earlier descents into madness. Scotland Yard never looked quite so eerie before or since, and the lighting and set-design helped to make credible what would otherwise have been a rather unlikely collapse from such a well-organised master criminal! While expressionism is generally (and rightly) considered to be primarily a matter of design, acting styles and the use of the body (and the way it was framed and photographed) in German films it often made the actor merely an extension of the set. In *Variety*, the oppressive mood of the prison set—an exercise yard shot from above, with the shuffling circle of prisoners, or corridors stretching off into infinity—is matched by the use of Emil Jannings's body, and the stress on his bowed shoulders and dejected back, which frequently fills the whole frame. The following year,

one finds F. W. Murnau—in Hollywood for his first American film, the classic *Sunrise*—grafting this introverted and physical acting style on to the most unlikely successor to Jannings, George O'Brien. O'Brien, a breezy personality most associated with action roles for John Ford, plays a potential wife-murderer who literally carries the weight of the world on his shoulders, and whose expressively laden back fills many of the frames as did Jannings's. Nor did this stylised form of acting die out entirely when sound and dialogue inevitably added subtleties and nuances to an actor's repertoire. In the late 1930s, German producer Erich Pommer, filming *St Martin's Lane* in England, cast Charles Laughton in a Jannings-type role—and back came those expressive close-shots of drooping shoulders again!

In Hollywood, expressionism, while not limited to certain studios, was certainly concentrated in them—and of course, in certain genres, such as the horror film and the gangster film. Its greatest impact was at Fox, where out of genuine homage to F. W. Murnau, such directors as Ford, Borzage, Howard, Walsh, Hawks and Dieterle frequently (and often with surprising success) tried to make films in his image. Even so essentially American a director as John Ford not only re-used some of Murnau's sets in his *Four Sons*, but he even slowed his characteristically snappy pace to match Murnau's tempo. And, of course, the art

F. W. Murnau, at right, behind two cameramen, directs George O'Brien in 1927's *Sunrise,* not the first but certainly the most influential American film to feature transplanted German expressionism.

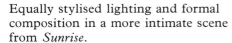

Equally stylised lighting and formal composition in a more intimate scene from *Sunrise.*

One of the extremely stylised carnival sets from *Sunrise.*

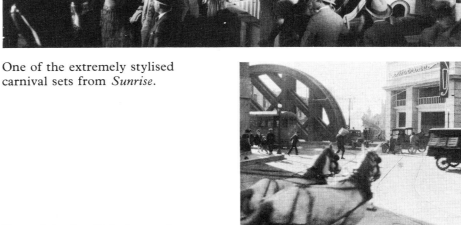

Part of the fanciful city set from *Sunrise.*

directors and cameramen who worked with these directors, creating images and sets in the German manner, continued to carry that influence into their work with other directors. The German dominance at Fox between 1927 and 1932 almost matched that in Britain in the late 1920s, although the Hollywood star system did enable the American examples to retain a recognisable identity.

Universal, with its influx of imported talent (e.g. Paul Leni, Paul Fejos, Karl Freund and James Whale) and its early-sound concentration on stylistic horror films, wasn't far behind. Although *The Man Who Laughs* was based on a Victor Hugo novel set in Britain in the Middle Ages, the décor was pure UFA, with entrances to buildings and castles retaining the low-ceilinged, tomb-like design that harked back to *Siegfried* and *Nosferatu*. Even the totally up-to-date *Broadway*, a 1929 musical-cum-gangster drama, mixed the old and the new—its bizarre night-club set was 50% art deco, and 50% throwback to Lang's equally bizarre (though less cheerful) nightclub in *Dr Mabuse* of seven years earlier. At other studios, the amount of expressionism was pretty much up to the talents and inclinations of individual directors. Paramount was geared primarily to turning out a glossy contemporary product, but on the other hand there was a great deal of Europe-orientated talent on their roster of creators: Lubitsch, von Sternberg, Mamoulian, Florey and, later on, Lang. Robert Florey's 1929 *The Hole in the Wall* (a Browning–Chaney type of thriller) was a fascinating early talkie ostensibly designed to introduce Claudette Colbert and Edward G. Robinson. Florey apparently went a little overboard in atmospheric by-play, and an entire *Cat and the Canary*-type sub-plot was completely eliminated before release, but enough remains, particularly in the area of set-design, to qualify it as a film with strong expressionist elements.

MGM's visual look was pure art deco; the mere mention of expressionism in a studio devoted to happy escapism would have horrified the studio heads, even if they had understood it! Individual directors however, did manage to sneak it through when resident art director Cedric Gibbons wasn't looking. In *The Crowd*, King Vidor's superb late silent, the hospital scenes (wherein the hero anxiously awaits the birth of his child) are surprisingly stylised and unreal in a film otherwise notable for its unforced realism. And, of course, when Fritz Lang came to the studio in 1936 for *Fury*, much of UFA's pictorial style came with him, and compositions in his lynch-mob scene are exact duplicates of the mob scenes in *Metropolis*. (This film, perhaps because of its commercial success, seems to have made an indelible impression on many directors. One finds obvious echoes from it in films as diverse as Hollywood's *The Bride of Frankenstein* and Britain's *The Great Barrier*.)

Warner Brothers had such an efficient assembly-line method of production and was so dependent on team-work that one wouldn't have expected expressionism to make many inroads there. On a large scale it didn't; certainly there was no continuing illustration of its influence, as there was at Fox and Universal (where it even infiltrated into a silent 'B' Western, *Wild Blood!*). But Warner had a large roster of extremely talented directors and art directors, many of whom—for example, Michael Curtiz, Joe May, Anatole Litvak, Robert Florey, Anton Grot and William Dieterle—had European backgrounds. One has only to look at Joe May's *Confession*, art-directed by Anton Grot (and a re-make of Pola Negri's German *Mazurka*) to realise that even at Warner—and in a Kay Francis vehicle to boot—expressionism had more than a casual foothold!

Perhaps the continuing influence on American film (and especially the usage of expressionist design) will be more apparent if we take a few specific chronological examples, bearing in mind that they represent only the tip of the filmic iceberg. The very first, expressionist influence on American film was almost certainly French, but from 1921 on there can be no question of the German dominance for this was the year of the American release of *The Cabinet of Dr Caligari* and, far from coincidentally, it was also the year of Nazimova's *Camille*, designed by

Natacha Rambova. From the point of view of design, it is a curious welding of the fledgling new art deco (not officially launched until 1925) with German expressionism. It opens in a gambling casino with interiors that look like Caligari exteriors. Camille's bedroom is perhaps even more bizarre, complete with windows that sustain the scrutinising-eyes motif that was a continuing expressionist theme. (Even the stage curtains in the nightclub in *Broadway* were covered with these eyes, surely a rather disconcerting adjunct to dining!) Incidentally, despite frequent claims that *The Cabinet of Dr Caligari* impressed all but influenced nobody, one finds it a constant source of design- or character-inspiration in Hollywood films, from the silent *The Bells* and *The Cat and the Canary*, to Robert Florey's talkie *The Murders in the Rue Morgue* (if not a re-make, then certainly a more than casual parallel). In 1928, at the height of Hollywood's filmic romance with Germany, one can point to two special highlights. *The Red Dance*, one of a then-current cycle of adventures and romances built around the Russian Revolution, was directed on brisk, no-nonsense lines by Raoul Walsh. Its sets were handsome and stylish, but only once do they branch off into expressionism. One sequence takes place in a Russian prison and mine, and here art director Ben Carré takes the prison expression of *Variety* several steps further. Instead of marching like somnabulists into tomb-like doorways, the prisoners now spiral downhill into a vertical shaft, a literal illustration of hell, lit from below with a never-quite-explained light. It seems an unusually expensively-created prison for the economical Russians, but there's no question of its visual effectiveness. If Raoul Walsh had neither asked for it nor expected it, he was undoubtedly impressed by it; he used all the prison footage again in his next foray into the Russian Revolution, the 1931 talkie *The Yellow Ticket*.

Even more derivative of German expressionism, and using it more consistently throughout the film, was 1928's *Street Angel*. It was a fairly patent attempt to weld the artistic success of *Sunrise* to the commercial success of *Seventh Heaven*, and it reunited the stars–director team of the latter: Janet Gaynor, Charles Farrell and Frank Borzage. So far as its plot was concerned, it was rather a silly and unduly protracted film, but visually it was breath-taking. Apart from containing direct references to *Tartuffe* and *Metropolis*, the sets, the lighting, the compositions and the camera mobility were all stunning. And for once, the expressionist elements were taken a step further than in the inspirational source. In *The Cabinet of Dr Caligari*, authority was expressed by a fussy, inattentive clerk on a high stool. Here, in a sequence where the heroine is sentenced to prison, the composition of the frame is dominated by the huge heads of the judge and the arresting officers, while perspective reduces the head of the heroine—and eventually just her forehead and eyes—almost to the size of a pin-head. If the plot of *Street Angel* had matched its visual elegance and imagination, it would have been one of the enduring classics of the American cinema.

In 1927 and 1929 respectively, Paul Leni, the former German art director, directed *The Cat and the Canary* and *The Last Warning* for Universal. Both were essentially fun movies in the 'old dark house' category, full of camera tricks and superb lighting. While *Cat* is undoubtedly the better film, *The Last Warning* contains some of the more innovative expressionist design— particularly the front of an allegedly haunted theatre, which takes on the appearance of a malevolent face, with brooding eyes and cruel grin. Both films also extended the use of expressionist design into macabre and mobile subtitles.

1929 also saw the production of Watson and Weber's experimental version of Poe's *The Fall of the House of Usher*, designed also to show the full capabilities of the camera and thus going out of its way to use distorting lenses, split screen, and other effects. Virtually undistilled expressionism, and yet another reminder of Caligari's omnipresence, *The Fall of the House of Usher*, a most effective evocation of the mood of Poe, underlines again that for the *consistent* application of expressionism in *one* film, one has to look outside the normal Hollywood channels.

1931's *The Bat Whispers* was another marvellous old-house chiller and, like director Roland West's other two talkies (the others, *Alibi* and *Corsair*, were both crime and gangster yarns), it was distinguished by remarkable pictorial compositions with, again, Fritz Lang's influence readily apparent throughout. 1932's *Six Hours to Live*, a lovely, unjustly forgotten film directed by William Dieterle, is, in truth, far more romanticist than expressionist. But there's one marvellous sequence, both human and warm, yet macabre at the same time, in a candle-festooned church that is clearly rooted in a similar sequence in Lang's *Destiny*. The Lang influence continues too in William K. Howard's *Mary Burns, Fugitive,* an excellent thriller of 1935. Howard, one of the most adept at utilising the German technique he admired so much in thoroughly American themes, had worked side by side with Murnau at Fox, admired him a great deal, and had been one of the pall-bearers at his funeral. *Mary Burns, Fugitive* was made at the height of the gangster and G-men cycle, yet it aims at a quiet, colder kind of thrill. A prison-break sequence is almost lyrical, the escapees finally being picked up by a small boat on a mist-covered lake. And in the gangsters' hideout, chief gangster Alan Baxter stretches himself out to sleep in a death-like trance. The angle and

lighting of the shot, the effect his appearance has on his cohorts, the cold brick background—suggesting a prison or a hospital rather than an apartment—all combine to create a scene which appears to be a direct homage to Lang and the memorable image of Mabuse in death in *The Last Testament of Dr Mabuse*. Apart from exerting his own considerable influence, Lang himself was of course extremely busy in Hollywood, infrequently so in the 1930s, but prolifically so from the 1940s on. Most of his thrillers—including *Fury, You Only Live Once* and *Manhunt*—had distinctly expressionist elements, but expressionism was particularly obvious in 1938's *You and Me*. One remarkable episode (in which paroled convicts gather on Christmas Eve to recall their days in prison, and the arrival, escape and death of 'Number One') combines visual and *aural* expressionism.

Although it could not be known at the time, 1940's *The Stranger on the Third Floor* unwittingly ushered in a new upsurge of expressionism in the Hollywood thriller. It was an unusual little 'B' film, directed by the Russian Boris Ingster, and had as its highlight an incredible dream sequence in which the hero imagines himself arrested for murder, convicted and sent to the electric chair. Because it was a cheap little film—and there was little money, or need, for big sets—this powerful sequence was created mainly by the adroit use of space and cunning

lighting. It is still one of the finest examples of the use of German expressionism in the Hollywood film—and its German origins are strengthened by the presence in the cast of Peter Lorre, virtually repeating his *M* characterisation. During World War II even more European life was pumped into Hollywood by the steady stream of refugee-directors and players: Renoir, Duvivier, Clair, Gabin and others from France, and a surprising number from Germany. Because of the relatively safe economy of war-time Hollywood, where almost anything could make money in a society hungry for constant and increased entertainment, many of the German producers and directors, including Seymour Nebenzal, Douglas Sirk and John Brahm, were given a free hand to make their own films in their own way—which often meant doom-ridden, expressionist films like the very peculiar *Voice in the Wind*. More importantly, the 1940s gave—if not birth, then certainly renewed life and a definite structure—to the *film noir* brand of film making. *Film noir* is too complex, important and fascinating to be dismissed in a few lines, but it is significant that the best of the *films noirs* were made by German film-makers such as Fritz Lang, Robert Siodmak and John Brahm. Even Frank Wisbar, working out of the poverty-row PRC studios, was able to remake his old German *Fahrman Maria* as *Strangler of the Swamp*. It was expressionist in theme and character, if not in design,

The expressionism of the German *Variety* taken to spectacular extremes in Raoul Walsh's *The Red Dance*.

Décor—and Boris Karloff's costuming—more than coincidentally reminiscent of *The Cabinet of Dr Caligari* in the 1925 film *The Bells*.

A corridor from Paul Leni's *The Cat and the Canary*.

Typical composition and mood lighting from Frank Borzage's *Street Angel*; Charles Farrell at rear.

William (then still Wilhelm) Dieterle directing Warner Baxter and Miriam Jordan in the lovely and very Gothic romantic film, *Six Hours to Live*.

and poor PRC must have been quite outraged to find that they had a minor classic on their hands instead of another addition to their *Dead Men Walk–Mad Monster* roster of cheap horror films. The expressionism of the *films noirs* was of a rather different, less obvious kind. Siodmak's *Criss Cross*, a top-notch 'caper' movie (almost a definitive *film noir* opus, and much more impressive now than it seemed in the mid 1940s) reverts to the kind of cold, calculated 'natural' expressionism of Murnau's *Nosferatu*.

After the emphasis on Germanic styles in the war years and the post-war period, the later decline in their use in favour of more documentarian and realistic methods of filmic story-telling made it seem as though expressionism in film design was almost an anachronism. Films like *Barrie Lyndon* veered more and more to authentic locations and buildings rather than the studio-created varieties, and the increasing dominance of colour films also helped to push expressionism (which seemed to belong far more to the black-and-white film era) into the background. But no genuine art form ever really vanishes. Even art deco (which can be disputed perhaps as a 'genuine' art form) seems to be in use again now that so many more films are being set in the 1930s, the period in which art deco itself reached its peak. Expressionism is still very much present in the European film, and perhaps by the end of 1979, when these notes are read, we'll know from films like Werner Herzog's remake of *Nosferatu,* or Wim Wenders's *Hammett* (now in preparation for shooting in San Francisco), whether the temporarily dormant German expressionist influence is alive and well once more.

Although *Manhunt* was set in London during World War II, Fritz Lang's underworld villains seemed to have been lifted bodily from *Dr Mabuse* and the Berlin of the 1920s.

Fritz Lang, whose Hollywood films always retained many direct echoes from his silent German classics, directs Joan Bennett in *Manhunt*.

Art-deco costuming and expressionist décor and design often inter-meshed, as in 1929's *Broadway*.

German lighting styles were prominent in British films too, as in David Lean's *Oliver Twist*.

The Hollywood Year

A review of 1978 in the Celluloid City
by Lennox Sanderson Jnr.

1978 was the year for Hollywood anniversaries. It marked the fiftieth birthday of both the Academy Awards and Mickey Mouse, and it was also the seventy-fifth anniversary of the incorporation of the city of Hollywood. All three events were celebrated in typical Hollywood fashion, with celebrities and ballyhoo, and each, in its own special way, was a successful happening. In addition, 1978 saw a number of Hollywood tributes to personalities as diverse as director David Butler and stuntman Yakima Canutt. As predictably as spring follows winter, the other major Hollywood Awards—the Emmys and the Golden Globes—were presented, and just as surely Hollywood's past seemed to hold the interest of the public at large far more than Hollywood's present.

The Hollywood year opens with the Golden Globe Awards, presented on 28 January by the Hollywood Foreign Press Association, which are perhaps not too well known outside the United States but which have importance not only in their own right but also as predictions as to which way the Academy Awards will go. Strangely enough, however, in 1978 the outcome of the Oscar race did not reflect the Golden Globe Awards, where the big winners were *The Turning Point, The Goodbye Girl, Julia* and *Equus.* The first was voted Best Motion Picture, Drama, and Herbert Ross received the Golden Globe for Best Director. *The Goodbye Girl* received the award for Best Picture in the Comedy and

Diane Keaton and Richard Dreyfuss with their Oscars for Best Actress and Best Actor.

Music field; Neil Simon received the Golden Globe for Best Screenwriting; his wife, Marsha Mason, was tied (with Diane Keaton for *Annie Hall*) for Best Actress in the Comedy and Music field, and Richard Dreyfuss received the Golden Globe for Best Actor in the same field. For their work in *Julia,* Jane Fonda won the Golden Globe for Best Actress in Drama and Vanessa Redgrave won for Best Supporting Actress. Similarly, for *Equus,* Richard Burton and Peter Firth received the male acting awards. Italy's *A Special Day* was voted Best Foreign Film. To no one's surprise, 'You Light Up My Life' was voted Best Original Song, and John Williams received the award for Best Original Score for *Star Wars*.

The winners in the television field were Ed Asner, Carol Burnett, Leslie Ann Warren and Henry Winkler, plus *Roots, All in the Family,* and the made-for-television feature, *Raid on Entebbe* (shown in GB as a regular cinema first feature). It was television which provided the 1978 Golden Globes with a little excitement, not so much for what took place but because of what NBC, which televised the show after a ten-year hiatus, decided to cut—chiefly the speeches of Richard Harris, making the Best Foreign Film Award, and Ed Asner.

The big event of 1978, the fiftieth annual Academy Awards presentation, took place at the Dorothy Chandler Pavilion of the Los Angeles Music Center on 3 April before an audience of 3,000 in the Pavilion and 300 million watching on television in fifty countries. Despite the absence of the big winner, Woody Allen, for Best Directing, Best Screenplay Written Directly for the Screen, and Best Picture, it was still a star-studded evening, with presenters including William Holden, Barbara Stanwyck, Greer Garson, Kirk Douglas, Raquel Welch, Joan Fontaine, Olivia de Havilland, Natalie Wood, Bette Davis, Charlton Heston, Gregory Peck, King Vidor, and Fred Astaire and Janet Gaynor, both of the last-mentioned receiving well-deserved standing ovations. Before presenting the Oscar for Best Actress to Diane

The controversial Vanessa Redgrave with her Oscar and John Travolta who presented it to her.

Keaton, the petite and still beautiful Miss Gaynor, who received the first Academy Award for Best Actress, commented, 'I am so happy that both the Academy and I survived to celebrate this golden anniversary.' The Academy Awards Show opened with a spectacular musical number, 'Look How Far We've Come,' sung and danced by Debbie Reynolds, substituting for Gene Kelly, and featuring thirty-seven former Oscar winners, among whom were George Cukor, Frank Capra, Ruth Gordon, Edith Head, Mickey Rooney, Claire Trevor and Gale Sondergaard. After Academy President and producer of the fiftieth Awards Show Howard W. Koch had welcomed everyone and had Gregory Peck and Bette Davis explain the complex rules, Bob Hope took over as master of ceremonies for

his record twenty-second appearance on the Academy Awards Show. Then the controversy began as Vanessa Redgrave received the Oscar for Best Supporting Actress for her role in *Julia,* and made a speech vowing to fight anti-semitism and fascism while at the same time referring to threats against her career and the Award by 'a small group of Zionist hoodlums'. She left the stage amid applause and boos. Later in in the show, Paddy Cheyefsky, presenting the Award for Best Screenplay, criticised Redgrave for exploiting the Academy Awards for her own personal political propaganda. Surprisingly the conservative Bob Hope made no comment.

The Oscars were a mixture of surprises and obvious choices. 'You Light Up My Life' had to be chosen

Best Original Song. John Williams had to win the Oscar for Best Music—Original Score for *Star Wars*—but that film, *Close Encounters of the Third Kind* and *The Turning Point* failed to win the Awards that most pundits thought they would receive. In fact, *The Turning Point* received no Oscars, *Close Encounters* won only one Oscar—to Vilmos Zsigmond for Best Cinematography—plus a Special Award for its sound effects, while *Star Wars* managed to garner six Oscars, plus a Special Award to Benjamin Burtt Jr for the creation of the alien, creature and robot voices. *Madame Rosa* was voted Best Foreign Language Film. The Jean Hersholt Humanitarian Award went to Charlton Heston, the Irving Thalberg Memorial Award went to past Academy president Walter Mirisch, while veteran film editor Margaret Booth received a well-deserved Honorary Academy Award from Olivia de Havilland. Richard Dreyfuss was voted Best Actor for *The Goodbye Girl*, and Jason Robards Best Supporting Actor for *Julia*. The biggest surprise of all was *Annie Hall* winning the Award for Best Picture over the more likely contenders: *Star Wars, Close Encounters, Julia* and *The Turning Point.*

The Emmy Awards were thirty years old on 17 September but, despite their being the USA's national television awards and television having an audience far larger than the cinema does or ever will have, they cannot muster the same appeal

to the American public as do the Oscars. For one thing, there are too many awards. Talk-show-host Johnny Carson once quipped that one of the Emmy categories was for the Best Show hosted by a midget named Marvin. It is not quite that ludicrous, but there are more than forty Emmys presented each year, not to mention countless local Emmys.

This year, the Hollywood Academy of Television Arts and Sciences invited Alexander H. Cohen and Hildy Parks, who had done such a wonderful job with the New York-based 'Tony' theatrical awards, to produce the show. Although it had much to recommend it—in particular only one, good opening production number—its running time of four and a half hours was far too long and it lost much of its audience both in television and at the Pasadena Civic Auditorium where it takes place. The American television networks obviously have little respect for the show, which was aired over CBS, with ABC programming the first episode of *Battlestar Galactica* and NBC screening a double bill of *Dumbo* and *King Kong* opposite it. As the Show's first presenter, Norman Lear, caustically commented, 'So proud are ABC and NBC of their own shows and stars who win Emmys on CBS tonight that they have scheduled against us a three-hour début of the most expensive new series ever made and the conclusion of *King Kong.*' Most would agree with Lear that it was

reminiscent of Dracula biting his own neck.

To add to Emmy's problems, the Show was pre-empted in part by President Carter's live press conference announcing the result of the Egyptian–Israeli peace conference at Camp David. Anyway, the big winners at the Emmy Awards were *All in the Family* and *Holocaust*, with the individual winners including Bette Midler, Carroll O'Connor, Jean Stapleton, Michael Moriarty, Ed Asner, Sada Thompson and Robert Vaughn. Perhaps appropriately Johnny Carson's *The Tonight Show*, in its seventeenth year, received its first-ever Emmy, when the following day it was announced that Carson would be the sole MC for the 1979 Academy Awards.

Only six years old, the American Film Institute's Life Achievement Award has gained much the same respect which the Academy Awards hold in the collective eyes of the film industry. On 6 March, at the Beverly Hilton, Henry Fonda followed in the illustrious footsteps of John Ford, James Cagney, Orson Welles, William Wyler and Bette Davis, as the sixth recipient of the Award. On hand to pay tribute to him were a host of Hollywood stars, including Barbara Stanwyck, Bette Davis, Charlton Heston, Gregory Peck, James Stewart, Lucille Ball, Richard Widmark, Richard Benjamin, Kirk Douglas, Richard Burton, Lillian Gish, James Garner, Ron Howard, Dorothy McGuire, Lloyd Nolan and Jack Lemmon. Lemmon eulogised

A group portrait of the winners from
the first Academy awards. Left to
right: Unidentified, Richard Arlen,
Unidentified, Douglas Fairbanks,
Benjamin Glazer, Janet Gaynor, Karl
Struss, Frank Borzage, Joseph
Farnham, Lewis Milestone, William
Cameron Menzies and Unidentified.

Fonda as 'the definitive American actor', but the 72-year-old star modestly noted, 'It's not how good you are, but how long you last.' Peter and Jane Fonda, along with the rest of the family, gave the evening a homely touch, despite the *de rigueur* black ties and Institute pomposity. Politics were not mentioned, but Henry Fonda did take the opportunity to recall his father, who would have replied to daughter Jane's critics, 'Shut up! She's perfect.'

The Los Angeles International Film Exposition, affectionately known as 'Filmex', is a year older than the AFI's Life Achievement Award and, like the AFI event, has been gaining yearly in stature and recognition. The 1978 Filmex programme lasted for twenty-three days in April, presenting the American premières of forty-two films, screening more than 150 features, and saluting personalities as varied as Roger Corman, Olivia de Havilland, Walter Lantz and Norman Jewison. The somewhat silly forty-eight-hour film marathon was this year, quite appropriately, devoted to Oscar-winning features and shorts. The festivities, which really are far too long and totally exhausting, opened with the première of *F.I.S.T.* and closed with the première of Burt Reynolds' *The End*.

Perhaps the high spot of this year's Filmex was the series titled 'Treasures from the Museum of Modern Art Film Archives', which included such rare, as far as Los Angeles is concerned, items as Raoul Walsh's first feature, *Regeneration* (1915), *Hail the Woman* (1921), *Souls for Sale* (1923) and Blanche Sweet's *Anna Christie* (1923). The greatest moment in the 1978 Filmex and one of the finest moments in the entire history of the festival was the presentation of an original nitrate print of D. W. Griffith's *Broken Blossoms*, with a full orchestra, under the direction of Fred Steiner, playing the original score. The harshest critic could not help but be moved by that evening's film, and I doubt whether Lillian Gish has received a more genuinely enthusiastic standing ovation than she received that night. The Directors Guild kicked off this year's Hollywood tributes on 1 July with a salute to veteran director David Butler, who has been turning out popular entertainment from *Sunny Side Up* in 1929 to television series of the fifties and sixties such as *Wagon Train* and *Bachelor Father*. A genuinely warm and friendly individual, who has never claimed his films to be works of art, Butler was greeted by friends and colleagues who included Will Rogers Jr, Shirley Temple, Bob Hope, Jane Withers, Buddy Ebsen, Jetta Goudal, Margaret O'Brien, George O'Brien, Jack Haley Sr and Dorothy Lamour. Introducing the programme, King Vidor emulated John Wayne in a current American television commercial by commenting, 'I've done one or two things in my life of which I'm not proud, but this isn't one of them.' John Cromwell and

Director David Butler meets old friends Jetta Goudal, art director and interior decorator Harold Grieve, Jane Withers and cinematographer Karl Struss.

Clarence Brown had received similar tributes from the Directors Guild in 1977.

The Academy of Motion Picture Arts and Sciences commenced a series of tributes to its past Honorary Oscar winners, with salutes to Groucho Marx, Pete Smith, Yakima Canutt, the 'Andy Hardy' series and Deanna Durbin. Coordinated by Anthony Slide, the tributes featured film clips, in some cases entire features and shorts, and panel discussions.

Needless to say, it was the Groucho Marx evening which brought out the crowds, with the Academy's 1,100 seat theatre filled to capacity. George Burns, opening the programme in his own inimitable and impeccable fashion, recalled, 'At a table there was about eight or ten of us. And somebody said to me, "George, who do you think is the funniest?" And I said, "Oh, the master, Charlie Chaplin." And Groucho resented that. He said, "Chaplin isn't the funniest man. I'm the funniest." I said, "Well, in that case I must be the funniest man in the world, because I'm funnier than you are." ' Following clips from *Animal Crackers, Horse Feathers, Monkey Business, A Night at the Opera, A Day at the Races* and *Love Happy*, together with a delightful sequence from Groucho's television series, *You Bet Your Life,* in which Phyllis Diller made her début, Fay Kanin moderated a panel discussion with Groucho's son, Arthur, Nat Perrin, Bronislau Kaper, John Guedel, who produced *You Bet Your Life,* and Morrie Ryskind. Ryskind, one of the great names in the field of humorous writing for stage and screen, who worked on *The Cocoanuts, Animal Crackers, A Night at the Opera* and *Room Service,* felt that not enough credit had been given to the Marx Brothers' writers, and insisted that much of Groucho's 'ad-libbing' was not ad-libbing at all but merely Groucho's following the script.

Yakima Canutt received his Honorary Academy Award in 1967, 'for achievements as a stuntman and for developing safety devices to protect stuntmen everywhere'. His fame is legendary. Not only was Yak one of the greatest stuntmen of all time—witness his amazing feat in John Ford's *Stagecoach*—but one of the film industry's finest second-unit

George Burns introducing the Groucho Marx tribute.

The distinguished humorous writer, Morrie Ryskind, at the Academy's tribute to Groucho Marx.

Gil Perkins, Yakima Canutt and Spencer Gordon Bennet reminisce with Charlton Heston about the early days of stunting at the Academy's tribute to Yakima Canutt.

directors, responsible for the action sequences in *Spartacus, El Cid, The Fall of the Roman Empire, Khartoum, A Man Called Horse, Rio Lobo* and, of course, the chariot race in the 1959 *Ben Hur*. The star of that film, Charlton Heston, was on hand to moderate the evening's proceedings, and director William Wyler was a surprise guest who paid tribute to Yakima Canutt's work, as did stuntmen Gil Perkins and Jack Williams and director Spencer Gordon Bennet.

Of the chariot race in *Ben Hur*, Heston recalled, 'The more chariots that got on the track, the more nervous I got about it, and finally I said to Yak one day, "You know, Yak, this is a pretty hot team, and with all the other chariots I don't know if I'm going to be able to cut this when we get to shooting it. It's going to be a heck of a problem." He said, "Look, Chuck, you just drive the chariot, I'll guarantee you're going to win the damn race."'

Yakima Canutt's advice to would-be stuntmen? 'You've got to remember to keep breathing.'

In 1932, Walt Disney received a Special Academy Award for the creation of Mickey Mouse, and on the occasion of the Mouse's fiftieth birthday the Academy was one of the places where tribute was paid to Mickey, with a screening of several of his classic cartoons including *Steamboat Willie* (1928), *Mickey's Gala Premiere* (1933) and *The Band Concert* (1935), with a commentary by veteran Disney animator Ward Kimball. On 13 November, Mickey Mouse became the first cartoon character to be honoured with a star on Hollywood Boulevard's Walk of Fame. That same day, Mickey left Los Angeles for a train trip across country—legend has it that Disney thought up the mouse character while travelling on the railroad—which was to include a tribute at the Library of Congress in Washington, DC, and a birthday party hosted by Amy Carter at the White House. It is doubtful whether any human film star could have generated the love and affection shown to Mickey Mouse on his golden anniversary. If anything typified the glamour, the excitement and the frenzied fan worship which was, and still is, Hollywood, it was the auction of some of Judy Garland's belongings on 27 November. Celebrities and fans, paying $25.00 just for the privilege of attending, bid outrageously for items such as Judy's personal scrapbook from *The Wizard of Oz* ($6,000); a photograph of President Kennedy autographed to Judy Garland ($5,750); the star's black silk jacket ($3,000); her personal microphone ($1,900), and her 1953 Mercedes-Benz ($60,000). The Hollywoodland Sign was erected in 1923 on Mount Lee, overlooking Hollywood Boulevard, to promote a real-estate development. The 'land' part of the Sign disappeared in the early thirties, and through the years the Sign had gradually deteriorated, while various efforts to restore it had been aborted through lack of funds

On the occasion of his fiftieth birthday, Mickey Mouse poses with veteran Disney animator Ward Kimball and screenwriter Fay Kanin, the first Vice-President of the Academy of Motion Picture Arts and Sciences.

and lack of interest on the part of the city of Los Angeles.

Not until 1978, and the seventy-fifth anniversary of the city of Hollywood, was the Hollywood Chamber of Commerce able to raise the necessary quarter of a million dollars needed for a new Sign. Nine individuals, including *Playboy* publisher Hugh Hefner, former cowboy turned Hollywood businessman Gene Autry, rock singer Alice Cooper and entertainer Andy Williams, each put up the money for one letter of the new Sign. Alice Cooper purchased one of the 'O's, and vowed he would drop an 'O' from his own name and be known as Alice Coper until the new Sign was built.

The new Hollywood Sign was to be unveiled on Saturday, 11 November as part of a television spectacular celebrating Hollywood's diamond jubilee. Unfortunately, the weather had other plans. High winds prevented a curtain from keeping the Sign covered, and torrential rain all but ruined the evening. Yvonne De Carlo had the dubious distinction of singing 'We're Still Here' at the base of the Hollywood Sign between showers, and she somehow managed to carry it off. Most people agreed that they were pleased the Hollywood Sign was back, looking in its prime again, but that they could have done without the accompanying festivities. The 1978 Hollywood year, to all intents and purposes, ended on 26 November with the annual Christmas Parade along Hollywood Boulevard, the largest parade in the forty-seven-

A composite shot showing the old Hollywood Sign, Mount Low minus the Sign, and the building of the new Hollywood Sign.

The building of the original Hollywood Sign in 1923. Two Mack Sennett starlets pose atop the tractor. It was the comedy producer's intention to build a mansion above the Sign.

year history of the event. Bob Hope, also celebrating his seventy-fifth birthday, was the Grand Marshall, and stars on hand included Angie Dickinson, Dorothy Lamour, Buddy Ebsen and Jane Withers.

The Awards aside, Hollywood landmarks remain much the same. There are few, if any, Hollywood premières any more; the film producers prefer the theatres of Westwood, with its close proximity to the UCLA campus, for their openings. But there are still crowds waiting outside the Pacific Dome on Sunset Boulevard and the Paramount on Hollywood Boulevard. The venerable Pantages Theatre, one of the last great super cinemas in Los Angeles, has become a home for theatrical productions, bringing new audiences to Hollywood and joining the ranks of other legitimate theatres in the neighbourhood, the Huntington Hartford and the Aquarius (which was once the Earl Carroll Theatre). During the last weeks of 1978, the Huntington

Hartford presented an English-style review, *Why Not Tonite?*, starring Hermione Baddeley, which was a disastrous flop despite a brilliant *tour de force* performance by Miss Baddeley.

Grauman's Chinese Theatre is now Mann's Chinese Theatre (named after owner Ted Mann, whose wife is actress Rhonda Fleming) but, thankfully, it has suffered no other changes aside from its name. The tourists still flock to see the footprints in the cement of its forecourt, the only recent additions to which have been R2D2 and C3PO from *Star Wars*.

The summer concerts at the Hollywood Bowl are still as popular as ever. The famous Brown Derby is still open on Vine Street. Musso-Frank Grill, the oldest restaurant in Hollywood, dating back to 1919, is as crowded and as over-priced as it has always been. The Hollywood Roosevelt Hotel, where the first Academy Awards were held on 16

May 1929, is still open for business, albeit the façade is looking a trifle woebegone. Those tourists who look carefully enough can still find nostalgia, such as the old Chaplin studios at Sunset and LaBrea, now the headquarters of A & M Records, or Don the Beachcomber's, its décor unchanged from when Joan Crawford and Ava Gardner, among others, spent their evenings there.

Hollywood, the place, has none of the glamour it once symbolised. Hollywood Boulevard has never seen poorer days, and one will look in vain for stars along its sidewalks or in its shops, restaurants and hotels. But perhaps times are changing for the better, and 1978 will mark a resurgence in the fortunes of the city of Hollywood. All those who have loved it at some time, and all those throughout the world to whom it is a name signifying the glory of the film industry, will join in wishing it a happy birthday and a happy recovery.

Jane Withers, the Honorary Councilwoman for Hollywood, poses with W. C. Fields's hat beside part of a seventy-fifth anniversary of Hollywood exhibition at the Academy of Motion Picture Arts and Sciences.

What A Carry On!

With the 30th 'Carry On' film released, the 31st is already planned to make the all-time series record even more remarkable

by James Cameron-Wilson

Bugsy Malone made more money in Britain than any previous British film, yet it still didn't get its production money back in this country. So how on earth did producer Peter Rogers and director Gerald Thomas manage to plan, film and sell *thirty* British comedies as indigenous to England as fish 'n' chips, Morecambe and Wise and saucy seaside-postcards? 'It's surprising the number of people who make the most successful films of all time,' Rogers told me over a cup of hot Dorchester coffee, 'and I certainly wouldn't try to analyse the success of the Carry Ons. They are only successful because audiences still go to see them, and I think if the audience knew why, they wouldn't go any more.'

It all began in 1958 when it was decided that the tone of a film entitled *The Ball Boys,* about British army conscription, was too serious. So they turned the film into a riotous comedy under the new title of *Carry on Sergeant,* at a modest cost of £72,000, with a cast comprising Eric Barker, Dora Bryan, Kenneth Connor, Shirley Eaton, William Hartnell, Charles Hawtrey, Bob Monkhouse, Bill Owen and the inimitable Kenneth Williams. There was nothing remarkable about it, it didn't break any new barriers of sexual awareness or cross any frontiers of unprecedented comedy technique; it just happened to have the right appeal at the right time. Despite its failure at the American box-office (probably because the subject-matter was too parochial for American audiences) Rogers decided to produce a sequel based on another serious project of his, about nursing. And so with Connor, Eaton, Hawtrey, Hattie Jacques, Terence Longdon, Owen and Williams again in the cast, and with the addition of Leslie Phillips, Joan Sims, Susan Stephen and Wilfrid Hyde White, and an improved budget of £75,000, Rogers went on to produce *Carry on Nurse* before the year was out. Not only was this second effort as successful in England as *Carry on Sergeant,* but it ran in America for two and a half years!

By this time Rogers began to think he had enough potential material to get him through another half-dozen films; and so a new comedy series was born. But nobody was aware that the Carry Ons were to continue well into the sixties, through the seventies and into the eighties! It was soon to be a case of: eat your heart out, Charlie Chan, Andy Hardy and even the ultra-prolific Old Mother Riley! A year later, the fourth Carry On, *Carry on Constable,* was joined by Sidney James (or just Sid James), who was to become the major star of the series if only through his top billing in the largest number of features. With the advent of 1962, *Carry on Cruising* found itself as the first Carry On in colour, and the series evened out into a more or less predictable run of comedies, only notable for their gradual progression into the realms of the double entendre.

In 1976 the Carry Ons met with

their first confrontation with the censor, when James Ferman insisted that *Carry on England* should carry a double 'A' certificate. But after a lot of fuss, five frames of a naked breast were removed and the film returned to its intended single 'A'. But it wasn't so much the 'tits and bums' the censor objected to, as the language and the more and more frequently occurring double meanings. Lines like 'rising to the occasion' or 'unable to come' were strictly double 'A' material, though Barbara Windsor was allowed to show what she liked in the way of flesh . . . providing it was in less than five frames, of course and Kenneth Williams got away with a particularly notorious four-letter word.

After *Carry on England*, Rogers cashed in on the 'That's Entertainment' phase and produced a compilation feature called, you guessed it, *That's Carry On*. And then there was *Carry on Emmannuelle* (it had to happen), this time with an immovable double 'A'. The series had turned thirty films of age. Thirty is a dangerous age, Cynthia, but number thirty-one is already on the way. *Carry on again Nurse* will be different from the rest inasmuch as it will have a brand-new cast—most likely to be picked from the cream of British pantomime—though the regular stars may feature in supporting cameos.

'And we can't stop at thirty-one,' Rogers exclaimed, 'it's such an uneven number. It'll be much better to stop at thirty-five.' Or forty-five?

Charles Hawtrey, Kenneth Williams and Hattie Jacques in *Carry on Doctor*.

Hattie Jacques, Barbara Windsor and Madeleine Smith in *Carry on Matron*.

Sidney James and Barbara Windsor in *Carry on Abroad*.

Or fifty-five?

The *Confession* films posed no serious threat, and it was admitted that if the *Carry Ons* had exploited their nudity, the *Confessions* couldn't have existed. And the *Carry Ons* probably won't get much further anyway, any more than the *Doctor* films did in the sixties, until they turned to television.

And the *Carry Ons* even captured that medium with their two successful TV specials going under the name of *Carry on Christmas*. Is there no end to the *Carry On* empire?

So, looking back over the twenty-one years, what were the lows, highs and changes?

Carry On Nurse, to this day, is still probably the most financially successful, though it will be years until one can fully measure the success of the subsequent returns, what with the complication of overseas sales, television sales, etc, all to be taken into account. *Carry on Cleo* was a turning-point, with both a successful run in the West End and a sudden acceptance by those ever-superior critics. And *Carry on England* was probably a low in terms of financial profit, but not enough to stem the flow of a myriad of upcoming sequels. Charles Hawtrey, Bill Owen and Leslie Phillips passed out of the series, and Sidney James and Peter Butterworth passed away completely. Barbara Windsor walked out of the last one because of the new extent of the nudity; and both Suzanne Danielle's and Kenneth

Williams' hind-quarters were bared, but surely not enough to make the BBC blush? And naturally the budgets increased from film to film, with *Carry on Emmannuelle* costing an inflated £320,000: too big a budget for the film to make back its money in England alone. But then there aren't the cinemas anymore. When *Carry on Sergeant* was made, there were some 3,000 independent picture houses in Great Britain alone, and now there are just a miserly 300. At most, Britain can only corner 3% of the current world market.

And so to the stars: the performers who made those terrible lines sound funny; the faces behind the double takes, the cast that worked so well together.

It is rather surprising that Sidney James endured so well as the star of the most successful series of films of all time. He couldn't knock out cracks like tennis balls *à la* Cary Grant and he couldn't make a telephone directory sound as funny as Frankie Howerd could. Perhaps he was just more identifiable as the ordinary, blue-collar chap in the pub. What happened to him happened to half the dads of the children who saw the films. But for me it was his laugh. Invariably the immense and homely Hattie Jacques would stand in as his long-suffering wife and be the butt of most of his jokes, and more especially of his laugh. In one film he said quite simply (jerking his thumb at Miss Jacques): 'This is my wife.' And laughed. It was one of the funniest pieces of comedy timing I

have ever seen.

A more recognisably favourite caricature must be Kenneth Williams: all nostrils, nasal entanglement and contorted elbows. Apologetic, snivelling and constantly taken by surprise, his was one of the most outrageous characterisations ever conceived, and as such he would carry it boldly into the public eye at both opening ceremonies and radio shows alike.

Joan Sims was more often than not the epitome of the prim, proper, and overweight, yet sexually repressed, matron; Barbara Windsor the bouncy, cheeky, exceedingly common girl who'd lost her way; Charles Hawtrey the bespectacled, skinny man darting about the general fracas like an inquisitive dormouse; Bernard Bresslaw the six-foot-six-inch 'heavy'; Peter Butterworth the fumbling, absent-minded, yet kindly gentleman who appeared to be perpetually lost; the coarse, diminutive Kenneth Connor; Jim Dale, Jack Douglas, Liz Fraser, Leslie Phillips, Patsy Rowlands, June Whitfield—and even Beryl Reid, Phil Silvers and Elke Sommer in one-off guest appearances.

But was it the cast that kept the series going for as long as it has (*Carry on England*, with Connor as the only regular favourite, didn't catch on), or was it its pre-sold reputation? We all enjoy a laugh, and the bluer the funnier, and while the children can roar at the custard-pie antics, adults can smile knowingly at the plethora of double entendres.

What A Carry On!

You know the sort of thing: Henry VIII to his tailor:
'I need a bit more length in my hose.'
'Oh, My Lord, you are too modest.' Et cetera.
Then, of course, popularity breeds popularity, and parents began to appreciate that the *Carry Ons* were neither pornographic nor violent, yet essentially English. And despite their Englishness they still did fantastic business in French-speaking Canada, Portugal, Singapore . . .
Part of their longevity must lie in Rogers's economic sense. He has always kept the budget down to a minimum: rises have only accommodated inflation and have not reflected success. When you consider that producer Ilya Salkind announced that if *Superman* only made $80 million it would be a financial disaster, you realise that it doesn't take long for a *Carry On* to get its money back in comparison. The entire gross of all the *Carry Ons* put together probably wouldn't amount to the budget of one Salkind film. And, like old soldiers, the *Carry Ons* will never die. If they did, we'd only have James Bond and the Hammer horror films to turn to; and with the threat that future Bond films will be shot outside England, and the flow of Hammer films practically at a halt, we would have no staple film diet left.
You may prefer the sophistication of Bond or you may, like most of the critics, enjoy kicking the *Carry Ons* for their lack of artistry. But, like home, it's what you kick most that will remain. The British film industry can always rely on the *Carry Ons* for production. And they may be vulgar, common and basic, but it's because of these that we mustn't knock them. Remember, the *Sun* sells more copies than any other newspaper.

Sid James, Jacki Piper and Richard O'Callaghan in *Carry on at your Convenience.*

Peter Butterworth and Charles Hawtrey in *Carry on up the Khyber.*

Patsy Rowlands and Kenneth
Williams in *Carry on Loving*.

Charles Hawtrey (as Sir Roger de
Loggerley) in *Carry on Henry*.

Judy Geeson and Patrick Mower in
Carry on England.

THE CARRY ON FILMS

All the following films have been
produced by Peter Rogers, and
directed by Gerald Thomas.

Carry on Sergeant (1958) with Bob Monkhouse,
William Hartnell, Kenneth Williams, Charles
Hawtrey, Shirley Eaton, Eric Barker, Dora Bryan,
Bill Owen, Kenneth Connor.

Carry on Nurse (1958) with Eaton, Connor,
Hawtrey, Hattie Jacques, Terence Longdon, Owen,
Leslie Phillips, Joan Sims, Susan Stephen, Williams,
Wilfrid Hyde White.

Carry on Teacher (1959) with Connor, Hawtrey,
Phillips, Sims, Williams, Jacques, Rosalind Knight,
Ted Ray.

Carry on Constable (1959) with Sidney James,
Barker, Connor, Hawtrey, Williams, Phillips, Sims,
Jacques, Eaton.

Carry on Regardless (1960) with James, Connor,
Hawtrey, Sims, Williams, Owen, Liz Fraser,
Longdon.

Carry on Cruising (1962) with James, Williams,
Connor, Fraser, Dilys Laye, Esma Cannon, Lance
Percival.

Carry on Cabby (1963) with James, Jacques,
Connor, Hawtrey, Cannon, Fraser.

Carry on Jack (1963) with Bernard Cribbins, Juliet
Mills, Hawtrey, Williams, Donald Houston, Cecil
Parker.

Carry on Spying (1964) with Williams, Cribbins,
Hawtrey, Barbara Windsor.

Carry on Cleo (1964) with James, Williams,
Connor, Hawtrey, Sims, Jim Dale, Amanda Barrie.

Carry on Cowboy (1965) with James, Williams,
Sims, Dale, Percy Herbert, Angela Douglas,
Hawtrey.

Carry on Screaming (1966) with Harry H.
Corbett, Williams, Fenella Fielding, Sims, Hawtrey,
Dale, A. Douglas, Peter Butterworth.

Don't Lose your Head (1966) with James,
Williams, Dale, Hawtrey, Sims, A. Douglas.

Follow that Camel (1967) with Phil Silvers,
Williams, Dale, Hawtrey, Sims, A. Douglas.

Carry on Doctor (1967) with Frankie Howerd,
James, Williams, Hawtrey, Dale, Windsor, Jacques,
Sims, Anita Harris, Bernard Bresslaw, Butterworth.

Carry on up the Khyber (1968) with James,
Williams, Hawtrey, Roy Castle, Sims, A. Douglas,
Terry Scott, Bresslaw, Butterworth.

Carry on Camping (1968) with James, Williams,
Hawtrey, Sims, Scott, Jacques, Windsor, Bresslaw,
Butterworth.

What A Carry On!

Carry on again Doctor (1969) with James, Williams, Hawtrey, Dale, Sims, Windsor, Jacques.

Carry on up the Jungle (1969) with Howerd, James, Hawtrey, Sims, Scott, Connor, Bresslaw, Jacki Piper.

Carry on Loving (1970) with James, Williams, Hawtrey, Sims, Jacques, Scott, Richard O'Callaghan, Bresslaw, Piper, Imogen Hassall.

Carry on Henry (1970) with James, Williams, Hawtrey, Sims, Scott, Windsor, Connor.

Carry on at your Convenience (1971) with James, Williams, Hawtrey, Sims, Jacques, Bresslaw, Kenneth Cope.

Carry on Matron (1971) with James, Williams, Jacques, Hawtrey, Windsor, Scott, Sims, Cope, Bresslaw, Connor.

Carry on Abroad (1972) with James, Williams, Hawtrey, Sims, Connor, Butterworth, Jimmy Logan, Windsor, June Whitfield, Jacques, Derek Francis, Sally Geeson, Carol Hawkins, John Clive, Jack Douglas.

Carry on Girls (1973) with James, Sims, Connor, Jacques, Bresslaw, Whitfield, Butterworth, Patsy Rowlands, Logan.

Carry on Dick (1974), with James, Windsor, Williams, Jacques, Bresslaw, Sims, Connor, Butterworth, J. Douglas.

Carry on Behind (1975) with Elke Sommer, Williams, Sims, Bresslaw, J. Douglas, Windsor, Davies, Connor, Fraser, Butterworth, Rowlands.

Carry on England (1976) with Connor, Davies, Patrick Mower, Judy Geeson.

That's Carry On (1977) compilation feature.

Carry on Emmannuelle (1978) with Suzanne Danielle, Williams, Connor, J. Douglas, Sims, Butterworth, Larry Dann, Beryl Reid, Henry McGee.

Kenneth Connor and Liz Fraser in *Carry on Cabby*.

Jim Dale and Kenneth Williams in *Carry on Cowboy*.

Carry On newcomer Suzanne Danielle and Howard Nelson in *Carry on Emmannuelle*, 30th and latest in the long *Carry On* line; and not the last by any means—*Carry On* No 31 is already being planned.

Awards and Festivals

With the continued proliferation of International Film Awards and Film Festivals of every kind it is no longer possible to pretend that the following is a complete record of the year's international prizes. But most, if not all, of the more important ones are given, along with some of the more interesting minor and specialised ones.

Cairo Film Festival—25 September–4 October 1978
Golden Nefertiti for Best Film: THE MAIN ACTOR, directed by Reinhard Hauff (West Germany)
Silver Nefertiti: TRAVEL OF THE STONE (Iran)
Special Jury Prize to GOOD FOR NOTHING, directed by Bernhard Sinkel (West Germany)
Jury Prize for Best Actor: MAHMOUD YASSINE

Karlovy Vary Festival—July 1978
Grand Prix (shared): SHADOWS OF A HOT SUMMER—Frantisek Vlacil (Czechoslovakia) and WHITE BIM WITH A BLACK EAR—Stanislav Rostotski (USSR)
Special Jury Prize (shared): A VILLAGE STORY—Mrinal Sen (India) and AUTOPSY OF CONSPIRACY—Mohamed Slim Riad (Algeria)
Other Prizes: IRISHMAN—Donald Crombie (Australia); FLIGHT—Roland Graef (German Democratic Republic); THE SAILOR'S RETURN—Jack Gold (GB); WHEN IT RAINS AND SHINES TOGETHER—Ferenc Andras (Hungary); US—Laila Mikkelsen (Norway)

Rose of Lidice Prize: OPERATION STADION—Dusan Vukotic (Yugoslavia)
Best Actor (shared): GIULIANO GEMMA in *The Iron Prefect* (Italy) and PETER FABER in *Doctor Vlimmen* (Holland)
Best Actress (shared): MARISOL in *A Few Days of the Past* (Spain) and MARIE-JOSE NAT in *A Simple Past* (France)

Locarno Film Festival—3–13 August 1978
Best Film—Golden Leopard: THE IDLERS OF THE FERTILE VALLEY (Greece), directed by Niko Panaytopoulos Silver Leopard: ROOM WITH A VIEW ON THE SEA (Poland), directed by Janusz Zaorsky Bronze Leopard: MELANIE MAYRON in Claudia Weill's *Girlfriends* (USA)

Montreal Film Festival—5 September 1978
Grand Prix des Amériques: LIGABUE, directed by Salvatore Nocita (Italy)
Premier Prix de Jury: IT IS DANGEROUS TO LEAN OUT OF THE WINDOW (Hungary)
Deuxième Prix de Jury: LA CIUTAT CREMADA (Spain)
Best Actress: GLENDA JACKSON in *Stevie* (GB)
Best Actor: FLAVIO PUCCI in *Ligabue* (Italy)
Prix de Presse Internationale: TYLER, directed by Ralph Thomas (Canada)
Grand Prix de Montréal for Shorts: APRÈS LA VIE (Canada)
Prix de Jury for shorts: PHENOME (France)

Awards and Festivals

The Festival of Animated Films at Ottawa—September 1978
Grand Prix: LA TRAVERSÉE DE L'ATLANTIQUE À LA RAME, directed by Jean-François Laguionie (France)
Special Jury Prize: THE METAMORPHOSES OF MR SAMSA, directed by Caroline Leaf (Canada)
Jury Awards to: WHY ME?, directed by Janet Perlman (Canada); POSTANOVKA & HYPOTEZA, directed by Henri Koulav (Bulgaria); RAPID EYE MOVEMENTS, directed by Jeff Carpenter (USA); WHEN I'M RICH, directed by Derek Phillips, Stan Hayward and Ted Rockley (GB)

San Sebastian Film Festival—September 1978
Golden Shell Award: ALAMBRISTA, directed by Robert Young (USA)
Silver Shell Award (shared): DOSSIER 55, directed by Michel Deville (France) and OLYAN MINT OTTHON, directed by Marta Meszaros (Hungary)
Best Director: MANUEL GUTIÉRREZ for *Somnambulists* (Spain)
Best Actor: JOSÉ SACRISTAN in *Autumn Flower* (Spain)
Best Actress: CAROL BURNETT in *A Wedding* (USA)
Best Spanish Language Film: THE PEDRALBES MURDERER, a Gonzalo Herralde documentary
Special Jury Prize: THE PLACE WITHOUT LIMITS, directed by Arturo Ripstein (Mexico)
Best Short Film: THE AGE OF SILENCE, directed by Gabriel Blanco (Spain)
International Catholic Film Award: ALAMBRISTA (USA)

Chicago Film Festival—14 November 1978
Gold Hugo: TO AN UNKNOWN GOD, directed by Jaime Chavarri (Spain)
Special Gold Hugo Jury Prize: A QUITE ORDINARY LIFE, directed by Imre Gyongyossy and Barna Kabay (Hungary)
Silver Hugo: THE KINGDOM OF NAPLES, directed by Werner Schroeter (Germany)
Bronze Hugos: MY WAY HOME, directed by Bill Douglas (GB); MEETINGS WITH ANNA, directed by Chantal Akerman (France)
Best First Feature (Silver Hugo): IDLERS OF THE FERTILE VALLEY, directed by Nicos Panayatopoulos (Greece)
Gold Plaque: UNFINISHED SCORE FOR PLAYER PIANO, directed by Nikita Mihalkov (USSR)
Silver Plaque: WHY NOT? directed by Coline Serreau (France)
Special Gold Plaque: JOHN CARPENTER for promise of talent in his direction of *Halloween* and *Assault on Precinct 13* (USA)

The 11th International Festival of Fantasy and Terror Films at Sitges—October 1978
Best Film: LONG WEEKEND, directed by Colin Eggleston (Australia)
Best Director: RICHARD FRANKIN, for *Patrick* (Australia)
Best Actress: CAMILLE KEATON in *Day of the Woman* (USA)
Best Actor: JOHN HARGREAVES in *Long Weekend* (Australia)
Best Screenplay: MARIO BAVA and GIUSEPPE MACCARI for *Shock* (Italy)
Best Photography: JAROSLAV KUCERA for *Adela Hasn't Supped Yet* (Czechoslovakia)

The Asian Film Festival at Sydney, Australia—October 1978
Best Film: RITES OF MAY, produced by Manuel de León (Philippines)
Best Actor: KEN TAKAKURA in *The Yellow Handkerchief*
Best Actress (shared): CHARO SANTOS in *Rites of May* and KIM JA OK for *Miss O's Apartment* (South Korea)
Best Direction: MASAHIRO SHINODA for *Melody in Gray* (Japan)
The Award for Overall Accomplishment: BELLS OF DEATH, produced by Tan Sri Runme Shaw (Malaysia)

The 21st Annual Australian Film Institute Awards—August 1978
Best Film: NEWSFRONT
Best Actor: BILL HUNTER in *Newsfront*
Best Actress: ANGELA PUNCH in *The Chant of Jimmie Blacksmith*
Best Supporting Actor: RAY BARRETT in *The Chant of Jimmie Blacksmith*
Best Supporting Actress: ANGELA PUNCH in the same film
Best Director: PHILLIP NOYCE for *Newsfront*
Best Cinematography: RUSSELL BOYD for *The Last Wave*
Best Editing: JOHN SCOTT for *Newsfront*
Best Original Screenplay: ANNE BROOKSBANK, BOB ELLIS and PHILLIP NOYCE for *Newsfront*
Jury Award for Best Film to: MOUTH TO MOUTH, directed by John Guigan

Australian Film Awards—October 1978
Best Film: NEWSFRONT

Best Direction: PHILLIP NOYCE for *Newsfront*
Best Actor: BILL HUNTER in *Newsfront*
Best Actress: GERALDINE FITZGERALD for *The Mango Tree*
Best Supporting Actor: CHRIS HAYWOOD in *Newsfront*
Best Supporting Actress: RUTH CRACKNELL in *The Chant of Jimmie Blacksmith*
Best Screenplay: PHILLIP NOYCE, ANNE BROOKSBANK and BOB ELLIS for *Newsfront*
Best New Talent: TOMMY LEWIS in *The Chant of Jimmie Blacksmith*

Mannheim Festival—November 1978
Grand Prize: ALYAM, ALYAM, directed by Ahmed el Maanouni (Morocco)
The Mayor's Prize: THEATRE GIRLS, directed by Claire Pollak and Kim Longinotto (GB)
Josef von Sternberg Prize: THE FLAT JUNGLE, directed by Johann van der Keuken (Holland)
Special Jury Prize: MATERNALE, directed by Giovanni Gagliardo (Italy)

Nyon Shorts Festival—November 1978
Golden Sesterce: THE MADONNA AND THE VOLCANO, directed by Mike Radford (GB)
Silver Sesterce: WITH BABIES AND BANNERS, directed by Lorraine Gray for Women's Labour History Film Project (USA)
Silver Sesterce: THE FLAT JUNGLE, directed by Johann van der Keuken (Holland)
Silver Sesterce: TIERRA Y LIBERTAD,
directed by Maurice Bulbulian (Mexico/Canada)
Special Jury Prizes: THEATRE GIRLS, directed by Claire Pollak and Kim Longinotto (GB) and CHRONIQUE DE LA VIE QUOTIDIENNE (8 TV episodes re-edited into one 5-hour documentary by Jacques Leduc and his National Film Board of Canada team)

Taormina Festival—August 1978
Grand Prix: THE KINGDOM OF NAPLES, directed by Werner Schroeter (West Germany)
Special Jury Award: TIES, directed by Istvan Gaal (Hungary)
Best Direction: PHILLIP NOYCE for his *Newsfront* (Australia) (also winning the award for the Best First Film)
Best Actor: REGINALDO FARIAS in *Lucio Flavio*, directed by Hector Babenco (Brazil)
Best Actress: ELENA KORENOVAIN in *Asya*, directed by Josif Heifitz (USSR)
Special Mention (Jury's Certificate of Merit): REASONS OF STATE, directed by André Cayatte (France)

Paris Film Festival—October 1978
Grand Prix: BLUE COLLAR, directed by Paul Schrader (USA)
Best Actress: GERALDINE CHAPLIN in *Remember My Name*, directed by Alan Rudolph (USA)
Best Actor: NINO MANFREDI in *In the Name of the Pope King*, directed by Luigi Magni (Italy)
Best Director: CHANTAL AKERMAN for *The Meeting of Anna*, a Belgian/French/German co-
production
International Critics' Award: KNIFE IN THE HEAD, directed by Werner Hauff (West Germany)
French Critics' Award: KNIFE IN THE HEAD

The 1978 German Film Awards—Film Strips in Gold and Silver
Gold: THE GLASS CELL, directed by Hans W. Geisendoerfer, based on the Patricia Highsmith novel
Silvers: Theodor Kotulla's DEATH IS MY TRADE; Wim Wenders's THE AMERICAN FRIEND; Niklaus Schilling's RHEINGOLD; Walter Bockmayer and Rolf Buehrmann's FLAMING HEARTS; Margarethe von Trotta's THE SECOND AWAKENING OF CHRISTA KLAGE, and Bernhard Sinkel's THE GOOD-FOR-NOTHING
Gold for Director: RAINER WERNER FASSBINDER for his *Despair*
Silver for Non-fictional Features: LUTZ MOMMARTZ for *The Garden of Eden* and ELFI MIKESCH for *I often think of Hawaii*

Italy's David di Donatello Award Winners for 1977–8—presented in Florence in July 1978
Best Film: Julia and Michael Phillips' CLOSE ENCOUNTERS OF THE THIRD KIND
Best Direction (shared): RIDLEY SCOTT for *The Duellists* and HERBERT ROSS for *Goodbye Girl*
Best Actress (shared): SIMONE SIGNORET in *Madame Rosa* and JANE FONDA in *Julia*
Best Actor: RICHARD DREYFUSS in *The Goodbye Girl*

Best Italian Film (shared): Franco Committeri's IN THE NAME OF THE POPE-KING and G. H. Lucari's I AM THE LAW
Best Direction: ETTORE SCOLA for *A Special Day*
Best Actress (shared): MARIANGELA MELATO in *The Cat* and SOPHIA LOREN in *A Special Day*
Best Actor: ARMANDO TROVAIOLI for *Wife-Mistress*

Leipzig Shorts and Documentary Festival—December 1978
Golden Doves: Malik Kajumov's PARANDSHA (USSR) and Carlos Aspurua's I SPEAK TO CARACAS (Venezuela)
Premium Prizes (Golden Dove): Ghalib Shaat's THE DAY OF THE LAND (PLO) (under 35 mins) and Frank Diamond's NICARAGUA (Netherlands) (over 35 mins)
Special Jury Prize: Lydia Chagoll's IN THE NAME OF THE FUEHRER (Belgium)
Silver Doves: DOLORES IN BILBAO (Spain) (under 35 mins) (no direction credit); Carlos Alvárez's INTRODUCTION TO CAMILO (Columbia) (under 35 mins); Jekaterina Vermisheva and Leonin Machnatch's THE QUIET AMERICAN (USSR) (over 35 mins); Larry Adelman's CONTROLLING INTERESTS (USA) (over 35 mins); THOSE ARE THE WEAPONS (Mozambique) (over 35 mins) (no direction credit); Jesús Liaz's 55 BROTHERS (Cuba)
Animation Prizes: Milos Macourek, Jaroslav Doubrava and Adolf Born's FROM THE LIVES OF CHILDREN

(Czechoslovakia) and Liviusz Gyulai's NEW HOUSE TENANTS (Hungary)

Winners at the Fantastic Film Festival at Avoriaz—January 1979
Grand Prix: PATRICK, directed by Richard Franklin (Australia)
Special Jury Prize: PHANTOM, directed by Don Coscarelli (USA)
Special Mention: THE NIGHT OF THE PROWLER, directed by Jim Sharman (Australia)
Critics' Prize: HALLOWEEN, directed by John Carpenter (USA)

Some of the top Awards at the new Miami Beach Film Festival—November 1978
Gold Venus for Best Film at the Festival: ABSOLUTION, directed by Elliott Kastner (USA)
Silver Venus: THE BOSS'S SON, directed by Bobby Roth (USA)
Silver Venus for Best Short Film: NOTES ON THE POPULAR ARTS (USA)
Best Actor: RICHARD BURTON in *Absolution*
Best Actress: GERALDINE CHAPLIN in *Remember My Name*
Best Director: ANTHONY PAGE for *Absolution*
Best Supporting Actor: ADOLPH CAESAR in *The Hitter*
Best Supporting Actress: RITA MORENO in *The Boss's Son*

The London Evening News Film Awards—28 November 1978
Best Film: STAR WARS, produced by Gary Kurtz
Best Actor: ALEC GUINNESS in *Star Wars*

Best Actress: NANETTE NEWMAN in *International Velvet*
Most Promising Male Newcomer: MICHAEL JACKSON in *Sweeney 2*
Most Promising Female Newcomer: LEA BRODIE in *Warlords of Atlantis*.
Best Comedy Film: THE REVENGE OF THE PINK PANTHER
Special Award: DAVID PUTTNAM for his outstanding services to British films

The Annual Awards made by the British Academy of Film and Television Arts for 1978—March 1979
Best Film: *Julia* directed by Fred Zinnemann
Best Actor: RICHARD DREYFUSS in *The Goodbye Girl*
Best Actress: JANE FONDA in *Julia*
Best Direction: ALAN PARKER for *Midnight Express*
Best Short Factual Film: HOKUSIA AN ANIMATED SKETCHBOOK by Tony White
Best Specialised Film: TWENTY TIMES MORE LIKELY by Robert Young
Robert Flaherty Award: THE SILENT WITNESS by David Rolfe
Best Screenplay: ALVIN SARGENT for *Julia*
Best Photography: DOUGLAS SLOCOMBE for *Julia*
Best Editing: GERRY HAMBLING for *Midnight Express*
Best Soundtrack: DON MACDOUGALL, RAY WEST, BOB MINKLER and DEREK BALL for *Star Wars*.
Best Art Direction: JOE ALVES for *Close Encounters of the Third Kind*
Best Supporting Actress: GERALDINE PAGE in *Interiors*

Best Supporting Actor: JOHN HURT in *Midnight Express*
Most Promising Newcomer: CHRISTOPHER REEVE in *Superman*
Anthony Asquith Award for most original music: JOHN WILLIAMS for *Star Wars*
Michael Balcon Award for the most outstanding contribution to British Cinema: the team of technicians who produced special effects never before attempted in *Superman*
The Academy's Fellowship Award: LORD GRADE

The 'Oscars'—The 1978–9 Academy of Motion Picture Arts and Sciences Awards
Best Film: THE DEER HUNTER, directed by Michael Cimino (EMI)
Best Direction: MICHAEL CIMINO for *The Deer Hunter*
Best Actor: JON VOIGHT in *Coming Home*
Best Actress: JANE FONDA in *Coming Home*
Best Supporting Actor: CHRISTOPHER WALKEN in *The Deer Hunter*
Best Supporting Actress: MAGGIE SMITH in *California Suite*
Best Photography: NESTOR ALMENDROS for *Days of Heaven*
Best Art Direction: PAUL SYLBERT, EDWIN O'DONOVAN and GEORGE GAINES for *Heaven Can Wait*
Best Editing: PETER ZINNER for *The Deer Hunter*
Best Original Musical Score: GIORGIO MORODER for *Midnight Express*
Best Screenplay written directly for the screen: WALDO SALT and ROBERT C. JONES for *Coming Home*

Best Screenplay based on material from another medium: OLIVER STONE for *Midnight Express*
Best Costume Design: ANTHONY POWELL for *Death on the Nile*
Best Foreign Language Film: GET OUT YOUR HANDKERCHIEFS (France)
Best Sound: RICHARD PORTMAN, WILLIAM MCCAUGHEY, AARON ROCHIN and DARRIN KNIGHT for *The Deer Hunter*
Best Live-Action Short: TEENAGE FATHER
Best Animated Short: SPECIAL DELIVERY (The National Film Board of Canada)
Best Documentary Feature: SCARED STRAIGHT (Golden West TV Productions)
Best Documentary Short: THE FLIGHT OF THE GOSSAMER CONDOR (Shedd Productions)
Special Award for Life Achievement: SIR LAURENCE OLIVIER

The Fantastic Film Festival at Avoriaz—January 1979
Grand Prix: PATRICK, directed by Richard Franklin (Australia)
Special Jury Prize: PHANTOM, directed by Don Coscarelli (USA)
Special Mention: NIGHT OF THE PROWLER, directed by Jim Sharman (Australia)
Critics' Prize: HALLOWEEN, directed by John Carpenter (USA)

The 7th Annual International Festival of Short, Documentary and Animation Films at Lille—January 1979
Fiction Grand Prix: LA BOÎTE DANS LE DÉSERT, directed by Brahin Tsaki (Algeria)
Animation Grand Prix: RAPID EYE MOVEMENT, directed by Jeff Carpenter (USA)
Documentary Grand Prix: EL DOMADOR (HORSE TAMER) directed by Joaquín Cortés (Venezuela)
Special Jury Prize to GENÈSE D'UN REPAS (ORIGINS OF A MEAL) directed by Luc Mollet (France)

The result of the 1978 *Motion Picture Digest* Quigley Publications Poll, in which cinema managers all over America vote for the stars they consider draw the most patrons into their cinemas, was as follows: 1. Burt Reynolds; 2. John Travolta; 3. Richard Dreyfuss; 4. Warren Beatty; 5. Clint Eastwood; 6. Woody Allen; 7. Diane Keaton; 8. Jane Fonda; 9. Peter Sellers, 10. Barbra Streisand. Some interesting sidelights on the poll are the drop from the top spot last year to 15th place this by Sylvester Stallone; the drop of Robert Redford from 5th to 12th place, and Mel Brooks from 7th to 11th.
Not even listed in the runners-up list this time are Robert de Niro (10th last year) and Al Pacino (8th last year). The steadiest star is Clint Eastwood who since starting in 5th place in the 1968 poll (reaching the top in 1972 and 1973) has always been hovering well up in the list. There was a big rise this time by Jane Fonda, from 21st place last year to 8th this, thanks to several good performances in good films.

Releases of the Year in Detail

Introduction Note: In this section you will find details of the films released in Great Britain between 1 July 1979 and the end of June 1980. The precise dating of some of the releases is rather difficult owing to the decreasing rigidity of the release pattern; the dates given are for general release not pre-release.

I have added where possible the date of the first London showing for films on 'floating' release as this is usually the first British showing.

Because of the advance work necessary for this annual, the dates given may have changed before publication. Any that are released later than stated or are rushed into release too late for this publication will be included with a note next year. (Those pending from last year are asterisked in this year's text.)

The normal abbreviations continue to operate as follows: Dir: for Director; Pro: for Producer; Ex Pro: for Executive Producer; Pro Sup: for Production Supervisor; Co Pro: for Co-Producer; Pro Co-Ord: for Production Co-Ordinator; Ph: for Photographer; Ed: for Editor; Art: for Art Director; Pro Des: for Production Designer, and M: for Music.

Abbreviations for the names of film companies are obvious: Fox for 20th Century-Fox and UA for United Artists, etc. EMI have joined with the Fox and Warner companies for the release of their films which creates another complication; where I have the name of the particular company I have used it.

The increasing number of co-productions between countries makes it difficult to always credit the correct origin exactly. The nationality of each film is noted whenever possible; those without any mention of source are to be understood as American.

Finally, unless otherwise specified, it can be assumed that each film has been made in Technicolor or a similar colour process.

When it comes to nationality of the film you will find that this is noted wherever it is possible to give it—those films without any mention of country of origin can be taken as being American—but in these days of increasing international co-productions between two, three and even four countries it is sometimes a little difficult to sort out where the proper credit is due.

Finally, unless otherwise specified (i.e. in black-and-white), it can safely be taken that the film is made in Technicolor or some similar colour process. Note: those few films which were unexpectedly released in June 1978, and therefore not included in the last *Film Review*, are included in this year's releases with an asterisk in front of the title, e.g. *The Medusa Touch*, and the actual date of release is included at the end of the entry in the normal way.

Across the Great Divide

Quite surprisingly tough children's Western about a brother and sister who decide to set out for Oregon to claim their land, and the non-too-villainous gambler who joins them. The wild is shown as really wild and formidable, with highly unfriendly grizzly bears, mountain lions, wolves and buffalo. Cast: *Robert Logan, Heather Rattray, Mark Edward Hall, George 'Buck' Flower, Hal Bokar, Frank F. Salsedo, Fernando Celis, Loren Ewing, Tiny Brooks, John Kauffman, James Elk, Stan Cowley.* Dir & Screenplay: Stewart Raffill. Pro: Arthur R. Dubbs. Ex Pro: Joseph C. Raffill. Ph: Gerard Alcan. Ed: R. Hansel Brown, Frank Decot & Ron Honanther. Art: Ronald Kent Foreman. M: Gene Kauer & Douglas Lackey. (Mavericks Inc–Pacific International.) Rel: Floating. 100 mins. Cert U.

*Adventures of a Plumber's Mate

Rough-and-ready British farce with a 'hero' who fits that category nicely and a story that is certainly the former. Cast: *Christopher Neil, Arthur Mullard, Stephen Lewis, Elaine Paige, Anna Quayle, Jonathan Adams, Graham Ashley, Neville Barber, Lindy Benson, Christopher Biggins, John Bott, Richard Caldicot, Dave Carter, Peter Cleall, Angela Daniels, Claire Davenport, Christine Donna, Prudence Drage, Kim Fortune, Leone Green, Linda Hartley, Mary Henry, Suzy Mandel, Derek Martin, David Rayner, Stephen Riddle, William Rushton, Vicki Scott, Tessa Skola, Jerold Wells, Nina West, William Whymper, Teresa Wood, John Wyman.* Dir: Stanley Long. Pro: Peter Long. Screenplay: Stephen D. Frances & Aubrey Cash. Pro Man: Hugh O'Donnell. Ph: Peter Sinclair. Ed: Jo Gannon. Art: Carlotta Barrow. M: Christopher Neil. (Salon Productions–Alpha Films.) Rel: 10 June 1978. 88 mins. Cert X.

Allonsanfan

Earlier effort (*circa* 1974) of the Taviani brothers, whose 1977 film *Padre Padrone* brought them international acclaim. A dense political, and visually elaborate, story of a left-wing aristocrat who is sent to prison in 1816 for his revolutionary beliefs which are less fervent on his release, and in fact he double-crosses his former allies and given them away to the authorities who shoot them down. But in the end the score is evened when the local militia shoot him too. Cast: *Marcello Mastroianni, Lea Massari, Mimsy Farmer, Laura Berti, Renata de Carmine, Bruno Cirino, Claudio Cassinelli, Benjamin Lev, Stanko Molnar, Biagio Pelligra, Alderico Casali, Luisa de Santis, Michael Berger, Raul Cabrera, Roberto Frau, Cirylle Spiga, Ermanno Taviani, Francesca Taviani, Stavros Tornes, Pier·Giovanni Anchisi, Luis La Torre, Carla Mancini, Bruna Righetti.* Dir & Screenplay: Paolo & Vittorio Taviani. Pro: Giuliani G. de Negri. Assoc Pro: Giuseppe Francone. Pro Sup: Bruno Liconti. Ph: Giuseppe Ruzzolini. Ed: Roberto Perpignani. Art: Giovanni Sabarra. M: Ennio Morricone. (Una Cooperative Cinematographica–Artificial Eye.) Rel: Floating; first shown London, June 1978. 111 mins. Cert AA.

The Amazing Captain Nemo

The adventures in three parts of Jules Verne's character who, after spending a century in suspended animation in his remarkable underseas craft *Nautilus* (following the end of his '20,000 Leagues Under the Sea' story), is revitalised by a couple of US Navy divers during some 1978 war-games exercises and proceeds to (a) save Washington from obliteration at the evil hands of fellow submariner *Burgess Meredith* with his rockets, (b) stop a looming disaster caused by atomic waste leaking on the sea-bed, and (c) discover Atlantis. Hilarious, simple, comic-strip stuff with remarkably good performances by *Jose Ferrer* (Nemo) and Meredith. Rest of cast: *Tom Hallick, Burr DeBenning, Lynda Day George, Mel Ferrer, Warren Stevens, Horst Buchholz, Med Flory, Randolph Roberts, David Westberg, Anthony McHugh, Stephen Powers, Yale Summers, Anthony Geary, Harvey Fisher, Art Ballinger, Richard Angarola, Peter Jason.* Dir: Alex March. Pro Ex: Arthur Weiss. Ex Assist to Pro: Art Volpert. Screenplay: Norman Katkov, Preston Wood, Robert Dennis, William Keys, Mann Rubin, Robert Bloch & Larry Alexander. Ph: Lamar Boren. Ed: Bill Brame. Art: Eugene Lourie & Duane Alt. M: Richard LaSalle. Underwater scenes directed by Paul Stader. (Warner.) Rel: 18 February. 102 mins. Cert U.

The American Soldier—Der amerikanische Soldat

Earlier (1970) and confusing Fassbinder film with all sorts of references to the American gangster film in its story about a character called 'The Killer' who returns to his native Germany from the USA and is recruited by the secret police to carry out a couple of assassinations. Cast: *Karl Scheydt, Elga Sorbas, Jan George, Margarethe von Trotta, Hark Bohm, Ingrid Caven, Eva Ingeborg Scholz, Kurt Raab, Marius Aicher, Gustl Datz, Marquhand Bohm, Rainer Werner Fassbinder, Katrin Schaake, Ulli Lommel, Irm Hermann.* Dir, Pro, Screenplay & Co-Art Dir (with Kurt Raab): Rainer Werner Fassbinder. Ph: Dietrich Lohmann. Ed: Thea Eymesz. M: Peet Raben. (Anti-teater–Cinegate.) Rel: Floating; first shown London, February 1979. 80 mins. No cert.

American Hot Wax

The story of American disc-jockey Alan Freed (played in the movie by *Tim McIntire*) and his popularising and championing of rock-and-roll in 1959, his fight against the authorities (who see it as a riot-creator) which results in a battle between cop and kids, and Freed's suspension from his DJ job. But rock-and-roll rolls—and—rocks on! Rest of cast: *Fran Drescher, Jay Leno, Laraine Newman, Carl Earl Weaver, Al Chalk, Sam Harkness, Arnold McCuller, Jeff Altman, Moosie Drier, John Lehne, Stewart Steinberg, Jack Edward Ellis, Richard Forbes, Stephen Pearlman, Keene Curtis, Pat McNamara, Will Thornbury, Hamilton Camp, Chuck Berry, Screamin' Jay Hawkins, Charles Greene, Kenny Vance, Jos*

Esposito, Bruce Sudano, Ed Hokenson, The Delights, Richard Roat, Marion Perkins, Matthew Tobin, Bobby Johnson, Red Keller, Elmer Valentine, Timmy and the Tangerines, Andrea Robinson, Gail Kantor, Patrica Clinger, Nils Lofgren, Mark Diamond, Al Maines, Artie Ripp, W. R. Yoakum, Charles Hallahan, Maurice Starr, John Hawker, Heather Lowe, Nora Denney, Garry Goodrow, Glenn Ash, Frank Campana, Buddy Micucci, Arnold Johnson, George Poulos, Doug Samha, Larry Hankin, Dina Ousley, Dianne Brooks, Denise Maynelli. Dir: Floyd Mutrux. Pro: Art Linson. Screenplay: John Kaye. Ph: William A. Fraker. Ed: Melvin Shapiro & Ronald J. Fagan. Assoc Pro: Fred T. Gallo. Art: Elayne Barbara Ceder. M: Kenny Vance. (Paramount–CIC.) Rel: 2 July 1978. 92 mins. Cert A.

Anger in his Eyes—Con la rabbia agli occhi
Routine small-time Italian gangster melodrama with the compensation of some delightful Naples backgrounds, where *Yul Brynner* as the invited American hit-man deals out death and is himself finally erased. Rest of cast: *Massimo Ranieri, Barbara Bouchet, Martin Balsam, Giancarlo Sbragia, Giacomo Furia, Sal Borgese, Loris Bazzocchi, Rosario Borelli, Luigi Williams, Renzo Marignano.* Dir: Antonio Margheriti. 2nd Unit Dir: Ignazio Dolce. Pro: Franco Caruso. Screenplay: Guido Castaldo & Giacomo Furia. Ph: Sergio D'Offizio. Ed: Mario Morra. Art: Luciano Puccini. M: Guido de Angelis & Maurizio De Angelis. (Giovine Cinematografica–Columbia/Warner.) Rel: 15 February. 98 mins. Cert AA.

Ashanti
Old-fashioned melodrama about a white doctor's (*Michael Caine*) black doctor wife (*Beverly Johnson*— début) who is kidnapped by slave-runner *Peter Ustinov* and forced into joining his caravan of young captives as it crosses the Sahara bound for the slave markets of Arabia. And the time for all this is the present! Luckily, determined doctor Caine gets the expert and skilled assistance of handsome sheikh *Kabir Bedi* in tracking, catching up with and finally disposing of the villains. And prominent in the cast is a scene-stealing camel. Rest of cast: *Omar Sharif, Rex Harrison, William Holden, Zia Mohyeddin, Winston Ntshona, Tariq Yunus, Tyrone Jackson, Jean-Luc Bideau, Johnny Sekka, Akosua Busia, Olu Jacobs, Marne Maitland, Eric Pohlmann.* Dir: Richard Fleischer. Pro: Georges-Alain Vuille. Screenplay: Stephen Geller; based on a novel by Alberto Vasquez-Figueroa. Ex Pro: Luciano Sacripanti. Assoc Pro: John C. Vuille. Pro Sup: Orazio Tassara. Ph: Aldo Tonti. Ed: Ernst Walter. Pro Des: Aurelio Crugnola. Art: Kuli Sander. M: Michael Melvoin. (Columbia.) Rel: 1 April. 117 mins. Cert AA.

Autumn Sonata
A beautifully-composed and marvellously-acted Ingmar Bergman chamber piece about the confrontation, between a star pianist and her married daughter, which blows up when after seven years the mother, having lost her lover, accepts the daughter's invitation to stay with her. What starts as a joyful reunion degenerates into unhappy recrimination as the emotionally-blocked daughter accuses her mother of rejecting her childish adoration because she was not even aware of it. A deep illustration of how lack of love can embitter, stunt and frustrate. A remarkably intelligent and human film, lit up by acting, directing and writing genius. Cast: *Ingrid Bergman, Liv Ullmann, Lena Nyman, Halvar Bjork, Georg Lokkeberg, Knut Wigert, Eva Von Hanno, Erland Josephson, Linn Ullmann, Arne Bang-Hansen.* Dir, Pro & Screenplay: Ingmar Bergman. Ph: Sven Nykvist. Ed: Sylvia Ingmarsdotter. Set Des: Anna Asp. M: Chopin, Bach & Handel played by Kabi Laretei, Claude Genetay & Frans Bruggen, Gustav Leonhardt & Anner Bylsma. (Personafilm GmbH, Munich–Suède-Film & Filmedis, Paris–Lew Grade & Martin Starger–ITC.) Rel: Floating; first shown London, March 1979. 92 mins. Cert AA.

Backroads
Impressive first feature film—made on a miniscule budget—by young Australian, Phillip Noyce. Basically one of the by now familiar road-chase films, this one has an original angle by making one of the fugitives a white crook (who steals their getaway car) and the other an Aborigine, and beneath the uninterrupted action there are attacks on white man's long and apparently consistent abuse of the continent's original inhabitants. Cast: *Gary Foley, Bill Hunter, Zac Martin, Terry Camilleri, Juliet McGregor.* Dir & Pro: Phillip Noyce. Assoc Pro: Elizabeth Knight. Screenplay: John Emery; with additional material by the director and members of the cast. Ph: Russell Boyd. Ed: David Huggett. M: Robert Murphy. (Backroads Productions–Scala). Rel: Floating; first shown London, August 1978. 60 mins. No cert.

Battlestar Galactica
A number of episodes of the popular American sci-fi television series strung together to make a two-hour movie with the added dimension of cinema-shaking Sensurround. A somewhat confusing story of the efforts of the villainous automatons to wipe out to the last man, woman and child the dozen **surviving** colonies of humans in space—giving opportunity for a number of spectacular spaceship battles and other exciting, if superficial, action. Cast: *Richard Hatch, Dirk Benedict, Lorne Greene, Ray Milland, Lew Ayres, Jane Seymour, Wilfrid Hyde White, John Colicos, Laurette Spang, John Fink, Terry Carter Jr, Maren Jensen, Tony Swartz, Noah Hathaway, Ed Begley Jr, Rick Springfield, Randi Oakes, Norman Stuart, David Greennan, Sarah Rush, David Matthau, Chip Johnson, Geoffrey Binney, Paua Coufos, Bruce Wright.* Dir: Richard A. Colla. Pro: John Dykstra. Screenplay & Ex Pro: Glen A. Larson. Sup Pro: Leslie Stevens. Ph: Ben Colman. Ed: Robert L. Kimble, Leon Ortiz-Gil & Larry Strong. Art: John E. Chilberg. M: Stu Philips & Glen Larson. Assoc Pro: Winrich Kolbe. (Larson–Universal–CIC.) Rel: 27 May. 118 mins. Cert U.

The Beast
Something of a celluloid curio from Walerian Borowczyk, who lifted an episode out of his previous French-made movie, *Immoral Tales*, after its first London Festival showing, and wove a full-length feature around it; twisting together the old *La Belle et la Bête* fable with the no less familar family-skeleton-in-the-cupboard theme, emerging with a story about a beautiful young girl waylaid and raped in the woods only to turn on her hirsute rapist and killing the beast with sheer ecstasy as she satisfies herself. This explains why many years later the heir of her family when he dies on the eve of his wedding to an American heiress, is discovered to have'a hairy tail! Often drily amusing and erotic to the edge of pornography without quite becoming so. Cast: *Sirpa Lane, Lisbeth Hummel, Elisabeth Kaza, Pierre Benedetti, Guy Tréjan, Dalio, Roland Armontel, Pascal Rivault, Jean Martinelli, Robert Capia, Hassan Falle, Marie and Stéphane Testanière, Anna Baldaccini, Mathieu Rivollier, Thierry Bourdon, Julien Hanany.* Dir, Screenplay & Ed: Walerian Borowczyk. Pro: Anatole Dauman. Ph: Bernard Daillencourt & Marcel Grignon. Art: Jacques d'Ovidio. M: Scarlatti. (Argos–New Realm.) Rel: Floating; first shown London, September 1978. 96 mins. Cert X (London GLC).

Beauty and the Beast
A re-make of the famous moral fairy story about the good little girl who grew to love the beast and when she kissed him found him to be a wonderful, handsome prince who was just suffering from a wicked witch's spell! Straightforward, quite well done but minor movie. Cast: *George C. Scott, Trish van Devere, Virginia McKenna, Bernard Lee, Michael Harbour, William Relton, Patricia Quinn.* Dir: Fielder Cook. Pro: Hank Moonjean. Ex Pro: Thomas M. C. Johnston. Screenplay: Sherman Yellen. Ph: Jack Hildyard & Paul Beeson. Ed: Freddie Wilson. Art: Elliott Scott. M: Ron Goodwin. (Hemdale.) Rel: Floating; first shown London, August 1978. 91 mins. Cert U.

Behind Convent Walls—L'Interno di un Convento
Another Walerian Borowczyk essay in erotica, based on the Stendhal novel *Promenades dans Rome*. Lovely amorous young nuns; a number of rough and certainly ready seductions; and lots of beautifully photographed explorations, typical of Borowczyk, of the female form. Cast: *Ligia Branice, Marina Pierro, Gabriella Giaccobe, Loredana Martinez, Mario Maranzana, Rodolfo Dal Pra, Howard Ross, Alessandro Partexano, Olivia Pascal, Gina Rovere, Dora Calindri, Francesca Balletta, Maria Cumari Quasimodo, Raymonde Carole Fouanon, Miana Mirisi, Simona Villani, Paola Arduini, Silvano*

Releases of the Year in Detail

Bernabei, Brid Cranitch, Stefania D'Amario, Elizabeth Jane Long, Imelde Marani; Patrizia Mauro, Paolo Morra; Mike Morris, Antonietta Patriarca, Elisabetta Pedrazzi, Rossella Pescatore, Valeria Pescatore, Paola Prosdogemi, Romano Puppo, Jole Rosa, Romana Monti, Greta Vayon. Dir, Ed & Screenplay: Walerian Borowczyk; based on the Stendhal novel Promenade dans Rome. Pro: Giuseppe Vezzani. Ex Pro: Marcello Lizzani & Renzo Ciabo. Ph: Luciano Tovoli. Art: Luciano Spadoni. M: Sergio Montori: the traditional Tuscan song sung by Ligia Branice. (Trust International Films–New Realm.) Rel: Floating; first shown London, February 1979. 95 mins. Cert X.

*The Betsy
High, wide and handsome adaptation of a typical Harold Robbins novel, a story of family feuds, sex, the greed for power, murder, incest and other (sexual) larks. Laurence Olivier, with odd accent, as the octogenarian motor-car magnate who wants to leave as his memorial a revolutionary new family car—and employing a young Italian racing-driver to build the job secretly when the company board, ruled by the old boy's grandson (who hates him because when he was a small boy he saw his mother in bed with him) turns down the idea. All very complicated, very familiar, and very well done. Rest of cast: Robert Duvall, Katharine Ross, Tommy Lee Jones, Jane Alexander, Lesley-Anne Down, Joseph Wiseman, Kathleen Beller, Edward Herrmann, Paul Rudd, Roy Poole, Richard Venture, Titos Vandis, Clifford David, Inga Swenson, Whitely Blake, Carol Williard, Read Morgan, Charlie Fields, Robert Phalen, Nick Czmyr, Norman Palmer, Fred Carney, Maury Cooper, Russell Porter, Teri Ralston, Warney H. Ruhl, Patrick J. Monks, William Roerick, William B. Cain, Edward C. Higgins, Mary Petrie, H. August Kuehl, Robert Hawkins, Sadie Hawkins, Anthony Streere. Dir: Daniel Petrie. Pro: Robert R. Weston. Screenplay: William Bast & Walter Bernstein; based on the Harold Robbins novel. Ph: Mario Tosi. Ed: Rita Roland. Pro Des: Herman A. Blumenthal. M: John Barry. Assoc. Pro: Jack Grossberg. (Allied Artists/Harold Robbins International–UA.) Rel: 25 June 1978. 125 mins. Cert X.

Between the Lines
Youth-oriented American film about an underground newspaper being taken over by a press baron, but neglecting the actual production side of the tale in order to concentrate on the personal stories of various members of the staff—their lives and their loves. Cast: John Head, Lindsay Crouse, Jeff Goldblum, Jill Eikenberry, Bruno Kirby, Gwen Welles, Stephen Collins, Lewis J. Stadlen, Michael J. Pollard, Lane Smith, Marilu Henner, Susan Haskins, Ray Barry, Douglas Kenney, John Korkes, Joe Morton, Richard Cox, Gary Springer, Charles Levin, Guy Boyd. Dir: Joan Micklin Silver. Pro: Raphael Silver. Screenplay: Fred Barron. Ph: K. V. Sickle. Ed: John Carter. Pro Des: Stuart Wurtzel. (Midwest Film Productions–

Essential.) First shown Octover 1978. 101 mins. Cert AA.

The Big Sleep
Re-make of the 1946 Raymond Chandler classic private-eye piece, now switched from Los Angeles to Britain and losing much of the essential Chandler atmosphere, if none of the witty lines, in the change of location. Now Robert Mitchum is the cynical but honest 'tec who becomes enmeshed in a highly complicated and convoluted case of blackmail and other crookery. Far below the original but if you can temporarily forget that (or are unable to make such comparisons) it is nevertheless a pretty entertaining thriller. Rest of cast: Sarah Miles, Richard Boone, Candy Clark, Joan Collins, Edward Fox, John Mills, Oliver Reed, James Stewart, Harry Andrews, Colin Blakely, James Donald, Diana Quick, Richard Todd, John Justin, Martin Potter, Simon Turner, Patrick Durkin, David Saville, Don Henderson, Roy Evans, Mike Lewin, David Jackson, Dudley Sutton, Derek Deadman, David Millet, Clifford Earl, Joe Ritchie, Michael Segal, Norman Lumsden, Nik Forster, Judy Buxton. Dir: Michael Winner. Pro: Michael Winner & Elliott Kastner. Screenplay: Michael Winner; from the story by Raymond Chandler. Pro Ex: Denis Holt. Assoc Pro: Bernard Williams. Ph: Robert Paynter. Pro Des: Harry Pottle. Art: John Graysmark. M: Jerry Fielding. (Lew Grade–Elliott Kastner/Jerry Bick–ITC.) Rel: 1 October. 99 mins. Cert AA.

Big Wednesday
A film which sets out to try and explain something of the mystique of surfing and takes a long time to do so. It tells the story of three young Americans, who can be viewed as layabouts; they spend all their days and nights on the beach practising and displaying their considerable abilities. Their friendship, born of the sport, survives war, friction and personal disaster and flowers at a moment that brings them altogether again when one of them is in danger of losing his life daring the waves. Cast: Jan-Michael Vincent, William Katt, Gary Busey, Patti D'Arbanville, Lee Purcell, Sam Melville. Dir: John Milius. Pro: Buzz Feitshans. Ex Pro: Alex Rose & Tamara Asseyev. Screenplay: John Milius & Dennis Aaberg. Ph: Bruce Surtees. Ed: Robert L. Wolfe (also Ed by Tim O'Meara). Pro Des: Charles Rosen. M: Basil Poledouris. 2nd Unit Dir: Terry Leonard. (A Team Production–Warner.) Rel: Floating. 119 mins. Cert. A.

*Bilitis
Still-photographer David Hamilton's first film, a very leisurely, nicely photographed and quite charming Emmanuelle-style piece of erotica set in the south of France and concerning a young girl's sensual awakening there while on extended holiday. Starring a youngster with great potential in Patti d'Arbanville. Rest of cast: Mona Kristensen, Bernard Giraudeau, Gilles Kohler, Mathieu Carrière. Dir: David Hamilton. Ex Pro: Sylvio Tabet. Assoc Pro: Jacques

Nahum. Screenplay: Catherine Breillat; inspired by Pierre Louys's 'The Songs of Bilitis' adapted by Robert Boussinot & Jacques Nahum. Ph: Bernard Daillencourt. Ed (and Technical Adviser): Henry Colpi. M: Francis Lai. (New Realm.) Rel: Floating; first shown London, June 1978. 93 mins.

Black and White in Colour
Drily amusing French film which takes two very small and isolated French and German colonial settlements in darkest Africa, circa 1915—who have been living in close harmony until they hear the news of the war—to show all the follies, farce and fever of conflict. Between the attacking French and the defending Germans the local blacks, co-opted to both sides are the only real sufferers, until the British march in and take over from everyone. Winner of the 1977 Oscar for 'Best Foreign Film'. Cast: Jean Carmet, Jacques Dufilho, Catherine Rouvel, Jacques Spiesser, Dora Doll, Maurice Barrier, Claude Legros, Jacques Monnet, Peter Berling, Marius Beugre Boignan, Baye Macoumba Diop, Aboubakar Toure, Dieter Schidor, Marc Zuber, Klaus Huebl, Mamadou Coulibaly, Memel Atchaori, Jean-François Eyou N'Geussan, Natou Koly, Tanoh Kouao and inhabitants of the Ivory Coast. Dir: Jean-Jacques Annaud. Pro: Arthur Cohn, Jacques Perrin & Georges Conchon. Ph: Claude Agostini, Set Dec: Max Douy. Ed: Françoise Bonnot. Assoc Pro: Jean-Michel Nakache. Pro Co: Gerard Crosnier & Timite Bassori. M: Pierre Bachelet. (Emanuel L. Wolf/Arthur Cohn–UA.) Rel: Floating; first shown London, November 1978. 92 mins. Cert A.

Blackboard Massacre (titled Massacre at Central High in America)
Nasty goings-on at school where David, after his leg is crushed by some bullies, sets out to kill the trio responsible for his limp. Ultimately he plans to blow up the school but when he has a sudden change of heart he just blows himself up in trying to put things right! Cast: Derrel Maury, Andrew Stevens, Kimberley Beck, Robert Carradine, Ray Underwood, Steve Bond, Steve Sikes, Lani O'Grady, Damon Douglas, Rainbeaux Smith, Dennis Kort, Jeffrey Winter, Thomas Logan. Dir & Screenplay: Renée Daalder. Pro: Harold Sobel. Ex Pro: Jerome Baumon. Ph: Bert Van Munster. Ed: Harry Keramidas. Art: Russell Tune. M: Tony Leonetti. (Evan–Tigon.) Rel: Floating. 88 mins. Cert X.

Blacks Britannica
Sobering and even somewhat frightening American-made documentary which examines the racist problem in Britain seen largely from the blacks' angle, coming up with a pretty clear statement of the coloured community's interpretation of its history in GB. Dir & Pro: David Koff. Assoc Pro: Musindo Mwinyipembe. Ph: William Brayne, Mike Davis & Charles Stewart. Ed: Tom Scott Robson. M: Steel Pulse. (Scala.) Rel: Floating; first shown London, July 1978. 57 mins. No cert.

Blood Relatives

Claude Chabrol's Canadian made whodunnit about the murder of a young girl and the sorting out of the various suspects by sombre detective *Donald Sutherland*; a film which starts beautifully but then slides gently downhill, losing both tension and credibility as it goes. Rest of cast: *Aude Landry, Lisa Langlois, Laurent Malet, Stéphane Audran, Walter Massey, Micheline Lanctot, Donald Pleasence, David Hemmings, Ian Ireland, Guy Hoffmann, Marguerite Lemir, Gregory Giannis, Jan Chamberlain, Tim Henry, Victor Knight, Jerome Tiberghien, Kevin Fenlon, Nini Balough, Terence Labrosse, Tammy Tucker, Robert King, Victor Desy, John Boyland, Howard Ryshpan.* Dir: Claude Chabrol. Pro: Denis Heroux & Eugène Lépicier. Ex Pro: Julian Melzack. Screenplay: Claude Chabrol & Sydney Banks; from the book by Ed McBain. Ph: Jean Rabier. Ed: Yves Langlois. Assoc Pro: Claude Léger. Pro Des: Ann Pritchard. (Classic Film Industries–Cinevideo–Filmel–Michael Klinger–Rank.) Rel: Floating. 94 mins. Cert X.

Blue Collar

A story about three US car-assembly-worker pals (one white, two black) who, unable—after their drugs-girls-and-booze parties!—to give their families such necessities as dental visits, decide to augment their income by breaking into and stealing their union's funds; then turning to blackmail when they uncover evidence of big-time financial mismanagement and gangster connections among the union's officers. But the film has so much to say, politically, racially and dramatically—and says it all in such needlessly foul language—that it is difficult to keep up with what is actually being said! Cast: *Richard Pryor, Harvey Keitel, Yaphet Kotto, Ed Begley Jr, Harry Bellaver, George Memmoli, Lucy Saroyan, Lane Smith, Cliff de Young, Borah Silver, Chip Fields, Harry Northup, Leonard Gaines, Milton Selzer, Sammy Warren, Timmy Martinez, Jerry Dahlmann, Denny Arnold, Rock Riddle, Stacey Baldwin, Steve Butts, Stephen P. Dunn, Speedy Brown, Davone Florence, Eddie Singleton, Rya Singleton, Vermettya Royster, Jaime Carreire, Victoria McFarland, Gloria Delaney, Rosa Flores, Crystal McCarey, Debra Fay Walker, Gino Ardito, Sean Fallon Walsh, Vincent Lucchesi, Jerry Snider, Colby Chester, Don Morse, William Pert, Tracey Walter, Almeria Quinn, Lee McDonald, Rodney Lee Walker, Glenn Wilder, Frank Orsatti, Matt (Jim) Connors.* Dir: Paul Schrader. Pro: Don Guest. Ex Pro: Robin French. Screenplay: Paul and Leonard Schrader. Assoc Pro: David Nichols. Ph: Sydney A. Glass. Ed: Tom Rolf. Pro Des: Lawrence G. Paull. M: Jack Nitzsche. (Universal–CIC.) Rel: Floating. 114 mins. Cert X.

The Boxer

Highly individualistic, stylish and in some ways poetic Japanese film relating the story of an ambitious young boxer and his relationship with the older man (who at the height of his success gave up the game) who he eventually succeeds in persuading to train him. Plenty of jump cuts, apparently unrelated scenes and various colour effects are used but they are made to add up to an impressive and visually stunning movie. Cast: *Kentaro Shimizu, Bunta Sugawara, Masumi Harukawa, Yoko Natsuki, Keiko Niitaka, Yoko Ran, Yataka Nemoto, Takeshi Wakamatsu, Salvadore Tali, Toshihiko Hino, Hajime Hirai.* Dir: Shuji Terayama. Pro: Yoshihiro Kojima. Screenplay: Shiro Ishimori, Masao Kishida & Shuji Terayama. Ph: Tatsuo Suzuki. Ed: Fumio Soda. Art: Tadayuki Kuwana. M: J. A. Seazer. (Toei Film Co–Marquee/World Wide Films.) Rel: Floating; first shown London, August 1978. 94 mins. Cert A.

The Boys from Brazil

Well-made, neatly-paced and quite brilliantly acted thriller with a basically pretty silly story about a fanatical Nazi medical scientist who, working in his South American hideaway, dreams up a plot (and achieves the means) to re-activate the old Nazi dream by creating 94 little Hitler clones around the world who in due course—identical in looks, character and evil—will take up the swastika and set off on their mission of world domination. But, luckily, between the plan and fruition stands a frail but equally dedicated old Jewish Nazi-hunter. Cast: *Gregory Peck, Laurence Olivier, James Mason, Lilli Palmer, Uta Hagen, Rosemary Harris, Jeremy Black, Steve Guttenberg, John Rubinstein, David Hurst, Anne Meara, Michael Gough, Linda Hayden, Guy Dumont, Bruno Ganz, Georg Marishka, Gunter Meisner, Jurgen Andersen, Wolf Kahler, Carl Duering, Walter Gotell, David Brandon, John Dehner, Denholm Elliott, Mervin Nelson, Monia Gearson, Joachim Hansen, Wolfgang Preiss, Raul Faustino Saldanha, Prunella Scales, Richard Marner, Gerti Gordon, Guida de Carlo.* Dir: Franklin J. Schaffner. Pro: Stanley O'Toole & Martin Richards. Ex Pro: Robert Fryer. Pro Sup: Ron Carr. Screenplay: Heywood Gould; based on the novel by Ira Levin. Ph: Henri Decae. Ed: Bob Swink. Pro Des: Gil Parrondo. Art: Peter Lamont. M: Jerry Goldsmith (song, 'We're Home Again' sung by *Elaine Paige*). (Lew Grade/Producer Circle Productions–ITC.) Rel: 18 March. 120 mins. Cert X.

The Brass Target

Thriller about the US Army which suggests that General Patton was murdered in 1945 (rather than killed in a road accident as has always been accepted) as a result of his taking on the personal investigation of the theft, by some of his own high-ranking officers, of 250 million dollars-worth of Nazi gold during its rail journey to Frankfurt bank vaults. Cast: *George Kennedy, John Cassavetes, Sophia Loren, Robert Vaughn, Patrick McGoohan, Bruce Davison, Edward Herrmann, Max Von Sydow, Ed Bishop, Lee Montague, Alan Tilvern, Sigfrit Steiner, Reinhold Olszewski, Heinz Bennent, Bob Cunningham, Bernard Horsfall, John Junkin, Brad Harris, Hal Galili, Claudia Butenuth, Osman Ragheb, Marshall Reynor,* Birgit Bergen, Drew Lucas, Peter Armstrong, Wolfgang Hiller, Dietrich Kerky, Sissy Weiner, Richard Kley, Ernst Zeiner, Martin Borger, Ray Le Clair, Jimmy Jackson, Hildegard Busse, Julian Panich, Lynn Ferren, Rene Schoenberg.* Dir: John Hough. Pro: Arthur Lewis. Ex Pro: Berle Adams. Pro Ex: Harold Nebenzal. Pro Sup: Dieter Minx. Screenplay: Alvin Boretz; based on the novel 'The Algonquin Project' by Frederick Nolan. Ph: Tony Imi. Ed: David Lane. Pro Des: Rolf Zehetbauer. M: Laurence Rosenthal. performed by the Graunke Orchestra. (Berle Adams/Arthur Lewis–MGM–CIC.) Rel: 25 March. 111 mins. Cert AA.

The Brute

Somewhat superficial examination (made in 1976) of the British social problem of wife-bashing, exemplified by the story of two such unfortunate young wives and mothers whose perverted hubbies periodically brutalise them. Cast: *Sarah Douglas, Julian Glover, Roberta Gibbs, Bruce Robinson, Suzanne Stone, Kenneth Nelson, Nicholas Barnes, Charlotte Cornwell, Jenny Twigge, Sylvester Morand, Jamie Farrar, Rickie Stewardson, David Millett, Clive Graham, Anne Godley, Carol Cleveland, Peter Bull, Betty Huntley Wright, John Franklyn Robbins.* Dir & Screenplay: Gerry O'Hara. Pro: John Quested. Assoc Pro: Julian Holloway. Pro Man: Edward Dorian. Ph: Dennis Lewiston (2nd Unit Ph: Alfie Hicks). Ed: Jerry Hambling. Art: Terence Pritchard. M: Ken V. Jones. (Tigon–Rank FD.) Rel: Floating. 89 mins. Cert X.

The Buddy Holly Story

Movie based on the real life-story of the well-known rock 'n' roll star who died in an airplane crash in 1959, introducing a dozen of his most popular numbers. Cast: *Gary Busey (as Buddy), Don Stroud, Charles Martin Smith, Bill Jordan, Maria Richwine, Conrad Janis, Albert Popwell, Amy Johnston, Jim Beach, John F. Goff, Fred Travalena, Dick O'Neil, Stymie Beard, M. G. Kelly, Paul Mooney, Bill Phillips Murry, Freeman King, Steve Camp, Jody Berry, Bob Christopher, Gloria Irricari, Rajah Bergman, Joe Renzetti, Gilbert Melgar, Gailaird Sartain, George Simonelli, Steve Doubet, Jack Dembo, Richard Kennedy, Arch Johnson, Neva Patterson, Anthony Johnson, Rod Grier, Peter Griffin, Maxine Green, Mary Hyland, Susan Morse, Buster Jones, Jerry Zaremba, Paul Carmello, Bill Lytle, Raymond Shockey, Loutz Gage, John Waldron, Alan Peterson, Jack Jozefson, Craig White.* Dir: Steve Rash. Pro: Fred Bauer. Ex Pro: Edward H. Cohen. Co-Ex Pro: Fred T. Kuehnert. Screenplay: Robert Gittler; from a story by Steve Rash & Fred Bauer. Assoc Pro: Frances Avrut-Bauer. Ph: Stevan Larner. Ed: David Blewitt. Pro Des: Joel Schiller. M: Joe Renzetti. (Innovisions/ECA Production-Entertainment Films.) Rel: 17 June. 114 mins. Cert A.

*Cain's Way

1969-made, minor Western set in the post-American Civil War period and concerning ex-Commander

Releases of the Year in Detail

Cain's (*Scott Brady*) tracking down the outlaw leader who killed his wife and son. Rest of cast: *John Carradine, Adair Jamison, Darwin Joston, Don Epperson, Robert Dix, Bruce Kimball, Russ McCubbin, Tereza Thaw, Valda Hansen, Tommy Davis, Tom Woytowich, Willis Martin, Andy Moon, Alen Elliot, Richard Scarso, Ruby Florence, John Crofton, Frank Saletri, Michael Perrota.* Dir: Kent Osborne. Ex Pro: Gerald Fine & Jerome Jackson. Pro: Ralph Luce & Budd Dell. Pro Co-Ord: Edward Gruskin. Screenplay: Will Denmark. Ph: Ralph Waldo. Ed: James Moore. Art: Coke Willis. (JC Productions–Alpha.) Rel: 10 June 1978. 88 mins. Cert X.

Camouflage
Leisurely, dialogue-developed Polish film about the verbal—though climactically physical—confrontation at an academic summer camp of an idealistic, liberal-minded young professor and his older, more cynical colleague who tries to prove to him that he will have to compromise if he is to get anywhere in his profession. A quietly amusing look at crusading youth coming up against the bitter realism of experienced middle age; fine performances by *Zbigniew Zapasiewicz* and *Piotr Garlicki.* Rest of cast: *Christin Paul, Marius Dmochowski, Magdalena Zawadska.* Dir and Screenplay: Krzysztof Zanussi. Pro: Witold Holtz, Grazyna Smuszowica Wybult and others. Ph: Edward Klosinski. Ed: Ursula Sliwinska, Ewa Smal. Art: Ta deusz Wybult, Maciez Putowski, Ewa Braun, Joanna Helanow, Stanislaw Rozewicz. M: Wojciech Kilar. (Tor Film Unit–Contemporary.) Rel: Floating; first shown London, November 1978. 100 mins. Cert AA.

Candido Erotico
A good example of the 'posh-porn' cinema: technically excellent, with well-photographed, interesting Danish backgrounds, attractive players, and a story about a young star of sexual acts in a Copenhagen sex club who, when he falls in love with and marries a pretty young girl, cannot consummate his marriage unless he has an audience—something his wife allows just once before she leaves him. Cast: *Lili Carati, Mircha Carven, Maxa Baxa, Ajita Wilson, Marco Guglielmi, Fernando Cerulli, Carlos Alberto Valles, Lionello Pio di Savoia, Filippo Perego.* Dir. Claudio de Molinis. Pro: Dino di Salvo. Screenplay: Romano Bernardi. Ph: Emilio Loffredo. Ed: Giancarlo Venarucci. M: Nico Fidenco. (Polo Films–Inter-Ocean Distributors.) Rel: Floating; first shown London, January 1979. 95 mins. Cert X.

California Suite
Thoroughly enjoyable, marvellously captivating Neil Simon adaptation of his own stage-play success, in which as a gesture to the changed medium he has added a fourth 'Act' and interwoven the stories a little. Best is *Walter Matthau*'s broadly farcical efforts to hide the blonde in his bed from surprise visitor, wife *Elaine May*; worst the untidy knockabout concerning the holiday of two black doctors (*Bill Cosby* and *Richard Pryor*). In between there's the wit of Oscar-loser *Maggie Smith* (who

actually won an Oscar for this performance) and hubbie *Michael Caine* as they recover from her disappointment and the acid-tongued fight between mother *Jane Fonda* and divorced husband *Alan Alda* for the possession of their daughter. But all the minor blemishes and occasional vulgarity are pushed into the background by the shining professionalism of the acting, and witty lines and general atmosphere of fun. Rest of cast: *Gloria Gifford, Sheila Frazier, Herbert Edelman, Denise Galik, David Sheehan, Michael Boyle, Len Lawson, Gino Ardito, Jerry Ziman, Clint Young, David Matathau, James Espinoza, Buddy Douglas, Armand Cerami, Joseph Morena, Brian Cummings, William Kux, Zora Margolis, Rita Gomez, Tina Menard, Lupe Ontiveros, Bert May, Eddie Villery, Army Archerd, Judith Hannah Brown, Gary Hendrix, Jack Scanlan, Bill Steinmetz, Paolo Frediani.* Dir: Herbert Ross. Pro: Ray Stark. Screenplay: Neil Simon; based on his own stage play. Ph: David M. Walsh. Ed: Michael A. Stevenson. Sup Ed: Margaret Booth. Pro Des: Albert Brenner. M: Claude Bolling. Assoc Pro & Pro Man: Ronald Schwary. (Columbia.) Rel: 22 April. 104 mins. Cert AA.

Capricorn One
Increasingly exciting story of an incredible but deadly space hoax in which, during the final countdown of a rocket destined for a Mars landing, the three crewmen are whisked away to a desert prison where they are informed by the scientist in charge that in order to cover up a late-discovered life-support failure (which would have meant the loss of any chances of further space-flights) he will simulate the landing and return, blackmailing the trio into taking part in the plan by acting out the landing and walk on the planet in front of cameras on a film-studio set. But when they realise that the plan also entails their disposal upon the rocket's deliberate malfunction during re-entry, they escape, pursued by two helicopters with murderous intent—a chase that leads to a brilliantly-achieved climactic battle between the choppers and a crop-dusting biplane piloted by *Telly Savalas!* A film so good in part that it might have been even better. Rest of cast: *Elliott Gould, James Brolin, Brenda Vaccaro, Sam Waterstone, O. J. Simpson, Hal Holbrook, Karen Black, David Huddleston, David Doyle, Lee Bryant, Denise Nicholas, Robert Walden, Jim Sikking, Alan Fudge, James Karen, Virginia Kaiser, Nancy Malone, Hank Stohl, Norman Bartold, Darrell Zwerling, Milton Selzer, Lou Frizzell, Chris Hyams, Seanna Marre, Paul Picerni, Barbara Bosson, Paul Haney.* Dir & Screenplay: Peter Hyams. Pro: Paul N. Lazarus III. Pro Man: Mike Rachmil. Ph: Bill Butler. Ed: Jim Mitchell. Pro Des: Al Brenner. Art: David M. Haber. M: Jerry Goldsmith. (Lew Grade/Associated General Films–ITC Film Dist.) Rel: 4 February. 123 mins. Cert A.

Carry on Emmannuelle
The 30th 'Carry On' film and the one in which the team largely departed from the usual cheerfully broad and blue-veined music-hall humour to indulge in

some indifferent jokes about sex illustrated by bare breasts and bottoms. A well-intentioned satire on the apparent nymphomania of all those other 'Emmanuelle' episodes, but which, because of less than inspired casting and spirit, never lives up to the promise of the subject. Cast: *Suzanne Danielle, Kenneth Williams, Kenneth Connor, Jack Douglas, Joan Sims, Peter Butterworth, Larry Dann, Beryl Reid, Henry McGee, Howard Nelson, Stanley McGeagh, Claire Davenport, Norman Mitchell, Albert Moses, Tricia Newby, Tim Brinton, Corbet Woodall, Robert Dorning, Bruce Boa, Michael Nightingale, Eric Barker, Malcolm Johns, Jack Lynn, Guy Ward.* Dir: Gerald Thomas. Pro: Peter Rogers. Screenplay: Lance Peters. Pro Man: Roy Goddard. Ph: Alan Hume (Camera Operator: Godfrey Godar.) Ed: Peter Boita. Art: Jack Shampan. M: Eric Rogers. (Thomas/Rogers–Hemdale International.) Rel: 2 December. 88 mins. Cert AA.

Casey's Shadow
A story of a lad, a horse and the big-race plan which fate seems determined to spoil; and the background is the ramshackle old house in the Louisiana bayou country where dad, *Walter Matthau*, makes a living by training a string of quarter (race) horses. Rest of cast: *Alexis Smith, Robert Webber, Murray Hamilton, Andrew E. Rubin, Stephan Burns, Susan Myers, Michael Hershewel, Harry Caesar, Joel Fluellen, Whit Bissell, Jimmy Halty, William Pitt DVM, Dean Turpitt, Sanders Delhomme, Richard Thompson, Galbert Wanoskia, William Karn, Ed Hyman, Thomas Caldwell, Bill Tackett, Tom Dawson, Robert Dudich, William Thomas, Warren Richardson, Ronald L. Schwary, Leonard Blach DVM, Justin Buford, Dean Cormier, Thelma Cormier, Ronald Benoit, Norman Faulk, Gene Norman, Paul Uccello, W. Patrick Scott, James Hutchinson Jr.* Dir: Martin Ritt. Pro: Ray Stark. Screenplay: Carol Sobieski; based on the short story *Ruidoso* by John McPhee. Ex Pro: Michael Levee. Ph: John A. Alonzo. Ed: Sidney Levin. Pro Des: Robert Luthardt. M: Patrick Williams. M Sup: Stewart Levine. (Ray Stark/Martin Ritt Production–Columbia.) Rel: 6 May. 94 mins. Cert A.

The Cat from Outer Space
Highly entertaining formula Disney farce-comedy which takes a satirical look at all those 'space' movies in a story about a communicating cat from another world, which crashlands its space capsule on earth and has to seek human aid for repairs. A most handsome and well-drilled feline and a supporting cast including some fine old-timers. Cast: *Ken Berry, Sandy Duncan, Harry Morgan, Roddy McDowall, McLean Stevenson, Jesse White, Alan Young, Hans Conried, Ronnie Schell, James Hampton, Howard T. Platt, William Prince.* Dir & Co Pro: Norman Tokar. Co Pro: Ron Miller. Screenplay: Ted Key. Ph: Charles F. Wheeler. Ed: Cotton Warburton. Art: John B. Mansbridge & Preston Ames. M: Lalo Schifrin. Assoc Pro: Jan Williams. 2nd Unit Dir: Arthur J. Vitarelli. (Disney.) Rel: 22 October. 98 mins. Cert U.

Catherine & Co—Catherine et Cie 1975
Franco-Italian film veering towards, and then against, the normal sex movie, with a slim story about an English girl (*Jane Birkin*) who goes to Paris, meets various men and decides to make herself into a company, with all her male friends as stockholders! Rest of cast: *Patrick Dewaere, Jean-Pierre Aumont, Vittorio Caprioli, Jean-Claude Brialy, Nathalie Courval, Mehdi, Henri Garcin, Jean Barney, Jacques Marin, Jacques Rosny, Dora Doll, Hélène Duc, Robert Favart, Alexandra Gorsky, Jacques Legras, Bernard Musson, Carlo Nell, Maurice Travail.* Dir. Michel Boisrond. Pro: Leo L. Fuchs. Assoc Pro: Volker Lemke. Screenplay: Catherine Breillat & Leo L. Fuchs; based on the novel by Edouardo de Segonzac. Ph: Richard Suzuki. Ed: Jacques Witta. Set Des: Jean Revel. (Viaduct Productions, Paris–PIC, Rome–Columbia/EMI/Warner.) Rel: Floating. 99 mins. Cert X.

The Chant of Jimmie Blacksmith
Bloody, violent, but brilliant Fred Schepisi adaptation of the Thomas Keneally book which in turn was motivated by a true Australian multi-murder case at the turn of the century, when a young half-caste aborigine—brought up and educated by a white clergyman and his wife and apparently a lively, ambitious, hard-working lad—is so cheated and otherwise ill-used by his several white bosses that he eventually takes an axe to a farmer's family and thus begins the saga of seven murders in seven months before he is caught and hanged. A sombre accusation of the rural Australian of the period, showing him as a bigoted, brutal and unfeeling racist. Another remarkable Australian production. Cast: *Tommy Lewis, Freddy Reynolds, Ray Barrett, Jack Thompson, Julie Dawson, Peter Carroll, Robyn Nevin, Don Crosby, Ruth Cracknell, Elizabeth Alexander, Peter Sumner, Tim Robertson, Jane Harders, Ray Meagher, Brian Anderson, Marshall Crosby, Matthew Crosby, Rosie Lilley, Katie Lilley.* Dir, Pro & Screenplay: Fred Schepisi; based on the book by Thomas Keneally. Pro Sup: Roy Stevens. Ph: Ian Baker. Ed: Brian Kavanagh. Pro Des: Wendy Dickson. M: Bruce Smeaton. (Fox.) Rel: 25 February. 125 mins. Cert X.

The Cheap Detective
Amusing comedy, from the same team that made *Murder by Death,* which gets a lot of the fun from references to classic old movies of the 1930s and 1940s, such as *Casablanca* and *The Maltese Falcon. Peter Falk,* with Bogart-type lisp, as the private eye suspected of murdering his partner, and stealing his wife, and having to solve the case in order to clear himself. Lots of witty Neil Simon lines, lovely ladies and some good performances. Rest of cast: *Ann-Margret, Eileen Brennan, Sid Caesar, Stockard Channing, James Coco, Dom Del DeLuise, Louise Fletcher, John Houseman, Madeline Kahn, Fernando Lamas, Marsha Mason, Phil Silvers, Abe Vigoda, Paul Williams, Nicol Williamson, Emory Bass, Carmine*

Caridi, James Cromwell, Scatman Crothers, David Odgen Stiers, Vick Tayback, Carole Wells, John Calvin, Barry Michlin, Richard Narita, Jonathan Banks, Lew Gallo, Lee McLaughlin, Zale Kessler, Jerry Ziman, Wally Berns, Bella Bruck, Henry Sutton, Maurice Marks, Joe Ross, Dean Perry, George Rondo, Ronald L. Schwary, Louis H. Kelly, Charles A. Bastin, Armando Gonzalez, Gary L. Dyer, Steven Fisher, Laurie Hagen, Lee Menning, Nancy Warren, Nancy Marlowe Coyne, Lynn Griffis, Paula Friel, Sheila Sisco, Lauren Simon, Cindy Lang, Tina Ritt, David Matthau, Gary Alexander, Michele Bernath, George F. Simmons, Joree Sirianni, Cornell Chulay. Dir: Robert Moore. Pro: Ray Stark. Screenplay: Neil Simon. Ph: John A. Alonzo. Ed: Sidney Levin & Michael Al Steven. Assoc Pro: Margaret Booth. Pro Des: Robert Luthardt. M: Patrick Williams. (Rastar–Columbia.) Rel: 15 October. 93 mins. Cert A.

The Chess Players
Delightful Satyajit Ray film about two Lucknow noblemen who are so obsessed with chess that they play it all day and every day and are unwilling to be made aware of the greater game in the background, with the British Governor-General deciding, in 1856, to forget the long-standing treaty of friendship with the small state of Oudh, and demanding that the poet–king step down and let the British take over. A witty, subtle and deeply observant comedy which is fair to all sides and passes no final judgement as to the rights and wrongs of the actions of all concerned. Beautifully acted by *Kumer* and *Saeed Jaffrey* as the chess players, *Amjad Khan* as the King and *Richard Attenborough* as the loyal but embarrassed carrier of the ultimatum, General Outram. Rest of cast: *Shabana Azmi, Farida Jalal, Amitabh Bachchan.* Dir & Screenplay: Satyajit Ray; based on the story by Munshi Premchand. Ph: Soumendu Roy. Ed: Dulal Dutta. Art: Bansi Chandragupta. M: Satyajit Ray. (Devki Chitra Productions–Connoisseur.) Rel: Floating; first shown London, January 1979. 128 mins. Cert A.

The Children of Theatre Street
Russian documentary, with commentary in English by Princess Grace of Monaco, about the young students of the Vaganova Choreographic Institute (more commonly called the Kirov School and formerly the Imperial Ballet School of Russia). Dir: Robert Dornhelm. (Columbia/EMI/Warner.) Rel: Floating. 93 mins. Cert U.

Chinese Roulette—Chinesisches Roulette
Fascinating, stylised Fassbinder film (made 1976) about a wealthy businessman who, saying he's off to Oslo for the weekend, takes his mistress to his country chateau—where he finds his wife with her lover. Then the couple discover that the confrontation has been engineered by their crippled daughter, who also turns up, to watch how they react to the situation, one which turns more sour when the mother kills her daughter's beloved governess. Highly artificial, full of paradox, and a thinly veiled

political attack on the bourgeoisie. Cast: *Margit Carstensen, Andrea Schober, Ulli Lommel, Anna Karina, Macha Meril, Alexander Allerson, Volker Spengler, Brigitte Mira, Armin Meier, Roland Henschke.* Dir & Screenplay & Pro: Rainer Werner Fassbinder. Assoc Pro: Jean-François Stevenin. Pro Sup: Christian Hohoff. Ph: Michael Ballhaus & Horst Knechtel. Ed: Illa von Hasperg. Art: Kurt Raab, Peter Müller & Helga Ballhaus. M: Peer Raben. (Albatros Produktion, Munich–Les Films du Losange, Paris–Cinegate.) Rel: Floating; first shown London, July 1978. 86 mins. Cert AA.

Close Encounters of the Third Kind
Steven (*Jaws*) Spielberg's remarkable science-fiction film about the visit to America made by some creatures from another planet in their fantastic spaceship—after various preparatory, investigatory flights by small scout ships. Not always completely clarified in earlier sequences but always magnificently visual and in the climactic scenes of the spaceship's arrival quite stunning, without ever losing a sense of humanity and wonder. The blockbuster which soon after first showings in America began to snap at the financially-successful heels of both *Jaws* and *Star Wars!* Cast: *Richard Dreyfuss, François Truffaut, Teri Garr, Melinda Dillon, Bob Balaban, Lance Hendriksen, Warren Kemmerling, Roberts Blossom, Phillip Dodds, Cary Guffey, Shawn Bishop, Adrienne Campbell, Justin Dreyfuss, Merrill Connally, George Dicenzo.* Dir & Screeplay: Steven Spielberg. Pro: Julia & Michael Phillips. Ph: Vilmos Zsigmond. Spec Ph Eff: Douglas Trumbull. M: John Williams. Dir Ph (additional American scenes): William A. Fraker, (add. sequences in India) Douglas Slocombe. Pro Des: Joe Alves. Ed: Michael Kahn. Assoc Pro: Clark Paylow. Additional Ph Dir: John Alonzo & Laszlo Kovacs. Art: Dan Lomino. Script Supervision: Charlie Bryant. Spec Eff Sup: Douglas Trumbull. UFO Ph: Dave Stewart. Project Co-ord: Mona Thal Benefiel. (Spielberg–Columbia–EMI–Warner) Rel: 6 August (included in *Film Review 1978–79* as a floating release). 135 mins. Cert A.

Coma
Highly incredible, if original and extremely entertaining medical whodunnit, with *Geneviève Bujold* as the pretty doctor at the Boston Memorial Hospital who, uneasy about the death of her best friend during a minor operation, begins an investigation which leads to the uncovering of a macabre plot by some of the higher management to kill off enough patients per year to satisfy a lucrative market in human spare parts. Written and directed by doctor Michael Crichton, who used the book by another doctor (Robin Cook) for his basis of the story; so the grisly scenes of operations can be taken as authentic even if some of the others—although often tense in the Hitchcock style—are far-fetched. Rest of cast: *Michael Douglas, Elizabeth Ashley, Rip Torn, Richard Widmark, Lois Chiles, Harry Rhodes, Gary Barton, Frank Downing, Richard Doyle, Alan*

Releases of the Year in Detail

Haufrect, Lance Le Gault, Michael MacRae, Betty McGuire, Tom Selleck, Charles Siebert, William Wintersole, Ernest Anderson, Harry Basch, Maury Cooper, Joni Palmer, Joanna Kerns, Kay Cole, Tom Borut MD, Philip Brooks MD, Benny Rubin, David Hollander, Dick Balduzzi, Gary Bisig, Kurt Andon, Wyatt Johnson, Mike Lally Snr, John Widlock, Duane Tucker, Del Hinkley, Paul Ryan, Michael Mann, Sarina C. Grant, David McKnight, Gerlad Bentson MD, Robert Burton, Ed Harris, Joe Bratcher, Martin Speer, Roger Newman, Paul Davidson, Amentha Dymally, Lois Walden, Sharron Frame, Sue Bugden, Susie Luner. Dir & Screenplay: Michael Crichton; the later based on the book by Robin Cook. Pro: Martin Erlichman. Ph: Victor J. Kemper. Pro Des: Albert Brenner. Ed: David Bretherton. Jefferson Institute Sequence Ph: Gerald Hirschfeld. M: Jerry Goldsmith. (MGM–CIC.) Rel: 12 November. 113 mins. Cert AA.

*The Comeback
Grand-Guignol-type, grisly thriller about a pop singer who comes back after five idle years in America to try to revive his former British glory but is immediately plunged into a plot to send him insane, murder his ex-wife and too curious friend, and wall up his girl-friend in the attic! Lots of laughable lines and incidents, gallons of gore, several rotting corpses and an acceptable performance by singer *Jack Jones* as singer Nick Cooper. A neat performance, too, by *David Doyle*. Rest of cast: *Pamela Stephenson, Bill Owen, Sheila Keith, Holly Palance, Peter Turner, Richard Johnson, Patrick Brock, June Chadwick, Penny Irving, Jeff Silk.* Dir & Pro: Peter Walker. Screenplay: Murray Smith. Ph: Peter Jessop. Ed: Alan Brett. Art: Mike Pickwoad. M: Stanley Myers. (Enterprise Pictures.) Rel: 17 June 1978. 100 mins. Cert X.

Coming Home
One of the Vietnam War cycle of movies, this one with a story about an enthusiastic US Army officer who goes off happily to fight but is disillusioned to find his wife has taken as a lover a paralysed young veteran in the hospital at which she is a voluntary worker. Well acted, ably directed but, finally, somehow unsatisfactory. Cast: *Jane Fonda, Jon Voight, Bruce Dern, Robert Carradine, Penelope Milford, Robert Ginty, Charles Dyphers, Teresa Hughes, Mary Jackson, Olivia Cole, Willie Tyler, David Clennon, Arthur Rosenberg, Lou Carello, Mary Gregory, Beeson Carrol, Bruce French, Richard Lawson, Kathleen Miller, Rita Taggert, Pat Corley, Ned Van Zandt, Dennis Rucker, Jonathan Banks, James Richardson, Tim Pelt, Claudie Watson, Sally Frei, Tony Santoro, Gwen Van Dam, Jim Klein, Toyko Ernie, Paul Bayardo, Stacy Pickren, James Kindelon, Joey Faustine, Kimberly Binion, Kirk Raymond, Bille Hale, Danny Tucker, Gary Downey, George Roberts, Bob Ott, Gary Lee Davis, Marc McClure.* Dir: Hal Ashby. Pro: Jerome Hellman. Screenplay: Waldo Salt & Robert C. Jones; from a story by Nancy Dowd. Ph: Haskell Wexler. Ed: Don Zimmerman. Assoc Pro: Bruce Gilbert. Pro Des: Michael Haller. (Jerome Hellman Enterprises/Jayne Productions–UA.) Rel: 15 October. 128 mins. Cert X.

Convoy
Sam Peckinpah turns from men to machines for his new excursion into the territory of celluloid violence, with a story about a convoy of belligerent truckers, headed by a character called 'Rubber Duck' (*Kris Kristofferson*), who for some reason is having a personal vendetta with the local sheriff (*Ernest Borgnine*). A running fight between the two leads to smashed cars, injured cops, overturned trucks, rough humour and some very odd moralising. With all the usual Peckinpah (slow motion) trade marks but less bloody, and well below the director's best efforts. Rest of cast: *Ali MacGraw, Burt Young, Madge Sinclair, Frankly Ajaye, Cassie Yates, Seymour Cassel.* Dir: Sam Peckinpah. Pro: Robert H. Sherman. Ex Pro: Michael Deeley & Barry Spikings. Screenplay: B. W. L. Norton: based on the C. W. McCall record of his song 'Convoy'. Ph: Harry Stradling Jr. Ed: Graeme Clifford. Pro Des: Fernando Carrere. (Columbia/EMI/Warner.) Rel: 27 August. 111 mins. Cert A.

The Courage of the People—(alternatively titled **The Night of San Juan**)—**El Coraje del Pueblo**
1971 Bolivian/Italian dramatised reconstruction of the massacre of Bolivian tin-miners and their families by soldiers during a strike in 1967 for higher wages and the release of the strikers' jailed leaders. Dir: Jorge Sandines. Pro: Ricardo Rada, Walter Achugar & Eduardo Pallero. Screenplay: Oscar Soria. (Ukamau Group, La Paz/RAi, Rome–The Other Cinema.) Rel: Floating; first shown London, January 1979. 91 mins. No cert.

Crash
Minor thriller about a 'death race' by cars and motor cycles across 1,000 miles of the roughest going in the Philippines, with the participants prepared to do anything to get the $100,000 first prize. Cast: *Joe Don Baker, Susan Sarandon, Larry Hagman, Alan Vint, Pavnelli Jones, Michel Pitton, Dana House, Logan Clarke, Bert Leroy, Bill Cross, Ben Leeman, Cachupoy, Eddie Mercado, Eazy Black, Dick Adair.* Dir: Alan Gibson. Pro: Fred Weintraub & Paul Heller. Assoc Pro: T. C. Wang. Screenplay: Michael Allin. Ph: Alan Hume. Ed: Allan Holzman. Art: Bill Sandell. M: Art Freeman. (Warner). Rel: 25 July. 78 mins. Cert A.

Cria Cuervos
Spanish. Carlos Saura's delicate, cloudy exploration of the strange fact-and-fiction world of a nine-year-old girl whose hoarded pot of poison she wields like God, killing her father, offering release to her stroke-stricken grandmother, attempting to murder her aunt and always living on the border between reality and imagination. Not an easy film but a compelling one, thanks considerably to the almost hypnotically fascinating performance of *Ana Torrent* as the child. Rest of cast: *Geraldine Chaplin, Conchita Perez, Maite Sanchez Almendros, Monica Randall, Florinda Chico, Hector Alterio, German Cobos, Mirta Miller, Josefina Diaz.* Dir & Screenplay: Carlos Saura. Pro: Elias Querejeta. Head of Pro: Primitivo Alvaro. Ph: Teodoro Escamilla. Ed: Pablo G. Del Amo. (Gala.) Rel: Floating; first shown London, July 1978. 110 mins. Cert AA.

The Cycle
Bitter Iranian black comedy about the local black market in blood, obtained from drug addicts, sold to the hospitals and often there used with fatal results. Used as the background to the story of a father and son who come to Tehran hoping to obtain a cure for the old man's lingering illness, instead of which he is contaminated and dies as the son slides into the city's corruption in order to get the money for the treatment. Cast: *Ezat Entezami, Ali Nassiriane, Frouzan, Said Kangarani, Bahman Forssi, Esmail Mohamadi.* Dir: Dariush Mehrjui. Pro: not named. Screenplay: D. Mehrjui; from a story by Golam Hossein Saedi. Ph: Hochang Baharlou. Ed: Talat Mirfendereski. No Art or M. credits. (Telfilm–Contemporary.) Rel: Floating; first shown London, September 1978. 102 mins. Cert AA.

Damien—Omen II
Gregory Peck, having realised his son is a little devil, literally, in the first *Omen* film and unsuccessfully trying to kill the kid—himself dying in the effort—takes no part in this sequel in which his business magnate brother (*William Holden*) is bringing up the orphan, sending him to a Chicago Military Academy where his own son of about the same age is being educated. It takes almost the entire film, the tragic death of the son and a number of devilishly unpleasant occurrences to convince Holden that he is nurturing a viper in his bosom, a realisation rapidly followed by his own demise at the hands of his Damien-obsessed wife. So Damien survives to carry on towards the holocaust promised by Satan, which we'll surely be witnessing in *Omen III*! And *Omen II* isn't as good as *Omen I*. Rest of cast: *Lee Grant, Jonathan Scott-Taylor, Robert Foxworth, Nicholas Pryor, Lew Ayres, Sylvia Sidney, Lance Henriksen, Elizabeth Shepherd, Lucas Donat, Alan Arbus, Fritz Ford.* Dir: Don Taylor. Pro: Harvey Bernhard. Screenplay: Stanley Mann & Michael Hodges; from a story by Harvey Bernhard based on the David Seltzer characters. Co-Pro: Charles Orme. Ph: Bill Butler. Ed: Robert Brown Jun. Pro Des: Philip M. Jefferies & Fred Harpman. M: Jerry Goldsmith. Assoc Pro: Joseph 'Pepi' Lenzi. (Fox.) Rel: 4 March. 107 mins. Cert X.

138

Damnation Alley

Spectacular slice of grand old Hollywood hokum about some survivors of atomic warfare—(General) *George Peppard*, insistently cheerful assistant *Jan-Michael Vincent* and Las Vegas pick-up *Dominique Sanda*—who trundle their way in their odd land-machine through lunar-like landscapes, under green-flecked skies, through fiery electric storms, hurricanes and floods to eventual green-fielded, blue-skied normality! Good clean fun almost every foot of the eventful way. Rest of cast: *Paul Winfield, Jackie Earle Haley, Kip Niven, Robert Donner, Seamon Glass, Trent Dolan, Mark L. Taylor, Bob Hackman, Erik Cord, Terence Locke, Marcia Holley*. Dir: Jack Smight. Pro: Jerome M. Zeitman & Paul Maslansky. Ex Pro: Hal Landers & Bobby Roberts. Assoc Pro: Maury Cohen. Screenplay: Alan Sharp & Lukas Heller; from the novel by Roger Zelazny. Ed: Frank J. Urioste. Ph: Harry Stradling Jun. Pro Des: Preston Ames. Art: William Cruse. M: Jerry Goldsmith. (Fox.) Rel: 21 January. 91 mins. Cert A.

*The Deadly Females

Minor British thriller about some housewives who, to earn a little extra money, become members of a sort of female Murder Inc, removing for cash unpleasant lovers and husbands. Episodic, far-fetched but in turn mildly amusing and, once, particularly horrifying. Cast: *Tracy Reed, Bernard Holley, Scott Fredericks, Heather Chasen, Brian Jackson, Roy Purcell, Jean Harrington, Olivia Munday, Jean Rimmer, Raymond Young, Lans Travers, Angela Jay, Gennie Nevinson, Graham Ashley, Rula Lenska*. Dir, Pro Ed & Screenplay: Donovan Winter. Ph: Austin Parkinson. (Donwin-Monarch.) Rel: Floating; first shown London, June 1978, though made in 1975. 105 mins. Cert X.

Dead Beat & Blood

Arts Council short film. Dir: Franco Rosso. (Rebel Movies/Arts Council.) Rel: Floating; first shown London, December 1978. 45 mins. No cert.

Dear Inspector—Tendre Poulet

A nice, simple, satirical French comedy about the first woman detective to serve at the Sûreté and her solving of a triple murder. Lots of Paris; delightful *Annie Girardot*, and solidly amusing *Philippe Noiret* as her Sorbonne-professor love. Rest of cast: *Catherine Alric, Hubert Deschamps, Paulette Dubost, Roger Dunas, Raymond Gerome, Guy Marchand, Simone Renant, Georges Wilson, Armelle Pourriche, Czarmiak, Maurice Illouz, Michel Norman, Georges Riquier, Alain David, J. P. Rambal*. Dir: Philippe de Broca. Pro: Alexandre Mnouchkine. Assoc Pro: Georges Dancigers & Robert Amon. Screenplay: Michel Audiard & Philippe de Broca; based on the novel *Le Commissaire Tanquerelle et le Frelon* by Jean-Paul Rouland & Claude Oliver; adapted by

Michel Audiard. Ph: Jean-Paul Schwartz. Ed: François Javet. Art: François de Lamothe. M: Georges Delerue. (Les Films Ariane/Mondex Films-Entertainment.) Rel: Floating; first shown London, December 1978. 105 mins. Cert AA.

Death on the Nile

First-class adaptation of the Agatha Christie whodunnit, with Hercule Poirot (*Peter Ustinov*, delightful) sorting out the murder suspects as the steamer paddles its way up the Nile. Some fascinating backgrounds, polished performances from a starry cast, tight direction. Rest of cast: *Jane Birkin, Lois Chiles, Bette Davis, Mia Farrow, Jon Finch, Olivia Hussey, I. S. Johar, George Kennedy, Angela Lansbury, Simon MacCorkindale, David Niven, Maggie Smith, Jack Warden, Harry Andrews, Sam Wanamaker*. Dir: John Guillermin. Pro: John Brabourne & Richard Goodwin. Screenplay: Anthony Shaffer. Assoc Pro: Norton Knatchbull. Ph: Jack Cardiff. Ed: Malcolm Cooke. Pro Des: Peter Murton. M: Nino Rota. (Nat Cohen–EMI.) Rel: 14 January. 140 mins. Cert A.

The Deer Hunter

Long, sincere and intermittently highly impressive, but flawed, effort to show the depths of love and loyalty which sometimes exist beneath the roughest of male friendships and the true, horrendous impact the Vietnam War had on the lives, loves and sanity of so many of those who took part in it. Some horrifying moments of brutal Vietnamese torture of their American prisoner, some bloody and beastly recurring sequences about the Russian roulette that was played by a leisurely East European-style wedding and reception sequence which takes up most of the film's three hours. And the winner of the 1979 Best Film Oscar. Cast: *Robert de Niro, John Cazale, John Savage, Christopher Walken, Meryl Streep, George Dzundza, Chuck Aspegren, Shirley Stoler, Rutanya Alda, Pierre Segui, Mady Kaplan, Amy Wright, Mary Ann Haenel, Richard Kuss, Joe Grifasi, Paul D'Amato, Father Stephen Kopestonsky, Tom Becker, Lynn Kongkham, Nongnuj Timruang, Po Pao Pee, Vitoon Winwitoon, Somasak Sengvilai, Phip Manee. Chai Peyawan, Mana Hansa, Sombot Jumpanoi, Ding Santos, Krieng Chaiyapuk, Ot Pakapoo, Chok Chai Mahasoke*. Dir Michael Cimino. Pro: Barry Spikings, Michael Deeley, Michael Cimino & John Peverall. Screenplay: Deric Washburn; from an original story by Michael Cimino, Deric Washburn, Louis Garfinkle & Quinn K. Redeker. Pro Consultant: Joann Carelli. Assoc Pro: Marion Rosenberg & Joann Carelli. Ph: Vilmos Zsigmond. Ed: Peter Zinner. Art: Ron Hobbs & Kim Swados. M: Stanley Myers; theme tune played by John Williams. Ex in charge of Pro: Elliott Schick. (EMI.) Rel: 1 April. 182 mins. Cert X.

*Derzu Uzala

Japan's famous director Akira (*Rashomon & Seven Samurai*) Kurosawa's Russian film (1975 Best

Foreign Language Film 'Oscar' winner) about a turn-of-the-century military explorer in eastern Siberia and the old hunter he meets and who, during three expeditions, becomes his friend and life-saver. A quiet, beautiful film with several remarkable action sequences and some outstanding acting performances, more especially by *Yuri Solomin* and *Maxim Minsuk* as the two main characters. Rest of cast: *M. Bechkov, V. Khrulev, V. Lastochkin, S. Marin, I. Sikhra, V. Sergiyavov, Y. Yakobsons, V. Khlestov, G. Polunik, V. Koldin, M. Tetov, S. Sinyavsky, V. Sverba, V. Ignatov, A. Pyatkov, V. Kremena, S. Chikmorov, S. Danilchenko, Dimm Korshikov, D. Netrebin, S. Zaitsev, N. Volkov, V. Kuryanov, Tsun Du-Go, Z. Mademilova, E. Erdniev, V. Prokhodko*. Dir: Akira Kurosawa. Pro: Eiti Mattsue. Screenplay: Akira Kurosawa & Yuri Gantman; based on the novels of Vladimir Klavdievic Arsenyev. Pro Man: Karlen Agadzhanov. Ph: Asakadzu Nakai, Yuri Gantman & Fyodor Dobronravov. Ed: V. Stepanovoi. Art: Yuri Raksha. M: Isaak Shvartz. (Mosfilm, Moscow–Toho, Tokyo–Curzon Films Dist.) Rel: Floating; first shown London, at the Curzon, June 1978. 141 mins. Cert U.

Despair

Rainer Werner Fassbinder's first 'international', or English-speaking, film and his most lavish and carefully stylish production yet: a psychological drama and murder-thriller, and something of a black comedy at the same time, scripted by Britain's Tom Stoppard. The story of a chocolate-manufacturer who becomes obsessed with existentialist despair and plots a way out by murdering a tramp he meets and taking his name. But he bungles the plot and slides into madness. A fascinating character-study always tinged with depravity; insistently Germanic in atmosphere, theme and treatment. A remarkable if studied performance by *Dirk Bogarde*. Rest of cast: *Andrea Ferreol, Volker Spengler, Bernhard Wicki, Alexander Allerson, Klaus Lowitsch, Peter Kern*. Dir: Rainer Werner Fassbinder. Pro: Peter Marthesheimer. Screenplay: Tom Stoppard; based on the novel by Vladimir Nabokov. Ex Pro: Lutz Hengst. Ph: Michael Lallhaus. Ed: Juliane Lorenz & Franz Walsch. Art: Rolf Zehetbauer. M: Peer Raben. (Bavaria Atelier–SFP–Geria Il–Gala.) Rel: Floating; first shown London, July 1978. 119 mins. Cert AA.

The Detour

Delightfully-photographed and imaginative half-hour film shot entirely on location in Malta, with a slim little story tying up the local hunting hounds with one of the ancient Egyptian god Anubis, the subject of one of the island's legends. Cast: *Nancy Clamatta, Adrian Rendle, John Galdes* and the dog, *Champion Ra of Attard*. Introduction spoken by *Peter Cushing*. Dir. & Pro: Rodney Holland. Ex Pro: Jeremy Holland. Story: John Branston & Rodney Holland. Ph: Ivan Strasburg. Ed: Tony Lawson. M: Adrian Wagner. (Barkrow–GTO Films.) Rel: 15 February. 34 mins. Cert U.

Releases of the Year in Detail

The Devil's Advocate
West German film about a 1958 investigation by devil's advocate Monsignor Meredith (*John Mills* as an Englishman suffering from inoperable cancer) on behalf of his Vatican superiors as to the validity or otherwise of the saintly legends built around a young English World War II deserter who, having taken refuge in a small Italian village, was accused as a collaborator and executed, but not before he apparently miraculously cured his son of blindness. Rest of cast: *Stéphane Audran, Jason Miller, Paola Pitagora, Daniel Massey, Leigh Lawson, Timothy West, Patrick Mower, Romolo Valli, Raf Vallone, Jack Hedley, Wimmi Riva, Hartmut Solinger, Janos Grapow.* Dir: Guy Green. Pro: Helmut Jedele. Ex Pro: Lutz Hengst. Pro Sup: Dixie Sensburg. Screenplay: Morris West; based on his own novel. Ph: Billy Williams. Ed: Stefan Arnsten. Pro Des: Rolf Zehetbauer. Art: Werner Achmann. M: Bert Grund. (Geria Films–Rank.) Rel: Floating; first shown London, May 1978. 109 mins. Cert AA.

Dogs
Minor league thriller about a pack of killer dogs who go on the rampage, turning from other animals to humans as prey. Cast: *David McCallum, George Wyner, Eric Server, Sandra McCabem, Sterling Swanson, Holly Harris, Fred Hice, Lance Hool, Jim Stathis, Debbie Davis, Barry Greenberg, Linda Gray, Dean Santoro, Larry Darbell, Elizabeth Kerr, Cathy Austin, Michael Davis, Russ Greive, Frank Paolasso, R. A. Rondell.* Dir: Burt Brinckerhoff. Pro: Allan F. Bodoh & Bruce Cohn. Ex Pro: Michael Leone. Assoc Pro: Mitchell Cannold & Joel Tator. Ex Pro. Supervisor: Jeff Sinclair. Screenplay: O'Brian Tomalin. Ph: Bob Steadman. Ed: John Wright. Art: No credits. M: Alan Oldfield. (Mar Vista/La Quinta Film Partners in assoc. with Bruce Cohn Productions–Enterprise.) Rel: Floating. 90 mins. Cert. AA.

Dog Soldiers
Oddly-titled piece which has nothing to do with dogs and, after the short, bloody Vietnam War introduction, very little to do with soldiers! A hard, rough drama about a war correspondent who decides to make his war pay off with a couple of kilos of pure heroin smuggled back to the USA but a pal. But the FBI narcotics agent and his two moronic assistants are quickly on the trail of the pal and the correspondent's wife (who becomes embroiled) and thereafter it's a chase, which ends with the couple besieged on a rugged mountain-top. Cast: *Nick Nolte, Tuesday Weld, Michael Moriarty, Anthony Zerbe, Richard Masur, Ray Sharkey, Gail Strickland, Charles Haid, David Opatoshu, Joaquin Martinez, James Cranna, Timothy Blake, Shelby Balik, Jean Howell, Jose Carlos Ruiz, John Durren, Bobby Kosser, Wings Hauser, Jonathan Banks, Michael Bair, Derrel Maury, Jan Burrell, Stuart Wilson, James Gavin, Bill Cross.* Dir: Karel Reisz. Pro: Herb Jaffe & Gabriel Katzka. Screenplay: Judith Rascoe & Robert Stone; based on the latter's book of the same title. Ph:

Richard H. Kline. Assoc Pro: Roger Spottiswoode & Sheldon Schrager. Sup Ed: John Bloom. M: Laurence Rosenthal. (UA.) Rel: 1 April. 125 mins. Cert X.

Dominique
Sombre little British thriller about the haunting to death of a man who drove his mentally unbalanced wife to suicide; a film full of foreboding, shadowy figures from the grave, unexplained noises and a general atmosphere of terror. Cast: *Cliff Robertson, Jean Simmons, Jenny Agutter, Simon Ward, Ron Moody, Judy Geeson, Michael Jayston, Flora Robson, David Tomlinson, Jack Warner.* Dir: Michael Anderson. Pro: Milton Subotsky & Andrew Donally. Ph: Ted Moore. Ed: Richard Best. Screenplay: Edward & Valerie Abraham; from a story by Harold Lawlor. Art: David Minty. M: David Whitaker. (Melvin Simon/Sword & Sorcery Production–Barber Dann Films.) Rel: June 24. 100 mins. Cert. AA.

The Domino Killings
Gene Hackman as the habitual criminal 'sprung' from jail after agreeing to repay the gang by a favour, which turns out to be the assassination of a national figure—an assignment he dodges and which leads to his girlfriend's death and his own name on the black list. . . . Rest of cast: *Candice Bergen, Richard Widmark, Mickey Rooney, Edward Albert Jr, Eli Wallach, Ken Swofford, Neva Patterson, Jay Novello, Joseph Perry, Ted Gehring, Robert Karnes, Claire Brennan, George Memmoli, George Fisher, Bob Herron, Denver Mattson, Charles Horvath, Wayne King, Jim Gavin, Kirk Mee, Laura Hippe, Farnsio de Bernal, Patricia Luke, Raquel Fitzpatrick, Anna Roth, Rosa Torres.* Dir & Pro: Stanley Kramer. Ex Pro: Martin Starger. Screenplay: Adam Kennedy; based on his own novel, *The Domino Principle.* Ph: Fred Koenekamp & Ernest Laszlo. Ed: John Burnett. Pro Des: William J. Creber. Art: Ron Hobbs. M: Billy Goldenberg. Assoc Pro: Terry Morse, Jr. (Lew Grade–Associated General Films in assoc with Martin Starger–ITC.) Rel: Floating. 100 mins. Cert AA.

Don's Party
Another rough, crudely credible Australian film, an adaptation of a play by David Williamson about a drunken and acrimonious 'party' held on the night of 25 October, 1969, when in the General Election of that day the Labour Party is surprisingly defeated. But it is sex, soured marriages, frustration and fear, rather than politics, which generate the bickering and brutality among the group of highly unpleasant and unsympathetically-drawn characters. And it is all so painfully and powerfully convincing. Cast: *Ray Barrett, Clare Binney, Pat Bishop, Graeme Blundell, Jeanie Drynam, John Hargreaves, Harold Hopkins, Graham Kennedy, Veronica Lang, Candy Raymond, Kit Taylor.* Dir: Bruce Beresford. Pro: Phillip Adams. Screenplay: David Williamson. Other credits not available. (Australian Film Commission–Miracle.) Rel: Floating. 90 mins. Cert X.

Don't Cry for Me Little Mother
German/Yugoslav (English speaking) film which does little to disguise the fact that its story, about a slum-born, small-part actress who uses her physical charms to climb from a general's bed into that of the president—as his wife!—and becomes the virtual leader of the country is based very firmly on South American history. An attractive performance of every citizen's lovely little mother by delightful *Christiane Kruger*, daughter of Hardy Kruger. Lots of explicit sex, some hints of sadism, and a most irritating technical way of telling the story by continually jumping from present to past and back again. Rest of cast: *Siegfried Rauch, Mark Damon, Ivan Desny, Anton Diffring, Elga Sorbas.* Dir: Radley Metzger. Assoc Pro: Ava Leighton. Screenplay: Brian Phelan. Ph: Hans Jura. Ed: Amedeo Salfa. M: George Craig. (Peter Carsten, Munich–Jahdran Films, Zagreb–Gala Film Dist.) Rel: Floating; first shown London, July 1978. 99 mins. Cert X.

A Dream of Passion
Melina Mercouri as an ageing, fading star who comes back to Greece to play in *Medea* and becomes involved with an American woman (*Ellen Burstyn*), jailed there for infanticide, using her for publicity purposes and then getting a guilt-complex about her action. Rest of cast: *Andreas Voutsinas, Despo Diamantidou, Dimitris Papamichael, Yannis Voglis, Phedon Georgitsis, Betty Valassi, Andreas Filippides, Kostas Arzoglou, Irene Emizra, Panos Papaionnou, Manos Katrakis, Nikos Galiatsos, Savvas Axiotis, Litsa Vaidou, Olympia Papadouka, Anna Thomaidou, Freddie Germanos, Stefanos Vlachos, Alexis Solomos.* Dir, Pro & Screenplay: Jules Dassin. Ph: George Arvanitis. Ed: George Klotz. Sets/Costumes (No other art credits): Dionysis Fotopoulos. M: Iannis Markopoulous. (ITC.) Rel: Floating; first shown London, February 1979. 110 mins. Cert X.

The Driver
Cold, spare, superficial but oddly compelling story of an (unexplained) deadly feud between ace crooks'-getaway driver, unhappy *Ryan O'Neal*, and dedicated and obsessed cop *Bruce Dern*, who sets the traps which always somehow fail to catch the proposed victim, in spite of double-crosses by Ryan's villainous mates, one of whom is almost as anxious to bring him down as the cop. And the title in this case tells—well, almost—all; a series of wild chases and automobile mutilations, as The Driver shows his expert car control. Rest of cast: *Isabelle Adjani, Ronee Blakely, Matt Clark, Felice Orlandi, Joseph Walsh, Rudy Ramos, Denny Macko, Frank Bruno, Will Walker, Sandy Brown Wyeth, Tara King, Richard Carey, Fidel Corona, Victor Gilmour, Nick Dimitri, Bob Minor, Angelo Lamonea, Patrick Burns, Karen Kleiman, Rhomas Myers, Bill McConnell, Peter Jason, William Hasley, Allan Graf.* Dir & Screenplay:

Walter Hill. Pro: Lawrence Gordon. Assoc Pro: Frank Marshall. Ph: Philip Lathrop. Pro Des: Harry Horner. Ed: Tina Hirsch & Robert K. Lambert. M: Michael Small. (EMI.) Rel: 8 October. 91 mins. Cert A.

Emanuelle and the Last Cannibals—Emanuelle e gli Ultimi Cannibali
Pretty frenetic Italian addition to the series, with a story of a search through the Amazon jungle by journalist Emanuelle—for a lost girl who is living with a tribe of man-eaters—with plenty of sex and violence. Cast: *Laura Gemser, Gabriele Tinti, Susan Scott, Donald O'Brien, Mónica Zanchi, Annamaria Clementi, Geoffrey Copplestone, Dirce Funari, Pierluigi Cervetti Vale, Bona Bono, Maria Gabrielle Mezzetti, Massimo Ciprari, Giuseppe Auci.* Dir: Joe D'Amato. Pro: Gianfranco Couyoumdjian. Pro Sup: Paolo Ganano. Screenplay: Romano Scandariato & Aristide Massaccesi. Ph: A. Massaccesi. Ed: Alberto Moriani. Art: Carlo Ferri. M: Nico Fidenco. (Fulvia Cinematografica/Gico Cinematografica/Flora Films–Entertainment.) Rel: Floating. 87 mins. Cert X.

Empire of Passion—Ai No Borei
A follow-up to Oshima's intensely erotic *Realm of the Senses*—and intended as the second film in a trilogy based on love and death—this story is again based on fact, and with stunning impact relates the passion of a young man for a woman twenty years his senior: a desire which leads to them murdering her husband, being haunted by his ghost, and eventually paying a horrible price for their crime. A mixture of sensualism and cruelty; stylish, poetic, absorbing and beautifully acted by *Kastuko Yoshiyuki* and *Tatsuya Fuji* as the lovers. Rest of cast: *Takahiro Tamura, Takuzo Kawatani, Akiko Koyama, Taiji Tonoyama, Sumie Sasaki, Eizo Kitamura, Masami Hasegawa, Kenzo Kawarazaki, Takaaki Sugiura.* Dir & Screenplay: Nagisa Oshima; based on a story by Itoko Nakamura. Pro: Anatole Dauman. Ph: Yoshio Miyajima. Art: no credit; set décor by Jusho Toda. Ed: Keiichu Uraoka. M: Toru Takemitsu. (Argos Films, Paris–Shibata Org, Tokoyo–Artificial Eye.) Rel: Floating; first shown London, January 1979. 106 mins. Cert X.

The End
Described by the releasing company as 'a black comedy about death', this somewhat messy mixture included not only authentic black comedy and wit but also broad farce, bad taste and vulgarity. A basically familiar story of a man who suddenly discovers he only has months to live and decides to avoid the painful End by self-destruction. But when after several farcical attempts to take his own life appears likely to succeed, he suddenly finds within him a fierce desire to live, if only temporarily. Compensations include a hilarious performance by *Dom DeLuise* as a happy murderer, cameos by

beloved old-timers *Myrna Loy* and *Pat O'Brien*, a subdued *Joanne Woodward* and neat comic timing by *Carl Reiner*. Burt Reynolds' direction of himself in the central role does him no favours! Rest of cast: *Sally Field, Strother Martin, David Steinberg, Norman Fell, Kirsty McNichol, Robby Benson, Louise Letourneau, Bill Ewing, Robert Rothwell, Harry Caesar, James Best, Peter Gonzales, Connie Fleming, Janice Carroll, Ken Johnson, Frank McRae, Alfie Wise, Edward Albrecht, Jerry Fujikawa, Jock Mahoney, Patrick Moody, Carolyn Martin, Queenie Smith, Jean Ann Coulter.* Dir: Burt Reynolds. Pro: Lawrence Gordon. Ex Pro: Hank Moonjean. Screenplay: Jerry Belson. Ph: Bobby Byrne. Ed: Donn Cambern. Pro Des: Jan Scott. M: Paul Williams. Assoc Pro: James Best. (Lawrence Gordon/Burt Reynolds Productions–UA.) Rel: Floating. 100 mins. Cert AA.

An Enemy of the People
Straightforward screen adaptation of Arthur Miller's (American) version of the Ibsen stage classic which in theme and arguments—about democracy, political dishonesty and the like—is as topical today as when it was written. Interesting technical qualities include low-toned lighting and an entire absence of bright colours, enhancing a real period atmosphere. *Steve McQueen* gives a remarkably good performance as the honest and ill-used Doctor Stockman, whose efforts to have the local polluted and poisonous spa waters—the basis of the town's prosperity—cleaned up, lead to abuse and physical violence, the loss of his job and the isolation of him and his family. Rest of cast: *Charles Durning, Bibi Andersson* (both brilliant), *Eric Christmas, Michael Cristofer, Richard A. Dysart, Michael Higgins, Richard Bradford, Ham Larsen, John Levin, Robin Pearson Rose.* Dir & Pro: George Schaefer. Ex Pro: Steve McQueen. Assoc Pro: Philip Parslow. Screenplay: Alexander Jacobs; based on the Arthur Miller adaptation of the Henrik Ibsen stage play. Ph: Paul Lohmann. Ed: Sheldon Kahn. Pro Des: Eugene Lourie. M: Leonard Rosenman. (Solar Productions–Enterprise Pictures.) Rel: Floating; first shown London, September 1978. 106 mins. Cert U.

Eraserhead
A quite extraordinary, surrealistic, black-and-white horror film as likely to draw cries of 'Rubbish' as to draw inordinate praise. A nightmare series of images telling no observable story but full of foul things with unlimited implications. At least completely original (if you push all thoughts of the old German expressionism to one side) and horribly compelling. Cast: *John Nance, Charlotte Stewart, Allen Joseph, Jeanne Bates, Judith Anna Roberts, Laurel Near, V. Phipps-Wilson.* Dir, Pro & Screenplay: David K. Lynch. Assist to Dir: Catherine Coulson. Ph: Frederick Elmes & Herbert Cardwell. Produced with the co-operation of the American Film Institute Centre for Advanced Film Studies. (Ben Barenholtz–Libra

Films.) Rel: Floating; first shown London, March 1979. 90 mins. Black-and-white. Cert X.

Every Which Way But Loose
Rough-hewn American comedy starring *Clint Eastwood*, as a genial truck-driver with a taste for bar-room brawls, and a monkey mate, and concerning his romantic pursuit of elusive lady singer *Sondra Locke*. Scenery and country music against a background of San Fernando Valley, California. Rest of cast: *Geoffrey Lewis, Beverly D'Angelo, Ruth Gordon, Walter Barnes, George Chandler, Roy Jenson, James McEachin, Bill McKinney, William O'Connell, John Quade, Dan Vadis, Gregory Walcott, Hank Worden, Jerry Brutsche, Cary Michael Cheifer, Janet Louise Cole, Sam Gilman, Chuck Hicks, Timothy P. Irvin, Tim Irvin, Billy Jackson, Joyce Jameson, Richard Jamison, Jackson D. Kane, Jeremy Kronsberg, Fritz Manes, Michael Mann, Lloyd Nelson, George Orrison, Thelma Pelish, William J. Quinn, Tom Runyon, Bruce Scott, Al Silvani, Hartley Silver, Al Stellone, Jan Stratton, Mike Wagner, Guy Way, George Wilbur, Gary Davis, Scott Dockstader, Orwin Harvey, Gene LeBell, Chuck Waters, Jerry Wills* and *Manis*, the monkey from the Bobby Berosini Performing Orangutan Show. Dir: James Fargo. Pro: Robert Daley. Screenplay: Jeremy Joe Kronsberg. Ph: Rexford Metz. Assoc Pro: Fritz Manes & Jeremy Joe Kronsberg. Ed: Ferris Webster & Joel Cox. Art: Elayne Ceder. M: Snuff Garrett. (Malpaso–Warner.) Rel: 31 December. 114 mins. Cert AA.

The Eyes of Laura Mars
Far too arty and contrived whodunnit about a sadomasochistic, stylish lady fashion-photographer who gets sudden visions of dreadful deaths just before they occur, becomes terrified as various colleagues meet bloody ends and falls in love with the detective in charge of the case . . . who is himself revealed as something of a strange character! Cast: *Faye Dunaway, Tommy Lee Jones, Brad Dourif, René Auberjonois, Raul Julia, Frank Adonis, Lisa Taylor, Darlanne Fluegel, Rose Gregorio, Bill Boggs, Steve Marachuk, Meg Mundy, Marilyn Meyers, Gary Bayer, Mitchell Edmonds, Michael Tucker, Jeff Niki, Toshi Matsuo, John E. Allen, Dallas Edward Hayes, John Randolph Jones, Al Joseph, Gerald Kline, Sal Richards, Tom Degidon, Paula Lawrence, Joey R. Mills, John Sahag, Hector Troy, Konrad Sheehan, Jim Lovelett, Harry Madsen, Bill Anagnos, Tammas Hamilton.* Models: *Anna Anderson, Deborah Beck, Jim Devine, Hanny Friedman, Winnie Hollman, Patty Oja, Donna Palmer, Sterline St Jacques, Rita Tellone, Kari Page.* Dir: Irvin Kershner. Pro: Jon Peters. Screenplay: John Carpenter & David Zelag Goodman; from the former's story. Ex Pro: Jack H. Harris. Ph: Victor J. Kemper. Assoc Pro: Laura Ziskin. Pro Ex: George Justin. Pro Des: Gene Callahan. Ed: Michael Kahn. Art: Robert Gundlach. M: Artie Kane (Columbia.) Rel: 25 February. 103 mins. Cert AA.

Releases of the Year in Detail

Fantasm
Australian pseudo-sex education lesson with
Professor Freud (Jugenot A. Freud) from Vienna
relating the case histories of nine of his patients.
Cast: *Dee Dee Levitt, Stan Stratton, John Green, Sam
Compton, Maria Arnold, Bill Margold, Kirby Hall,
Robert Savage, Helen O'Connell, Wendy Cavenaugh,
Gretchen Gayle, Con Convert, Mara Lutra, Uschi
Digard, Maria Weston, John Holmes, Maria
Gavin, Gene Alan Poe, Shayne, Rick Partlow, Sam
Wyman, Paul Wyman, Serena Clement St George,
Robin Spratt, Lyman Britton, Thomass Blaz, Gary
Dolgin, Mitch Morrill, William Wutke, Kirby Adams,
Sue Doloria, Al Wood, Rene Bond, Ronnie Scholes, Al
Williams.* Dir: Richard Bruce. Pro: A. L. Ginnane.
Ex Pro: Leon Gorr & Ted Mulder. Screenplay: Ross
Dimsey; from an idea by A. I. Ginnane. Ph: Vincent
Monton. Ed: Tony Patterson. Art: Craig Stevens. No
Music credit. (TLN Film Productions–Butcher's.)
Rel: Floating. 85 mins. Cert X.

Firepower
Complicated crookery compiled by Michael Winner,
who gives this vaguely (earlier) Bond-type story some
top-drawer technical qualities such as superb
photography, lush Caribbean backgrounds and
entertaining fast tempo. Difficult to follow but nicely
relaxing to watch! *James Coburn* as the very unofficial
US agent assigned to the task of bringing back to
Uncle Sam's justice a millionaire crook who has
taken refuge on a Caribbean island, where he's
guarded by a small army of crooks. *O. J. Simpson* as
Coburn's black aide, *Eli Wallach* as a helpful
gangster and *Sophia Loren* as the widow who appears
to change sides twice every reel. Rest of cast:
*Anthony Franciosa, George Grizzard, Vincent
Gardenia, Fred Stuthman, Richard Caldicot, Frank
Singuineau, Bill Abbot, George Touliatos, Andrew
Duncan, Hank Garrett, Billy Barty, Conrad Roberts,
Jake La Motta, Vincent Beck, Dominic Chianese, Paul
D'Amato, Paul Garcia, Richard Roberts, William
Trotman, Paula Laurence, Victor Mature.* Dir, Pro &
Story (the last with Bill Kerby): Michael Winner.
Screenplay: Gerald Wilson. Ph: Robert Paynter
(Caribbean), Dick Kratina (USA) & Richard Kline
(2nd Unit). Ex Ed: Max Benedict. Ed: Arnold Crust.
Pro Des: John Blezard (Caribbean) & Robert
Gundlach (USA). M (& saxophone solos): Gato
Barbieri. (Michael Winner–Lew Grade–ITC.) 20
May. 104 mins. Cert AA.

The First Great Train Robbery
The story of a Raffles-like thief's (*Sean Connery*)
attempt to steal £25,000 of gold bullion from a
moving train in 1855. A meticulously planned,
brilliantly organised though finally unsuccessful
crime. A wonderful reconstruction of England of the
period, beautifully photographed. Rest of cast:
*Donald Sutherland, Lesley-Anne Down, Alan Webb,
Malcolm Terris, Robert Lang, Wayne Sleep, Michael
Elphick, Pamela Salem, Gabrielle Lloyd, James*
*Cossins, John Bett, Peter Benson, Janine Duvitski,
Agnes Bernelle, Frank McDonald, Brian de Salvo, Joe
Cahill, Pat Layde, Derek Lord, Rachel Burrows.* Dir
& Screenplay: Michael Crichton; based on his novel
The Great Train Robbery. Pro: John Foreman.
Starling Productions Executive: Stanley Sopel. Pro
Man: Al Burgess. Ph: Geoffrey Unsworth. Pro Des:
Maurice Carter. Ed: David Bretherton. M: Jerry
Goldsmith. Art: Bert Davey. (Dino de
Laurentiis–UA.) Rel: 4 February. 110 mins. Cert A.

The First Time—La Première Fois
Claude Berri's less than subtle contribution to the
considerable, and variable, list of French films made
on the subject of awakening sex. A little more crude
than most of its predecessors, but often amusing in
spite of the not-very-engaging youngsters seeking
their first sexual encounter. Cast: *Alain Cohen,
Charles Denner, Zorica Lozic, Delphine Lévy, Claude
Lubicki, Philippe Teboul, Jérôme Lobb, Bruno
Rosenker, Daniele Schneider, Maryse Raymond, Carine
Rivière, Danielle Minazzoli, Roland Blanche, Joel
Moskowitz.* Dir & Screenplay: Claude Berri. Pro Ex:
Ralph Baum. Ph: Jean César Chiabaut. Ed:
Dominique Daudon. Art: Alexandre Trauner. M:
René Urtreger. (Lira Films/Renn Productions–Gala.)
Rel: Floating; first shown London, February 1979. 84
mins. Cert X.

F.I.S.T.
In his second film *Sylvester Stallone* plays Johnny
Kovak, the poor boy who becomes the big union
leader (of the Federation of Interstate Truckers,
hence F.I.S.T.) of the turbulent 1930s, accepts help
from the gangsters and finally pays for that mistake
with his life. A thinly-veiled parallel of the true story
of Jimmy Hoffa, boss of the Teamsters Union. Too
long and too pedestrian ever to match the obviously
epic proportions envisaged and not enhanced by
Stallone's often mumbled and lumpish performance
as Kovac. Rest of cast: *Rod Steiger, Peter Boyle,
Melinda Dillon, David Huffman, Tony Lo Bianco,
Kevin Conway, Cassie Yates, Peter Donat, Henry
Wilcoxon, John Lehne, Richard Herd, Tony Mockus,
Elena Karam, Ken Kercheval, Robert Lipton, Joe
Tornatore, Brian Dennehy, Frank McRae, Patrick
Hughes, James Karen, Rozsika Halmos, John Bleifer,
Stuart Gillard, Earl Montgomery, Charles Gradi,
Hugo Bolba, Alphonse Skerl, Ron Delagardelle, Henry
Wills, Nada Rowand, Andy Romano, Richard
Dioguardi, Sam Chew, Bill Zuckert, Harry Basch,
Robert Cortleigh, Reid Cruickshanks, Sidney Clute,
Martin Braddock, Sandy Ward, Walt Davis, Michael
Twain, Tony Crupi, Herman Poppe, J. Murphy, Mary
Horan, Barry Atwater, Judson Pratt.* Dir & Pro:
Norman Jewison. Ex Pro: Gene Corman. Assoc Pro:
Patrick Palmer. Screenplay: Joe Eszterhas &
Sylvester Stallone from the former's story. Ph:
Laszlo Kovacs. Ed: Graeme Clifford. Sup Ed: Tony
Gibbs. Art: Angelo Grahame. Pro Des: Richard
MacDonald. M: Bill Conti. (Jewison–UA.) Rel: 5
November. 130 mins. Cert A.

Fist of Fury Part 2—Ching-Wu Men Su-Tsi
Minor kung-fu movie which starts with a montage of
stills from the original Bruce Lee film, *Fist of Fury,*
and goes on to fall fat short of it. Cast: *Bruce Li, Lo
Lieh, Tien Feng, Lee Quinn, Shikamura Yasuyoshi,
Jimmy Nam, Chen Hui-Lou, Chou Chien, Shin Nam,
Shiu Yu, Kam Tao, Miao Shao-Hsiu, Lee Kin-Ming,
Cheng Hai-Ching, Shun Chio-Bo, Lee Fa Yuen, Lee
Keung.* Dir: Li Tso-Nan. Pro: Jimmy Shaw.
Screenplay: Chang Hsin-Yi. Ph: Yip Ching-Bui. Ed.
Leung Wing-Chai. Art: Wu Shui-Ping. M: Chow
Fuk-Leung. (Hong Kong Alpha–Inter Ocean.) Rel:
20 August. 104 mins. Cert X.

FM
The hectic, chaotic life behind the 'mikes' at a small
Los Angeles radio-station and the confrontation
between the managing disc-jockey and the advertising
director who wants to slot in some corny US Army
recruiting spots—a struggle that leads to the staff
staging a sit-in and final victory when their public
turn up to support them. Cast: *Michael Brandon,
Eileen Brennan, Alex Karras, Cleavon Little, Martin
Mull, Cassie Yates, Norman Lloyd, Jay Fenichel,
James Keach, Joe Smith, Tom Tarpey, Linda
Ronstadt, Kevin Cronin, Jimmy Buffett, Gary
Richrath, Tom Petty, Alan Gratzer, Reo Speedwagon,
Bruce Hal, Neal Doughty.* Dir: John A. Alonzo. Pro:
Rand Holston. Co Pro: Robert Larson. Screenplay:
Ezra Sacks. Ph: David Myers. Ed: Jeff Gourson. Pro
Des: Lawrence G. Paull. Title song composed and
sung by *Steely Dan.* In-concert sequences: Linda
Ronstadt and Jimmy Buffett etc. (Universal–CIC.)
Rel: Floating. 105 mins. Cert A.

Force Ten from Navarone
In a sense, a sequel to the Carl Foreman war-
spectacular of the early sixties, *The Guns of
Navarone,* with some of the same characters (now
played by different actors) in a story about a
combined American-British mission to Yugoslavia to
kill a German agent among the partisans and to blow
up a very important bridge there, something
spectacularly achieved in the end by the British major
Robert Shaw (one of his last screen appearances prior
to his sudden death), explosives-expert sergeant
Edward Fox, American lootenant *Harrison Ford* and
coloured sergeant *Carl Weathers.* Good fun and first-
class hokum. Rest of cast: *Barbara Bach, Franco
Nero, Richard Kiel, Alan Badel, Michael Byrne,
Philip Latham, Angus MacInnes, Michael Sheard,
Petar Buntic, Leslie Schofield, Antony Langdon,
Richard Hampton, Paul Humpeletz, Dicken Ashworth,
Christopher Malcolm, Nick Ellsworth, Jonathan Blake,
Roger Owen, Frances Mughan, Mike Sirett, Graham
Crowther, Jim Dowdall, Michael Osborne, Edward*

142

Peel, Michael Josephs, Jurgen Andersen, David Gretton, Paul Jerrico, Edward Kalinski, Robert Gillespie, Wolf Kahler, Hans Kahler, Ramiz Pasic. Dir: Guy Hamilton. Pro: Oliver A. Unger. Co-Pro: John R. Sloan & Anthony B. Unger. Screenplay: Robin Chapman; from the screen story by Carl Foreman; based on the Alistair MacLean novel. Ph: Chris Challis. Assoc Pro: David Orton. Ed: Ray Poulton. Pro Des: Geoffrey Drake. Art: Fred Carter. M: Ron Goodwin. (Columbia.) Rel: 7 January. 117 mins. Cert A.

Foul Play
Mildly amusing conventional comedy-thriller about a girl who becomes innocently involved with a plot of a fanatical anti-religious sect to murder the Pope while he's attending a New York Opera performance of the *Mikado*, and although she knows that she is on *the* list of the sect's victims she cannot at first convince the cops of the seriousness of the situation because each time she's a witness of a murder the corpse and the clues have vanished by the time the law arrives. *Goldie Hawn* as delightful as ever as the girl; newcomer, American comedian *Chevy Chase* as the handsome and smitten cop (without any chance to prove his prowess as a comedian). Rest of cast: *Burgess Meredith, Rachel Roberts, Eugene Roche, Dudley Moore, Marilyn Sokol, Brian Dennehey, Marc Lawrence, Chuck McCann, Billy Barty, Don Calfa, Bruce Solomon, Cooper Huckabee, Pat Ast, Frances Bay, Lau Cutell, William Frankfather, John Hancock, Barbara Sammeth, Queenie Smith, Hope Summers, Irene Tedrow, Ion Teodorescu, Janet Wood.* Dir & Screenplay: Colin Higgins. Pro: Thomas L. Miller & Edward K. Milkis. Ph: David M. Walsh. Assoc Pro: Peter V. Herald. Ed: Pembroke Herring. Pro Des: Alfred Sweeney. M: Charles Fox. (Paramount–CIC.) Rel: 28 January. 116 mins. Cert A.

The French Way
Interesting if not entirely satisfactory French film about a crippled writer who gets vicarious pleasure by organising and advancing the career of a bank-clerk acquaintance by means of various helpful ladies. A somewhat uneasy mixture of black comedy and social satire and never particularly convincing—but always essentially Gallic and generally good fun. Cast: *Jane Birkin, Jean-Louis Trintignant, Romy Schneider, Jean-Pierre Cassell, Florinda Bolkan, Georges Wilson, Henri Garcin, Michel Vitold, Dominique Constanza, Jean-François Balmer, Georges Beller, Betty Berr, Carlo Nell, Pierre Gualdi, Adrienne Servantil, Yvette Delaune, Salvino di Pietra, Dominique Marcas, Guy Michel, Madeleine Ganne, Yves Bureau, Leoni Collet, Frédérique Nort, Françoise Burgi, Madeleine Damien, Gérard Lemaire, Jacques Verlier, Christine Boisson, Jean-Pierre Maurin, Arlette Balkis, Renée Legrand, Gisèle Casadesus, Mary Marquet, Andre Reybag, Pippo Marisi, Robert Andre, Claude Marcault, Jean-Pierre Moreux, Roger Muni, Raoul Curet, Rachell*

Cathoud, Marie-Christine Carliez, A. Blancheteau. Dir: Michel Deville. Pro: Leo L. Fuchs. Assoc Pro: Roger Debelmas. Pro Sup: Leoda Guignier. Screenplay: Christopher Frank; based on a novel by Roger Blondel. Ph: Claude Lecomte. Ed: Raymond Guigot. Art: Pierre Lefai. (Viaduct Productions, Rome/TRAC, Rome–Rebel Films–Watchgrove Ltd.) Rel: Floating; first shown London, July 1978. 104 mins. Cert X.

F.T.A.
Sort of home-movies-type documentary about the provocative Jane Fonda/Donald Sutherland show with which they toured the GI camps during late 1971–early 1972, dispensing anti-war (more especially anti-Vietnam war) sentiments in sketches, monologues and songs. What comes across on the screen is sincerity, but very little else. Taking part: *Jane Fonda, Donald Sutherland, Len Chandler, Pamela Donegan, Rita Martinson, Holly Near, Paul Mooney, Michael Alaimo, Yale Zimmerman.* Dir: Francine Parker. Pro: Francine Parker, Jane Fonda & Donald Sutherland. Screenplay: Robin Menken, Michael Alamo, Rita Martinson, Holly Near, Len Chandler, Pamala Donegan, Jane Fonda, Donald Sutherland & Dalton Trumbo. Ph: Juliana Wang, Eric Saarinen & Joan Weidman. M: Aminadav Aloni. (Duaque Film Production for Free Theatre Associates–ICA.) Rel: Floating; first shown London, November 1978. 94 mins. Cert X.

Full Circle
Macabre little thriller about a young mother who feels a great guilt complex when her daughter chokes to death. She leaves her mercenary husband, rents a haunted house and, after allowing a disastrous seance to take place there, starts to investigate the circumstances of the haunting—an investigation which leads to her death. Always ambiguous, a little slow. Cast: *Mia Farrow, Keir Dullea, Tom Conti, Jill Bennett, Robin Gammell, Cathleen Nesbitt, Anna Wing, Edward Hardwicke, Mary Morris, Pauline Jameson, Peter Sallis, Arthur Howard, Damaris Hayman, Susan Porrett, Sophie Ward, Hilda Fenemore, Yvonne Edgell, Nigel Havers, Denis Lill, Ann Mitchell, Michael Bilton, John Tinn, Robert Farrant, Elizabeth Weaver, Susan Hibbert, Julian Fellows, Oliver Maguire, Samantha Gates.* Dir: Richard Loncraine. Pro: Peter Fetterman & Alfred Pariser. Screenplay: Dave Humphries; based on the adaptation by Harry Bromley Davenport of Peter Straub's novel. Ex Pro: Julian Melzack. Assoc Pro: Hugh Harlow. Ed: Ron Wisman. Ph: Peter Hannan. Art: Brian Morris. M: Colin Towns. (A UK/Canadian Official Co-Production–Fetter Productions/Classic Film Industries–CIC.) Rel: Floating. 98 mins. Cert AA.

The Fury
Surely you known what psychokinesis is? Well, you should. It's the simple little business of willing others suddenly to bleed or yourself to take occasional trips

up to the ceiling! Unlikely? Well, this film certainly suggests so, with its wild if plushly-produced tale about a young man with The Power who is abducted and kept under cover by a *very* secret US government agency who want to use him to experiment upon—something not liked by dad *Kirk Douglas*, who tries to free him with the help of a young girl with the same bloody talents. And it is all very involved, gruesome and, to be honest, pretty silly. Rest of cast: *John Cassavetes, Carrie Snodgress, Charles Durning, Amy Irving, Fiona Lewis, Andrew Stevens, Carol Rossen, Rutanya Alda, Joyce Easton, William Finley, Jane Lambert.* Dir: Brian de Palma. Pro: Frank Yablans. Ex Pro: Ron Preissman. Assoc Pro: Jack B. Bernstein. Screenplay: John Farris. Ph: Richard H. Kline. Ed: Paul Hirsch. Pro Des: Bill Malley. M: John Williams. (Fox.) Rel: 14 January. 118 mins. Cert X.

Game of Death
A film of some historical importance in that it was while he was making it—presumably quite early on— that kung-fu star *Bruce Lee* died. Five years later, completely re-structured to fit the new situation, the film uses for the most part another actor in Lee's role but cuts in the already completed climactic series of amusingly violent confrontations between him and various villains. Rest of cast: *Gig Young, Dean Jagger, Hugh O'Brian, Colleen Camp, Robert Wall, Mel Novak, Kareem Abdul Jabbar, Danny Inosanto, Hung Kim Po, Roy Chiao, Tony Leung, Jim James, Russell Cawthorne, David Hu, Peter Gee, Don Barry, Jess Hardie, Lee Hau Lung, Albert, Roz Hudson, Eddie Lye, Peter Nelson, Stephen Nicholson.* Dir: Robert Clouse. Pro: Raymond Chow. Assoc Pro: Andre Morgan. Ph: Godfrey Godar. Ed: Alan Pattilo. Art: Catherine Chang. M: John Barry. (Paragon Films–Golden Harvest–EMI.) Rel: 2 July. 94 mins. Cert X.

Germany in Autumn—Deutschland im Herbst
Fassbinder's political statement about Germany under the threat of urban terrorists and consequent anti-terrorist measures in the autumn of 1977 (at the time of the Schleyer and Kapler kidnappings, the Mogadishu highjacking and the terrorists' suicides in jail) by way of a collection of contributions from a number of young directors in addition to Fassbinder's own amusing segment. Cast: *Wolfgang Baechler, Heinz Bennent, Wolf Biermann, Joachim Bissmeyer, Caroline Chaniolleau, Hans Peter Cloos, Otto Friebel, Hildegard Friese, Michael Gahr, Vadim Glowna, Helmut Griem, Horatius Haeberle, Hannelore Hoger, Petra Kiener, Dieter Laser, Horst Mahler, Lisi Mangold, Eva Meier, Enno Patalas, Franz Priegel, Werner Poosardt, Leon Rainer, Katja Rupe, Walter Schmiedinger, Gerhard Schneider, Corinna Spies, Eric Vilgershofer, Franziska Walser, Angela Winkler, Manfred Zapataka, Kollaktiv 'Rote Rube'.* Dir: Heinrich Boll, Alf Brustellin, Hans Peter Cloos, Rainer Werner Fassbinder, Alexander Kluge, Maximiliane Mainka, Beate Mainka-Jellinghaus, Edgar Reitz, Katja Rupe, Volker Schlondorff, Peter

Releases of the Year in Detail

Schubert, Bernhard Sinkel, Peter Steinbach. Pro: Theo Hinz & Ebarhard Junkersdorf. Ph: Heidi Genee, Mulle Gotz-Dickopp, Tanja Schmidbauer & Christian Warnk. (Pro-Ject Filmproduktion in Filmverlag der Autoren, Munich/Hallelujah Film, Munich/Kairos Film, Munich–Scala.) Rel: Floating; first shown London, November 1978. 123 mins. No cert.

The Getting of Wisdom
Another remarkable Australian film: an adaptation of the autobiographical novel by Ethel Richardson based on her schooldays in Melbourne in the late 1800s. Completely unsentimental and beautifully-composed story of the musically gifted young daughter of an outback, widowed postmistress, who has to come to terms with the big-city environment and her more sophisticated fellow-pupils but triumphs in the end without ever surrendering her gritty individualism. A superb collaboration of script, director and players, with an outstanding performance by young *Susannah Fowle*. Rest of cast: *Barry Humphries, Sheila Helpmann, Patricia Kennedy, John Waters, Jan Friedl, Monia Maugham, Candy Raymond, Dorothy Bradley, Hilary Ryan, Kim Deacon, Alex Longman, Jo-Anne Moore, Kerry Armstrong, Celia de Burgh, Amanda Ring, Janet Shaw, Sigrid Thornton, Kay Ecklund, Karen Sutton, Maggie Fitzpatrick, Julie Blacke, Diana Greentree, Max Fairchild.* Dir: Bruce Beresford. Pro: Philip Adams. Screenplay: Eleanor Witcombe; based on the novel by Henry Handel Richardson (Ethel Richardson). Ph: Donald McAlpine. Ed: William Anderson. Pro Des: John Stoddard. M: No credits. (Southern Cross Films, Melbourne–Tedderwick Ltd.) Rel: Floating. 100 mins. Cert A.

The Giant Spider Invasion
Minor 1975 American film (only reaching a GB release in late 1978) which is revealed as a lesser spin-off from the 'Jaws' cycle of animal, vegetable and insect frighteners. About a giant spider 'exploded' into Wisconsin activity and preferring to sup off people rather than waste time with silly little flies! Cast: *Barbara Hale, Steve Brodie, Leslie Parrish, Alan Hale, Robert Easton, Kevin Brodie, Christiane Schmidtmer, Bill Williams, Tain Bodkin, Paul Nentzen, William W. Gillett, Diana Lee, J. Stewart Taylor, David B. Hoff.* Dir: Bill Rebane. Pro: Bill Rebane & Richard L. Huff. Ex Pro: William W. Gillett Jun. Assoc Pro: Jack Willoughby & Dick Plautz. Screenplay: Richard L. Huff & Robert Easton; from the former's story. Ph: Jack Willoughby. Ed: Barbara Pokras. Art: Ito Rebane. (Cinema Group 75/Transcentury Pictures–Hemdale.) Rel: 5 November. 76 mins. Cert A.

Girlfriends
Starting off as a thirty-minute short, but gradually expanded during its three years of production into very much a one-off, commendably original feature, this film has something to say about women

struggling to find a reasonable place of their own in the world, and about true friendship between members of the female sex. All rather casual and real and very well acted. Cast: *Melanie Mayron, Eli Wallach, Anita Skinner, Jean de Baer, Christopher Guest, Ken McMillan, Bob Balaban, Gina Rogak, Russell Horton, Amy Wright, Tania Berezin, Kathryn Walker, Roderick Cook, Viveca Lindfors, Kristofer Tabori, Mike Kellin.* Dir: Claudia Weill. Pro: Claudia Weill & Jan Saunders. Screenplay: Vicki Polon. Ph: Fred Murphy. Ed: Suzanne Pettit. Art: Patrizia von Brandenstein. M: Michael Small. (Warner.) Rel: 8 April Floating. 87 mins. Cert AA.

The Girls—Gehenu Lamai
The story of two Ceylonese sisters and their divergent dreams of romantic fulfilment. The first attempt at direction by the wife of Sri Lanka's best-known male director, providing a fascinating glimpse of women in a far different culture from that of the Western world. Dir: Sumitra Peries. (Scala.) Rel: Floating; first shown London, November 1978. 103 mins. Black-and-white. No cert.

Go Tell the Spartans
Superior Vietnam war film set in the early days of that disaster, when the American military presence was of some 12,000 'military advisers', among whom is the highly efficient Major Barker (*Burt Lancaster*, in one of his best performances for some time), trying to use his small company to defend a very large patch of territory and finally coming unstuck when the Vietcong attack and overrun a small outpost fort in the jungle. Some good performances, assured direction and unflagging pace add up to an absorbing if conventionally-modelled movie. Rest of cast: *Craig Wasson, Jonathan Goldsmith, Marc Singer, Dennis Howard, David Clennon, Evan Kim, John Megna, Hilly Hicks, Dolph Sweet, Clyde Kusatu, James Hong, Denice Kumagai, Tad Horino, Phong Diep, Ralph Brannen, Mark Carlton.* Dir: Ted Post. Pro: Allan F. Boddoh & Mitchell Cannold. Screenplay: Wendell Mayes; based on the book by Daniel Ford. Ex Pro: Michael Leone. Ph: Harry Stradling Fun. Ed: Millie Moore. Art: Jack Senter. M: Dick Halligan. (Mar Vista Productions–1977 Spartan Film Partners Ltd–UA.) Rel: 9 July. 114 mins. Cert X.

Grease
Very loud, fast-paced (even frenetic) musical based on the Broadway stage success aimed at, and largely starring, youngsters and hitting that target well enough to take it to record-breaking success on both sides of the Atlantic. Every number whammed across as if it were a masterpiece by a youthful cast that almost flogs itself to death to please. Lots of pretty girls, and new cult star *John Travolta* as the college lad who meets an Australian girl while on holiday, falls in love with her, says goodbye for ever—and then finds she's a new girl at his college. With old-timers *Eve Arden* and *Sid Caesar* stealing the acting (comedy) honours. Rest of cast: *Olivia Newton-John,*

Stockard Channing, Jeff Conaway, Barry Pearl, Michael Tucci, Kelly Ward, Didi Conn, Jamie Donnelly, Dinah Manoff, Susan Buckner, Lorenzo Lamas, Fannie Flagg, Dick Patterson, Eddie Deezen, Darrell Zwerling, Ellen Travolta, Annette Charles, Dennis C. Stewart. Guests: *Eve Arden, Frankie Avalon, Joan Blondell, Ed Byrnes, Sid Caesar, Alice Ghostley, Sha-Na-Na.* Dir: Randal Kleiser. Pro: Robert Stigwood & Allan Carr. Screenplay: Bronte Woodard (adapted by Allan Carr from the stage musical by Jim Jacobs & Warren Casey). Ph: Bill Butler. Ed: John F. Burnett. Pro Des: Phil Jefferies. M Sup: Bill Oakes. (Paramount–CIC.) Rel: 17 September. 111 mins. Cert A.

The Great Gundown
Doom-laden, death-filled Western in the 'Spaghetti' tradition which begins with murder and ends with a scalping, between which there are countless killings and a cold, inhuman disregard for life. But all the continual violence is beautifully set and paced against superbly scenic backgrounds. With *Robert Padilla* as the gaunt and grim Mari ('The Savage') tracking down the villain in his lair and taking awful revenge on him for having been the cause of his wife's death. Rest of cast: *Malila St Duval, Richard Rust, Steven Oliver, David Eastman, Stanley Adams, Rockne Tarkington, Michael Christian, Michael Green, Owen Orr, Ted Markland, Haydee Dubarry, Walter Barnes, Lucas Andreas, Gene Borkan, John Bellah, Darrell Cotton, A. J. Solari, Frank Packard, Stephen Whittaker, Don Megowan, John Chilton, Don McGovern, Patrick Hawley, Doodles Weaver, Kid Chessell, Virgil Frye.* Dir: Paul Hunt. Pro: Paul Nobert. Screenplay: Steve Fisher; from a story by Robert Padilla & Paul Hunt. Ex Pro: John Leuthold. Pro Ex: Michael Bennett. Ph & Assoc Pro: Ronald V. Garcia. Art: No credit. M: Alan Caddy & Robert Fallon. (Sun Productions–Bordeaux Films International.) Rel: Floating. 98 mins. Cert X.

The Greek Tycoon
Thinly disguised story of a famous Greek shipowner and his romance with a US President's widow. Very carefully tailored and set against beautifully photographed Grecian backgrounds, the film was lush, lovely and pretty empty. A masterful performance by *Anthony Quinn* as the Greek millionaire. Rest of cast: *Jacqueline Bisset, Raf Vallone, Edward Albert, James Franciscus, Camilla Sparv, Marilu Tolo, Charles Durning, Luciana Paluzzi, Robin Clarke, Kathryn Leigh Scott, Roland Culver, Tony Jay, John Bennett, Katharine Schofield, Joan Benham, Linda Thorson, Guy Deghy, Jill Melford, Lucy Gutteridge, Zozo Saeountzaki, Nasis Kedrakas, John Denison, Carolle Rousseau, Danos Lygizos, Cassandra Harris, Particia Kendall-John, Sandor Eles, Beaulah Hughes, Vicki Michelle, Carol Royle, Mimi Denissi, Athene Fielding, Bonnie George, Charles Maggiore, Jeff Pomerantz, Richard Fasciano, John Bolt, Henderson Forsythe, Michael Prince, Gordon Oas-Heim, William Stelling, John Hoffmeister,*

Carinthia West, Dimitri Nikolaidos, Dimos Starenios, John Ioannou, David Masterman. Dir: J. Lee Thompson. Pro: Allen Klein & Ely Landau. Screenplay: Mort Fine; from a story by Nico Mastorakis, Win Wells & Art Fine. Co-Pro: Nico Mastorakis & Lawrence Myers. Ex Pro: Mort Abrahams, Peter Howard & Les Landau. Assoc Pro: Eric Rattray. Ph: Tony Richmond. Pro Des: Michael Stringer. Ed: Alan Strachan. M: Stanley Myers (Title themes by John Kongos.) (Abkco–Universal–CIC.) Rel: 29 October. 107 mins. Cert AA.

Halloween
Brilliant young John Carpenter follows up his college-made cult movie *Dark Star* and the later, outstanding thriller *Assault on Precinct 13* with this modestly-made but brilliant horror piece about a homicidal maniac who escapes after twenty years to return to the town in which, as a boy of six, he stabbed his sister to death, with the idea of adding several more young people to his list of victims. Carpenter's magic is to bring terrible menace to everyday scenes and familiar objects and to create ever-increasing tension as the white-masked killer stalks his prey and maniacally destroys them. Cast: *Donald Pleasence, Jamie Lee Curtis, Nancy Loomis, P. J. Soles, Charles Cyphers, Kyle Richards, Brian Andrews, John Michael Graham, Nancy Stephens, Arthur Malet, Mickey Yablans, Brent Le Page, Adam Hollander, Robert Phalen, Tony Moran, Will Sandin, Sandy Johnson, David Kyle, Peter Griffith, Jim Windburn, Nick Castle.* Dir, Screenplay (with Debra Hill) & M: John Carpenter. Pro: Debra Hill. Ex Pro: Irwin Yablans. Ph: Ray Stella. Set Décor: Craig Stearns. Script Supervisor: Louise Jaffe. Ed: Tommy Wallace, Charles Bornstein. (Miracle.) Rel: Floating. 91 mins. Cert X.

Harlan County USA
Overlong, generally interesting, intermittently absorbing American Oscar-winning feature documentary which in relating the events of the Kentucky coal miners' strike of 1973–4 sets them in perspective by looking back at past events on the labour scene in general and the coal-mining industry in particular. Dir: Barbara Kopple. (The Other Cinema.) Rel: Floating; first seen at opening of London Scala cinema in June 1978. 103 mins. 16mm. Cert A.

How to Score
Interesting 30-minute movie about the way in which musical scores are integrated into a film's soundtrack with—as an illustration—guitarist John Williams masterminding the recording of Patrick Gowers's composition for the Trevor Howard–Glenda Jackson movie *Stevie*. Howard gives a commentary about the technical know-how and the advances that have been made in recent years. Dir & Pro: Robert Enders. (Enterprise Pictures.) Rel: Floating; first shown London, September 1978. 30 mins. Cert U.

Heaven Can Wait
A re-vamping of the Harry Segall play which has previously served for the 1941 screen-comedy success *Here Comes Mr Jordan*, with Robert Montgomery as the boxer who due to a holy error is escorted right up to the pearly gates before it is realised he shouldn't be there and has in fact years left to live—so he is rushed back to earth with kindly guide Mr Claude Rains to find the first available spare body, which turns out to be that of a business tycoon just murdered by his wife and her lover. Now it is *Warren Beatty* as the football star who finds himself in this peculiar situation and *Julie Christie* as the girl who persuades him to accept the unacceptable shell, at least till something more suitable comes along! James Mason is the benevolent guardian angel. Still, an amusing predicament and a lively comedy. Rest of cast: *Jack Warden, Charles Grodin, Dyan Cannon, Buck Henry, Vincent Gardenia, Joseph Maher, Hamilton Camp, Arthur Malet, Stephanie Faracy, Jeannie Linero, Harry D. K. Wong, George J. Manos, Larry Block, Frank Campanella, Bill Sorrells, Dick Enberg, Dolph Sweet, R. G. Armstrong, Ed V. Peck, John Randolph, Richard O'Brien, Joseph F. Makel, Will Hare, Lee Weaver, Roger Bowen, Kenne Curtis, William Larsen, Morgan Farley, William Bogert, Robert E. Leonard, Joel Marston, Earl Montgomery, Robert C. Stevens, Bernie Massa, Peter Tomarken, William Sylvester, Lisa Blake Richards, Charlie Charles, Nick Outin, Jerry Scanlan, Jim Boeke, Marvin Fleming, Deacon Jones, Les Josephson, Jack T. Snow, Curt Gowdy, Al DeRogatis.* Dir: Warren Beatty & Buck Henry. Pro: Warren Beatty. Screenplay: Elaine May & Warren Beatty; based on a play by Harry Segall. Ex Pro: Howard W. Koch Jun & Charles H. Maguire. Ph: William A. Fraker. Ed: Robert C. Jones & Don Zimmerman. Pro Des: Paul Sylbert. M: Dave Grusin. (Paramount–CIC.) Rel: 1 October. 101 mins. Cert A.

Herbie Goes to Monte Carlo
A further adventure of the Volkswagen with a magical mind of its own, now involved in his owner *Dean Jones'* plan to win the Paris to Monte Carlo rally-race; in a love affair with a pretty Lancia; and the crooks who have dropped their loot into his petrol tank! Rest of cast: *Don Knotts, Julie Sommers, Roy Kinnear, Jacques Marin, Xavier Saint Macary, François Lalande.* Dir: Vincent McEveety. Pro: Ron Miller. Screenplay: Arthur Alsberg & Don Nelson. M: Frank De Vol. No other credits. (Disney.) Rel: 20 August (included in *Film Review 1978–79* as a tentatively late June release). 105 mins. Cert U.

The Hills Have Eyes
A promising thriller, about an American family on holiday who blunder into a desert bombing range and are marooned there with a broken axle, which sinks into excessive bloodiness and beastliness when they are besieged by a family of cannibalistic freaks who

after eating their dog (raw), proceed to rape the daughter, burn the father alive, shoot the mother and run off with the baby, to be cooked as a change of diet! Initially some extremely good tension; remarkable scenic backgrounds. Cast: *John Steadman, Janus Blythe, Arthur King, Russ Grieve, Virginia Vincent, Susan Lanier, Dee Wallace, Brenda Marinoff, Robert Houston, Martin Speer, James Whitworth, Michael Berryman, Lance Gordon, Corda Clarke;* and dogs *Flora & Striker.* Dir, Ed & Screenplay: Wes Craven. Pro: Peter Locke. Ph: Eric Saarinen, (2nd Unit Ph: Tim Wawrzeniak & Bob Eber). Art: Robert Burns. M: Don Peake. (Blood Relations Co–New Realm.) Rel: 1 April. 90 mins. Cert X.

Hitler—A Career
Largely culled from newsreel and other clips, this German documentary follows the story of the dictator from his early agitating in Austria to his rise to power in Germany—against a terrifying background of the way in which one loud-mouthed, cynical power-seeker could influence a whole nation to become unspeakably evil. Though playing down the full horrors of war and the concentration camp, the film is still a pretty devastating example not only of how it happened then then, but also how it could as easily happen here, or anywhere, today or tomorrow! Pro: Joachim C. Fest and Christian Herrendoerfer based on the former's book. (Werner Rieb–Interart–GTO Films.) Rel: Floating; first shown London, November 1978. 155 mins. Cert A.

Hollywood on Trial
1976 American-made feature documentary about the Joseph McCarthy, reds-under-the-beds days of Hollywood. A series of newsreel cuts, still photographs and interviews about the witch-hunting, smearing and persecution that went on at the time; and the infamous black-list which was compiled to bar suspects from working at their business. Narrated by *John Huston.* With contributions from *Walter Bernstein, Alvah Bessie, Lester Cole, Gary Cooper, Howard Da Silva, Walt Disney, Edward Dmytryk, Millard Lampell, Ring Larnder Jr, Joseph McCarthy, Albert Maltz, Ben Margolis, Louis B. Mayer, Adolphe Menjou, Zero Mostel, Otto Preminger, Ronald Reagan, Martin Ritt, Gale Sondergaard, Robert Taylor, Leo Townsend, Dalton Trumbo.* Dir: David Helpern Jun. Pro: James Gutman. Assoc Pro: Frank Galvin & Jurgen Hellwig. Ph: Barry Abrams. Writer: Arnie Reisman. Ed: Frank Galvin. (Gutman/Helpern Jun Productions–Cinema Associates/October Films–Contemporary.) Floating; first shown London, October 1978. 102 mins. No cert.

Hooper
High-spirited and entertaining hokum, if a somewhat superficial look at Hollywood stuntmen with the story of the greatest, Hooper (*Burt Reynolds*), who nurses

old wounds, chances new ones and is always trying to create records of danger and daring while looking back over his shoulder to see what young daredevil is likely to try and wrest his crown from him. Rest of cast: *Jan-Michael Vincent, Sally Field, Brian Keith, John Marley, James Best, Adam West, Alfie Wise, Robert Klein.* Dir: Hal Needham. Pro: Hank Moonjean. Screenplay: Thomas Rickman & Bill Kerby; from a story by Walt Green & Walter S. Herndon. Ex Pro: Lawrence Gordon. Ph: Bobby Byrne. Ed: Donn Cambern. M: Bill Justis. (Burt Reynolds/Lawrence Gordon–Warner.) Rel: 5 November. 99 mins. Cert A.

L'Hotel de la Plage
Gently satirical comedy (though far less biting than the same director's look at a British seaside resort in his earlier *A Nous Les Petites Anglaises*) about the French on holiday in Brittany in August, with a little romance, a little wife-cheating (and as much hubby-cheating!) and everyone determined to have a good time. Cast: *Sophie Barjac, Myriam Boyer, Daniel Ceccaldi, Michèle Grellier, Bruno Guillain, Francis Lemaire, Robert Lombard, Bruno du Louvat, Guy Marchand, Jean-Paul Muel, Anne Parillaud, Michel Robin, Martine Sarcey, Bernard Soufflet.* Dir & Screenplay: Michel Lang. Pro: Marcel Dassault. Ex Pro: Alain Poiré. Ph: Daniel Gaudry. Ed: Helene Plemiannikov. Art: no credit. M: Mort Shuman. (2000 Gaumont–Gala.) Rel: Floating; first shown London, September 1978. 111 mins. Cert AA.

The Hound of the Baskervilles
Would-be comic British re-hash of the Conan Doyle Sherlock Holmes classic which does nobody concerned any great credit. Cast: *Peter Cook, Dudley Moore, Denholm Elliott, Joan Greenwood, Terry-Thomas, Max Wall, Irene Handl, Kenneth Williams, Hugh Griffith, Dana Gillespie, Roy Kinnear, Prunella Scales, Penelope Keith, Spike Milligan, Lucy Griffths, Jessie Matthews, Rita Webb, Mohammed Shamsi, Patsy Smart, Geoffrey Moon, Josephine Tewson, Vivien Neves, Jacquie Stevens, Anna Wing, Henry Woolf, Molly Maureen, Helena McCarthy, Ava Cadell, Sidney Johnson, Pearl Hackney.* Dir: Paul Morrissey. Pro: John Goldstone. Ex Pro: Michael White & Andrew Braunsberg. Assoc Pro: Tim Hampton. Screenplay: Peter Cook, Dudley Moore & Paul Morrissey; based on the Conan Doyle story. Ph: Dick Bush & John Wilcox. Ed: Richard Marden & Glenn Hyde. Pro Des: Roy Smith. M: Dudley Moore. (Michael White Ltd–Hemdale.) Rel: 5 November. 85 mins. Cert A.

House Calls
Delightful comedy, with plenty of witty lines—and only an occasional lapse of good taste—about a middle-aged medico who, when his wife dies, decides to sow the wild oats he had previously kept gathering dust in the cupboard of marital fidelity but quickly finds himself preferring the attentions of a not-so-young lady to the young chicks he had set his mind

on! Beautifully-timed performances in the lead roles by *Walter Matthau* and *Glenda Jackson*; and great support from *Art Carney* as a doddering doctor. Rest of cast: *Richard Benjamin, Candice Azzara, Dick O'Neill, Thayer David, Anthony Holland, Reva Rose, Sandra Kerns, Brad Dexter, Jane Connell, Lloyd Gough, Gordon Jump, William J. Fiore, Taurean Blacque, Charlie Matthau, Ken Olfson, Len Lesser, Nancy Hsueh, Lee Weaver, Susan Batson, Alma Beltran, Pamela Toll, Anita Alberts, Enzo Gagliardi, Bob Goldstein, Bernie Kuby, Patch Mackenzie, Maurice Marks, Sally K. Marr, Harlee McBride, Judith Brown, David Bond, Walter D. O'Donnell, Kyle Oliver, George Sasaki, Roberto Trujillo, Kedric Wolfe, Michael Mann, Dave Morick, John Pleshette, Jack Griffin.* Dir: Howard Zieff. Pro: Alex Winitsky & Arlene Sellers. Ex Pro: Jennings Lang. Screenplay: Max Shulman, Julius P. Epstein, Alan Mandel & Charles Shyer. Ph: David M. Walsh. Ed: Edward Warschilka. Pro Des: Henry Bumstead. M: Henry Mancini. (Jennings Lang Productions–Universal–CIC.) Rel: 13 August. 98 mins. Cert A.

The Humanoid
Italian-made, English-speaking science-fiction lark, reminiscent of greater, such spectaculars right down to the comedy robot mascot. About the power-hungry villain's plans to take over the Earth by means of his robot army and invincible Humanoid, a captured earth-man turned into a controlled creature. All good, clean, very simple fun! Cast: *Richard Kiel, Corinne Clery, Leonard Mann, Barbara Bach, Arthur Kennedy, Ivan Rassimov, Marco Yeh, Massimo Serato.* Dir: George B. Lewis. Pro: Giorgio Venturini. Screenplay: Adriano Bolzoni & Aldo Lado; based on the former's story. 2nd Unit Dir: Enzo Castellari. Ph: Silvano Ippoliti. Ed: Mario Morra. Scenic Designer: Enzo Bulgarelli. Special Effects Supervisor: Anthony N. Dawson. Pro Sup: Cecilia Bigazzi. M: Ennio Morricone. (Merope–Columbia.) Rel: May 27. 99 mins. Cert. A.

Ice Castles
The struggle of Iowan small-town girl *Lynn-Holly Johnson* to achieve world ice-skating fame, and how this interferes with her private—and romantic—life! Rest of cast: *Robby Benson, Colleen Dewhurst, Tom Skerritt, Jennifer Warren, David Huffman, Diane Reilly, Craig T. McMullen, Kelsey Ufford, Leonard Lilyholm, Brian Foley, Jean-Claude Bleuze, Teresa Willmus, Diana Holden, Michelle McLean, Carol Williams, Mary Schuster & Staci Loop, Patti Elder, Jim Nickerson & Dee Ingalls.* Dir: Donald Wrye. Pro: John Kemeny. Ex Pro: Rosilyn Heller. Co Pro: S. Rodger Olenicoff. Screenplay: Donald Wyre & Gary L. Baim; from the latter's story. Ph: Bill Butler. Ed: Michael Kahn & Maury Winetrobe. Pro Des: Joel Schiller. M: Marvin Hamlisch. (International Cinemedia Center Productions–Columbia.) Rel: 6 May. 109 mins. Cert A.

I Never Promised You a Rose Garden
A commendably restrained picture of life within a women's mental asylum, highlighted by the story of a teenager who in three years, after trying to commit suicide on more than one occasion, is helped by a sympathetic woman doctor towards a more or less normal life. Beautifully acted, often moving and never needlessly shocking or sensational. Cast: *Bibi Andersson, Kathleen Quinlan, Ben Piazza, Lorraine Gary, Darlene Craviotto, Reni Santoni, Susan Tyrrell, Signe Hasso, Norma Alden, Martine Bartlett, Robert Viharo, Jeff Conaway, Dick Herd, Sarah Cunningham, June C. Ellis, Diane Varsi, Patricia Singer, Mary Carver, Barbara Steele, Cynthia Szigetti, Carol Androsky, Elizabeth Dartmoor, Cherry Davis, Lynne Stewart, Carol Worthington, Margo Burdichevsky, Gertrude Granor, Helen Venit, Jan Burrell, Irene Roseen, Nancy Parson, Leigh Curran, Donald Bishop, Samatha Harper, Dolores Quentin, Pamela Seaman.* Dir: Anthony Page. Pro: Michael Hausman. Screenplay: Gavin Lambert; based on the novel by Joanne Greenberg. Ph: Bruce Logan. Ed: Garth Craven. Pro Des: Toby Rafelson. (Roger Corman–Imorh Productions–New World Pictures.) Rel: Floating. 96 mins. Cert X.

In Praise of Older Women
Adaptation of Stephen Vizinczey's best-seller novel about a sexually hungry young man's progression from one woman to another, first in his native Hungary and then, after the revolution there, in Canada. Cast: *Tom Berenger, Karen Black, Susan Strasberg, Helen Shaver, Marilyn Lightstone, Alexandra Stewart, Marianne McIsaac, Alberta Watson, Ian Tracey, Monique Lepage, Louise Marleau, Jill Frappier, Mignon Elkins, Joan Stuart, John Bayliss, Jon Granik, Budd Knapp, Earl Pennington, Michael Kirby, Bronwen Mantel, Wally Martin, Arden Ryshpan, Tibor Polgar, Julie Wildman, Julie Morand, Griffith Brewer, Walter Bolton, Martha Parker, Robert King, Arthur Grosser, Jeanette Casenave, Alexander Godfrey, Tina Shuster, Danny Brainin, Casey Stephens, Peter Gottlieb.* Dir: George Kaczender. Pro: Robert Lantos & Claude Héroux. Ex Pro: Stephen J. Roth & Harold Greenberg. Screenplay: Paul Gottlieb; based on the novel by Stephen Vizinczey. Ph: Miklos Lente. Ed: George Kaczender & Peter Wintonick. Art: Wolf Kroeger. Assoc Pro: Howard R. Lipson. M: Tibor Polgar. (Canadian Film Development Corp–Famous Players & TSM Investments Ltd–Warner.) Rel: Floating. 110 mins. Cert X.

Interiors
Woody Allen in Bergman-type mood—and *very* serious—in a family-relationships piece about a pallid, vague and artistic woman, her solid husband (who gently forsakes her for another, more florid, more vulgar, more satisfying woman) and the three frustrated, artistically striving, guilt-conscious

daughters. Coldly impressive; good acting against a sterile and often silent background, and an inevitable progression towards final tragedy. Cast: *Kristin Griffith, Marybeth Hurt, Richard Jordan, Diane Keaton, E. G. Marshall, Geraldine Page, Maureen Stapleton, Sam Waterton.* Dir & Screenplay: Woody Allen. Pro: Charles H. Joffe. Ex Pro: Robert Greenhut. Ph: Gordon Willis. Ed: Ralph Rosenblum. Pro Des: Mel Bourne. (Jack Rollins/Charles H. Joffe–UA.) Rel: Floating. 91 mins. Cert AA.

International Velvet

Bryan Forbes's (he wrote, directed and produced) sequel to the 1945 film, *National Velvet*, which launched the 12-year-old Elizabeth Taylor on her starry film career. Now *Nanette Newman* as the character, Velvet Brown (grown up and living with a novelist) faced with a problem when her brother's young daughter comes to live with her after the girl's parents are killed in a road crash. But Sarah, the girl, is won over, takes a great interest in horses and becomes a dedicated trials and show-jumping rider with a fierce ambition to win Olympic honours for Britain. And the sequel shares with the original great visual beauty, warmth and charming performances. Rest of cast: *Tatum O'Neal, Christopher Plummer, Anthony Hopkins, Peter Barkworth, Dinsdale Landen, Sarah Bullen, Jeffrey Byron, Richard Warwick, Daniel Abineri, Jason White, Martin Neil, Douglas Reith, Dennis Blanch, Norman Wooland, Susan Jameson, Brenda Cowling, James Smilie, David Tate, Ronald Chenery, Geoffrey Drew, Stephanie Cole, Margaret John, David Wilkinson, Emma Forbes, Paul Rosebury, Chris Quentin, John May, Marsha Fitzalan, Susan Hamblett, Russell Lodge, Pam Rose, George Hillsden, Trevor Thomas, Jack Dearlove, Jean Lockhart, Ernest Hare, Kenneth Benda.* Riders: *Alastair Martin Bird, Tad Coffin (USA), Bruce Davidson (USA), Tom Davies, Marsha Fitzalan, Jan Gay, Susan Hamblett, Tony Hill, Jane Holderness-Roddam, Virginia Holgate, Stephen Hoye, Russell Lodge, Angela Meade, Richard Meade, Gareth Milne, Roger Plowden, Michael Plumb (USA), Peter Pocock, Suzanne Roquette, Julian Seaman, Georgina Simpson, Stewart Stevens, Nigel Tabor, Mary Ann Tausky (USA), Diana Thorne, Nicholas Wilkinson & The Garth South Berks. Pony Club.* Dir, Pro & Screenplay: Bryan Forbes; suggested by Enid Bagnold's novel *National Velvet*. Assoc Pro: John L. Hargreaves. Ph: Tony Imi. Pro Des: Keith Wilson. Ed: Timothy Gee. M: Francis Lai, arranged by Jean Musy. (Bryan Forbes–MGM–CIC.) Rel: 20 August. 127 mins. Cert A.

Invasion of the Body Snatchers

A large, long and elaborate delayed sequel to the excellent little mid fifties thriller about pods from outer space which engulf earthlings and emerge as complete copies—but lacking any human feelings. And how San Francisco public-health inspector *Donald Sutherland* and his lady, *Brooke Adams,* discover what is going on and try to avoid going the way of everyone else. An excellent example of the maxim that bigger is not always better, though there's enough chasing, macabre touches and other thrills to keep most people reasonably happy. Rest of cast: *Leonard Nimoy, Veronica Cartwright, Jeff Goldblum, Art Hindle, Lelia Goldoni, Kevin McCarthy, Don Siegel, Tom Luddy, Stan Ritchie, David Fisher, Tom Dahlgren.* Dir: Philip Kaufman. Pro: Robert H. Solo. Screenplay: W. D. Richter; based on the book *The Body Snatchers* by Jack Finney. Ph: Michael Chapman. Ed: Douglas Stewart. Pro Des: Charles Rosen. M: Denny Zeitlan. (Solo/Kaufaman–UA.) Rel: 25 March. 116 mins. Cert X.

It Lives Again

Uneven, but fascinating, sequel to *It's Alive*—again about monster mutant babies who start killing almost the moment they are born. And a more serious note is struck by one of the characters' defence of the horrors by saying that as they are God's creatures they must have been sent to earth for some reason and should not, as official policy has it, be killed as quickly as possible. Cast: *Frederic Forrest, Kathleen Lloyd, John P. Ryan, John Marley, Andrew Duggan, Eddie Constantine, James Dixon, Dennis O'Flaherty, Melissa Inger, Victoria Jill, Bobby Ramsen, Glenda Young, Lynn Wood.* Dir, Pro & Screenplay: Larry Cohen. Assoc Pro: William Wellman Jun. Pro Ex: Peter Sabiston. Ph: Fenton Hamilton. Ed: Curt Burch, Louis Friedman & Carol O'Blath. Art: No credit. M: Bernard Herrmann. (Larco Productions–Warner.) Rel: 3 December. 91 mins. Cert X.

I Wanna Hold Your Hand

American Beatlemania, 1964. The striving of a group of enthusiastic fans from Maplewood, New Jersey, to get into the Ed Sullivan television show on which the group are scheduled to appear. Cast: *Nancy Allen, Bobby Di Cicco, Marc McClure, Susan Kendall Newman, Theresa Saldana, Wendie Jo Sperber, Eddie Deezen, Christian Juttner, Will Jordan, Read Morgan, Claude Earl Jones, James Houghton, Michael Hewitson, Dick Miller, Vito Carenzo, Luke Andreas, Roberta Lee Carroll, Sherry Lynn, Irene Arranga, Carole H. Field, Nancy Osborne, Newton Arnold, Wil Albert, Troy Melton, Nick Pellegrino, Martin Fiscoe, Marilyn Moe, Michael Ross Verona, Marilyn Fox, Kristine DeBell, Gene LeBell, Victor Brandt, Roger Pancake, Kimberly Spengel, Bob Maroff, Ivy Bethune, Craig Spengel, Frank Verroca, Derek Barton, Edward Call, John Malloy, Larry Pines, Dave Adams, Poppy Lagos, Robyn Petti, Paula Watson, Leslie Hoffman, Chuck Waters, Rick Sawaya, Jim Nickerson, George Sawaya, The Romanos.* Dir: Robert Zemeckis. Pro: Tamara Asseyev & Alex Rose. Ex Pro: Steven Spielberg. Screenplay: Robert Zemeckis & Bob Gale (who is also named Assoc Pro). Ph: Donald M. Morgan. Ed: Frank Morririss. Art: Peter Jamison. All the songs performed by the Beatles. (Universal–CIC.) Rel: 2 July. 99 mins. Cert A.

J. A. Martin, Photographer—J. A. Martin, Photographe

1976 French–Canadian film about a couple who, after fourteen years of marriage and having had five children, realise their relationship is going on the rocks and set out together on the husband's annual photographic tour of the backwoods hoping that the experience will rekindle their former love for each other. Cast: *Marcel Sabourin, Monique Mercure, Marthe Thierry, Catherine Tremblay, Mariette Duval, Denis Hamel, Stéphane L'Ecuyer, Jacques Bilodeau, Colette Courtois, Marthe Nadeau, André St-Denis, Denise Prouix, Robert Des Roches, Guy L'Ecuyer, Charlie Beauchamp, Luce Guilbeault, Denis Drouin, Madeleine Pageau, Eric Gaudry, Yvan Canuel, Germaine Lemyre, Jean Lapointe, Walter Massy, Denis Robisbon, Henry Raimer, Jean Mathieu, Pierre Gobeil, Pierre Daigneault, Paul Cormier, Bobby Lalonde, Jocelyn Berube, Yvon Leroux, Louise Dubigue, Gaetan Giard, Colette Berthiaume, Jean-Louis Berthiaume, Francine Durault, Jean-Paul Lebel, Mireille Machado, René Rivest, André St Pierre, Monique St Pierre, François Berd, Christine Breton, Colette Dorsay.* Dir: Jean Beaudin. Pro: Jean-Marc Garand. Screenplay: Jean Beaudin & Marcel Sabourin. Ph: Pierre Mignot. Ed: Jean Beaudin & Hélène Girard. Art: Vianney Gauthier. M: Maurice Blackman. (National Film Board of Canada–Contemporary.) Rel: Floating; first shown London, November 1978. 101 mins. No cert.

Jaws 2

Exploitative follow-up to the tremendous box-office success of the original *Jaws*, of primary interest to those who missed or liked it well enough to ask for a second helping, which is exactly what this film is. Set some time after *Jaws*, the small seaside Amity community have almost forgotten the bloody attack on them by the giant shark and are concentrating on swelling the visitor traffic when another giant fish strikes, starting with a couple of skin-divers, going on to a pretty water-skier and then attacking a small flotilla of boats crewed by local youngsters. When the shark smashes the helicopter sent to their rescue, police chief *Roy Scheider* once again goes into battle and produces the spectacular duel climax. Rest of cast: *Lorraine Gary, Murray Hamilton, Joseph Mascolo, Jeffrey Kramer, Collin Wilcox, Ann Dusenberry, Mark Gruner, Barry Coe, Susan French, Gary Springer, Donna Wilkes, Gary Dubin, John Dukakis, G. Thomas Dunlop, David Elliott, Marc Gilpin, Keith Gordon, Cynthia Grover, Ben Marley, Martha Swatek, Billy Van Zandt, Gigi Vorgan, Jerry M. Baxter, Jean Coulter, Daphne Dibble, Christine Freeman, April Gilpin, William Griffith, Greg Harris, Coll Red McLean, Susan O. McMillan, David Owsley, Allan L. Paddack, Oneida Rollins, Frank Sparks, Thomas A. Stewart, David Tintle, Jim Wilson, Kathy Wilson.* Dir: Jeannot Szwarc. Pro: Richard D. Zanuck & David Brown. 2nd Unit Dir: Joe Alves. Screenplay:

Releases of the Year in Detail

Carl Gottlieb & Howard Sackler; based upon the characters created by Peter Benchley. Ph: Michael Butler. Ed: Neil Travis. Pro Des & Assoc Pro: Joe Alves. Art: Gene Johnson & Stewart Campbell. M: John Williams. (Zanuck/Brown–Universal–CIC.) Rel: 24 December. 117 mins. Cert A.

Julia
Infinitely subtle, intelligently directed, beautifully acted adaptation of the Lillian Hellman story about her lasting friendship with the woman who gives the film its title. Julia is a girl of strong character who grows up to work—in the years immediately before the war—for the smuggling out of Germany of some of the people who are likely to become targets for Nazi nastiness, and at one point she enmeshes Miss Hellman in her plots persuading her to carry a small fortune in a case through customs into Berlin—an adventure which, presumably, leads a little later to Julia's death. Absorbing, brilliantly directed drama, with outstanding performances by *Jane Fonda* (as Lillian), *Vanessa Redgrave* (as Julia—which brought her the 1978 Oscar for Best Supporting Actress) and *Jason Robards* (as writer Dashiell Hammett, with whom Miss Hellman lived and who helped her in her career with advice and support). Rest of cast: *Maximilian Schell, Hal Holbrook, Rosemary Murphy, Meryl Streep, Dora Doll, Elisabeth Mortensen, John Glover, Lisa Pelikan, Susan Jones, Cathleen Nesbitt, Maurice Denham, Gerard Buhr, Stefan Gryff, Phillip Siegel, Milly Urquhart, Antony Carrick, Ann Queensberry, Edmond Bernard, Jacques David, Jacqueline Staup, Hans Verner, Christian de Tiliere.* Dir: Fred Zinnemann. Pro: Richard Roth. Screenplay: Alvin Sargent; based on the story by Lillian Hellman. Ex Pro: Julien Derode. Assoc Pro: Tom Pevsner. Ed: Walter Murch. Ph: Douglas Slocombe. Pro Des: Gene Callahan, Willy Holt & Carmen Dillon. M: Georges Delerue. (Richard Roth/Fred Zinnemann–Fox.) Rel: 10 September (included in *Film Review 1977–78* as April release but this was the pre-release date). 117 mins. Cert A.

Just a Gigolo
A very odd German-made film with the good things in it never quite adding up to a good movie; but for various reasons consistently fascinating and certainly never boring. *David Bowie* (thin, cold and far from having any human passions, walking through his part with the withdrawn dignity of a waxwork breathed into half-life) as the young Prussian officer who arrives at the front just too late to become the war-hero which was his ambition, and, in the familiar, desperate and degraded Germany of the twenties and thirties drifts into the job of being just a gigolo! Authentic Hollywood glamour from *Kim Novak*, the old star magic like *La Dietrich*, delightful directorial touches (like the macabre black humour of the old hero's funeral), beautiful tonal photography and good technical qualities. Rest of cast: *Sydne Rome, David Hemmings, Maria Schell, Curt Jürgens, Erika Pluhar,*

Rudolf Schundler, Hilde Weissner, Werner Pochath, Bela Erny, Friedhelm Lehmann, Rainer Hunold, Evelyn Künneke, Karin Hardt, Gudrun Genest, Ursula Heyer, Christiane Maybach, Martin Hirthe, Rene Kolldehoff, Gunter Meisner, Peter Schlesinger. Dir: David Hemmings. Pro: Rolf Thiele. Screenplay: Joshua Sinclair. Pro Man: Lutz Winter. Ph: Charly Steinberger. Pro Des: Peter Rothe. Ed: Susan Jaeger & Fred Srp ('Release Version': Maxine Julius). Musical numbers sung and played by *The Manhattan Transfer, Pasadena Roof Orchestra & The Ragtimers.* M: Gunther Fischer; 'Revolutionary Song' by David Bowie. (Leguan Films, Berlin–Tedderwick.) Rel: 18 February. 105 mins. Cert AA.

Kentucky Fried Movie
A series of sketches, all parodies of American TV programmes, the intervening commercial or cinema films and adding up to a pretty thin ration of laughter. All presented by the Los Angeles Kentucky Fried Theatre. Contents include shafts aimed at the Breakfast Television Show, the Sex Film Trailer, the Martial Arts movies and, in Feel-A-Round, the novelty techniques. Cast: Members of the Theatre Company. Dir: John Landis. Pro: Robert K. Weiss. Ex Pro: Kim Jorgensen. Assoc Pro: Larry Kostroff. Pro Co-Ord: Alice West. Screenplay: David & Jerry Zucker & Jim Abrahams. Ph: Steven M. Katz (additional Ph: Bob Collins). Ed: George Folsey Jr. (Additional Ed: Lee Burch). Art: Rick Harvel. (Kentucky Fried Theatre Productions–Alpha.) Rel: Floating; first shown London, April 1979. 84 mins. Cert X.

The Lady Vanishes
Re-make of the famous, 1938, Hitchcock thriller about a British governess who vanishes from a transcontinental train where everyone seems anxious to deny her very existence and on which before very long a lot of very unpleasant and mysterious high-speed events take place. Cast: *Elliott Gould, Cybill Shepherd, Angela Lansbury, Herbert Lom, Arthur Lowe, Ian Carmichael, Gerald Harper, Jean Anderson, Jenny Runacre, Vladek Sheybal, Madlena Nedeva, Wolf Kahler, Madge Ryan, Rosalind Knight, Jonathan Hackett, Barbara Markham, Hillevi, Garry McDermott, Jacki Harding.* Dir: Anthony Page. Pro: Tom Sachs. Ex Pro: Michael Carreras, Arlene Sellers & Alex Winitsky. Screenplay: George Axelrod; based on a screenplay by Frank Launder & Sidney Gilliat and the novel *The Wheel Spins* by Ethel Lina White. Ph: Douglas Slocombe. Ed: Russel Lloyd. Pro Des: Wilfred Shingleton. Art: Bill Alexander & George von Kieseritzky. M: Philip Martell. (Hammer Films–Rank.) Rel: 3 June. 97 mins. Cert A.

The Last Snows of Spring—Ultima Neve di Primavera
Sad little Italian film—seen fleetingly in London in 1977 and recorded as a floating release in *Film Review* of that year—about a busy father's sudden realisation of just how much his small son means to

him, but it comes too late, as the little chap is found to be dying of blood-cancer. Cast: *Bekim Fehmiu, Agostina Belli, Renato Cesti, Nino Segurini, Margherita Horowitz, Margherita Melandri, Carla Mancini, Fillipo de Gara, Raika Juri, Giovanni Petrucci.* Dir: Raimondo del Balzo. Pro: Enzio Doria. Screenplay: Antonio Troiso & Raimondo del Balzo. Ph: Roberto d'Ettore Piazzoli. Ed: Angelo Curi. Pro Des: Gisella Longo. M: Franco Micalizzi. (GTO Films.) Rel: 21 January. 90 mins. Cert A.

The Last Supper
Cuban production about the sugar plantations and the harsh treatment of the slaves who worked on them in the 18th century, illustrated by the story of one paternalistic owner whose sense of guilt allied to his religious ties causes him to invite a dozen of his slaves to dine with him on Maundy Thursday, but when they refuse to work on Good Friday and turn against the foreman, the owner lops off the heads of those he considers to be the ringleaders. The heart of the film is the long supper sequence with its many implications. Cast: *Nelson Villagra, Luis Alberto García, Silvano Rey, José Antonio Rodríguez, Samuel Claxton, Mario Balmaseda.* Dir: Tomás Gutiérrez Alea. Pro: Santiago Yapur & Camilo Vives. Screenplay: Tomás González, Maria Eugenia Haya & Tomás Gutiérrez Alea. Ph: Mario García Joya. Ed: Nelson Rodriguez. Art: Carlos Arditi. M: Leo Brouwer. (Connoisseur.) Rel: Floating; first shown London, March 1979. 113 mins. Cert AA.

The Last Waltz
Very loud, Martin Scorsese film record of the final concert as a group given by *The Band,* led by *Robbie Robertson,* at the end of the summer of 1976 at Winterland, the venue in which they made their successful big-time début in rock music in 1969. A programme of their biggest hits over a period of twenty years, performed by them and various guest artists like *Bob Dylan.* Cast: *Robbie Robertson, Rick Danko, Levon Helm, Garth Hudson, Richard Manuel* (The Band); *Ronnie Hawkins, Dr John, Neil Young, The Staples, Neil Diamond, Joni Mitchell, Paul Butterfield, Muddy Waters, Eric Clapton, Emmylou Harris, Van Morrison, Bob Dylan, Ringo Starr, Ron Wood* and all (the guests). Dir: Martin Scorsese. Pro: Robbie Robertson. Ph: Michael Chapman. Pro Des: Boris Leven. Ed: Yeu-Bun Yee & Jan Roblee. Ex Pro: Jonathan Taplin. The songs: 'Don't Do It', Theme from 'The Last Waltz', 'Up on Cripple Creek', 'The Shape I'm In', 'It Makes No Difference', 'Stagefright', 'The Weight', 'Old Time Religion', 'The Night They Drove Old Dixie Down', 'Evangeline', 'Genetic Method/Chest Fever', 'Ophelia'. (Scorsese–UA.) Rel: 30 July. 117 mins. Cert U.

The Last Wave
Fascinatingly original if finally not completely satisfying Peter (*The Cars That Ate Paris, Picnic at*

Hanging Rock) Weir—Australian—film about a young lawyer, assigned the defence of some aborigines accused of murder, who becomes increasingly and disturbingly involved with them, their tribal secrets, 'magic' and stories of long-past civilisations. Unfortunately the opening atmosphere of tension and threat becomes increasingly dispelled towards the end, when the story reaches situations for which there can be no satisfactory explanation. Cast: *Richard Chamberlain, Olivia Hammett, Gulpilil, Frederick Parslow, Vivean Gray, Nandjiwarra Amagula MBE, Walter Amagula, Roy Bara, Cedric Lalara, Morris Lalara, Peter Carroll, Athol Compton, Hedley Cullen, Michael Duffield, Wallas Eaton, Jo England, John Frawley, Jennifer de Greenlaw, Richard Henderson, Merv Lilley, John Meagher, Guido Rametta, Malcolm Robertson, Greg Rowe, Katrina Sedgwick, Ingrid Weir.* Dir: Peter Weir. Pro: Hal McElroy & James McElroy. Screenplay: Peter Weir, Tony Morphett & Petru Popescu; from the original idea by Weir. Ph: Russell Boyd. Ed: Max Lemon. Art: Neil Angwin. M: Charles Wain. (McElroy & McElroy Productions in assoc with Derek Power–The South Australian Film Corp & Australian Film Commission–UA). Rel: Floating; first shown London, August 1978. 106 mins. Cert AA.

The Late Show
The most successful attempt yet to recapture the style and, more especially, the spirit of those classic private-eye films of the forties and thereabouts; with a highly involved and complicated story of murder, solved with dogged persistence and brilliant calculation by 'retired' private 'tec Ira Wells, dragged back into the business when his old pal and ex-partner turns up at his flat dying from a bullet in the belly. The ageing but still on occasion highly active Ira is helped by the kookie lady whose cat's abduction turns out to be all part of the plot. Delightful performances by *Art Carney* and *Lily Tomlin*. Rest of cast: *Bill Macy, Eugene Roche, Joanna Cassidy, John Considine, Ruth Nelson, John Davey, Howard Duff.* Dir & Screenplay: Robert Benton. Pro: Robert Altman. Assoc Pro: Robert Eggenweiler & Scott Bushnell. Ph: Chick Rosher. Ed: Lou Lombardo & Peter Appleton. M: Ken Wannberg. (Warner.) Rel: 16 July (included in *Film Review 1978–79* as a floating release). 93 mins. Cert AA.

Lebanon . . . Why?
A documentary examination of the problem of the two opposing, Christian and Moslem, factions in Lebanon, made during the 1975 war by a young man who had only recently completed his training at a film school but took his cameras out into the war-torn streets and for three years recorded what he saw there, always asking an agonised Why? And never getting the same reply twice! (Spot Anta Films–Oppidan Films.) Rel: Floating; first shown London, July 1978. 90 mins. Cert A.

The Legacy
Wildly incredible, old-fashioned English (Hammer-like) thriller about a young American girl lured to England by the promise of a big design job. Once here she, and her boy-friend, are further lured to the Old Dark House whose aged—if young-looking—owner, on the edge of death, has to choose from the girl and the other five selected 'heirs' which is the best one to take over his business empire and his occult powers . . . and there's a lot of fun in all this which was surely never intended! Cast: *Katharine Ross, Sam Elliott, Roger Daltrey, Charles Gray, Lee Montague, Hildegarde Neil, John Standing, Margaret Tyzack, Marianne Broome, Patsy Smart, William Abney, Mathias Kilroy.* Dir: Richard Marquand. Pro: David Foster & Larry Turman. Ex Pro: Arnold Kopelson. Pro Sup: Ted Lloyd. Ph: Dick Bush. Pro Des: Disley Jones. Ed: Anne Coates. M: No credit. (Columbia.) Rel: 1 October. 102 mins. Cert X.

*Legend of the Lawman
1975 American film (called *Part 2 Walking Tall* in that country) and in fact a direct sequel to the first film about an unshakably honest sheriff, based on the true story of Buford Pusser of McNairy County, Tennessee, who died in a mysterious (and some think skilfully engineered) car accident in 1974. Cast: *Bo Svenson, Luke Askew, Noah Beery, John Chandler, Robert Doqui, Bruce Glover, Richard Jaeckel, Brooke Mills, Logan Ramsey, Angel Tompkins, Lurene Tuttle, Leif Garrett, Dawn Lyn, William Bryant, Lloyd Tatum, Levi Frazier Jun, Red West, Jon R. Wilson, Ken Zimmerman, Archie Grinalds, Allen Mullikin, Libby Boone, Jimmy Moore, Frank McRae, Gary M. Darling.* Dir: Earl Bellamy. Pro: C. A. Pratt. Pro Sup: J. E. Pommer. Screenplay: Howard B. Kreitsek. Ph: Keith Smith. Ed: Art Seid. Art: Phil Jefferies. M: Walter Scharf. (Bing Crosby Productions–Avco/Embassy–Fox–Rank.) Rel: 17 June 1978. 109 mins. Cert AA.

Lemon Popsicle
Nostalgic Israeli film about youth in the 1950s, enlivened with a succession of some twenty-five big musical hits of the period. Cast: *Yiftach Katzur, Anat Atzmon, Jonathan Segal, Zachi Noy, Deborah Kidar, Ophelia Shtrall, Denis Bouzaglo, Rachel Steiner, Menache Warshavsky.* Dir: Boaz Davidson. Pro: Yoram Globus & Menahem Golan. Screenplay: Boaz Davidson & Eli Tabor. Ph: Adam Greenburg. Ed: Alain Jackubowicz. Art: no credit but set-dressing credits to A. Roshko & A. Gershony. M (supervision): Jack Fishman. (Entertainment Film Dist.) Rel: 12 March. 95 mins. Cert X.

Leopard in the Snow
The romance of the lady lost in a Northumberland blizzard and the former racing driver, now hermit invalid, she meets exercising his leopard in the snow! Anglo-Canadian production and the first of a possible series of similar movies promised by publishers Mills & Boon. Cast: *Keir Dullea, Susan Penhaligon, Kenneth More, Billie Whitelaw, Jeremy Kemp, Gordon Thomson.* Dir: Gerry O'Hara. Pro: John Quested & Chris Harrop. Screenplay: Anne Mather & Jill Hyem; based on the novel of the same title by Anne Mather. Ph: Michael Reed. Ed: Eddy Joseph. Art: Anthony Pratt. M: Kenneth V. Jones. Ex Pro: W. Lawrence Heisey. (Seastone Productions Ltd/Leopard in the Snow Ltd–Enterprise Pictures.) Rel: 9 July (included in *Film Review 1978–79* as a floating release). 94 mins. Cert A.

Lola Montes
A revival in its rarely-seen original version of the 1955 Max Ophuls's/Franco-German classic: a lush, stylised and artificial, but fascinatingly decorative and imaginative, treatment and framing of the story of the notorious lady who could number a King (of Bavaria) among her myriad lovers. Cast: *Martine Carol, Peter Ustinov, Anton Walbrook, Ivan Desny, Will Quadflieg, Oscar Werner, Lise Delamre, Henri Guisol, Paulette Dubost, Willy Eichberger, Beatrice Arnac, Helena Manson, Jacques Fayer, Daniel Mandaille, Pieral, Willy Rosner, Friedrich Domin, Werner Finck, Gustav Waldau.* Dir: Max Ophuls. Screenplay: Max Ophuls, Annette Wademant & Franz Geiger; based on the book *La Vie Extraordinaire de Lola Montes* by Cecil St Laurent. Dialogue: Jacques Natanson. Ph: Christian Matras. Ed: Madeleine Gug. Sets: Jean d'Eaubonne & Willy Schatz. M: Georges Auric. (Gamma Films–Florida–Oska Films Paris–Artificial Eye.) Rel: Floating; first shown London, August 1978. 110 mins. Cert A.

Love and Bullets
Routine cops-and-robbers piece with *Charles Bronson* as the small-time cop grimly determined to smash the big-boss, 'Godfather'-type crook who has invaded his Phoenix, Arizona, territory; and, when the villain's girl-friend (with whom the cop has fallen in love) is murdered by the gang, the cop steps outside the law to bring a holocaust of an end to the man and his empire. And it's about on the level of any of next week's familiar TV series episodes. Rest of cast: *Jill Ireland, Rod Steiger, Strother Martin, Henry Silva, Bradford Dillman, Ray Lefre, Lon Carli, Richard Brose, Andy Romano, Robin Clarke, Bill Gray, Richard Graydon, Alan Bryce, Cliff Pellow, Chip Lucia, Joe Rainer, Michael Parrent, Ramon Chavez, James Keane, Gene Earle, Jerry Thor, Raynold Gideon, John Hallam, Sidney Kean, Lorraine Chase, Alex Mayo, Karen Wyeth, J. Kenneth Campbell, Zoren Veltman, Urs Keller, Hans Kronig, Sapp Gruber.* Dir: Stuart Rosenberg. Pro: Pancho Kohner. Screenplay: Wendell Mayes. Pro Man: Hal Klein. Pro Sup: Basil Rayburn & George Casati. Ph: Fred Koenekamp & Anthony Richmond. Ed: Michael Anderson, Tom Priestley & Lesley Walker. Pro Des: John De Cuir. Art: Colin Grimes. M: Lalo Schifrin. (Lew Grade–ITC.) Rel: Floating. 95 mins. Cert A.

149

Releases of the Year in Detail

Love Letters from Teralba Road
With a background of read extracts from some letters actually found in a Sydney flat, this Australian film relates the story of the relationship between a storeman in Newcastle (Australia) and the wife he beats up and who leaves him. Cast: *Bryan Brown, Kris McQuade, Joy Hruby, Kevin Leslie, Gia Carides, Pat Jones, Don Chapman, Ashe Venn, Stuart Green.* Dir & Screenplay: Stephen Wallace. Pro: Richard Brennan. Ph: Tom Cowan. No other credits available. (Scala.) Rel: Floating; first shown London, August 1978. 50 mins. No cert.

Ludwig
Luchino Visconti's film about the last, mad, King of Bavaria who ruined his country with his passion for building incredibly elaborate castles and palaces, was finally deposed, confined and then died mysteriously. Visconti uses this story as his excuse for a slow-moving, episodic but superbly beautiful movie, using the screen as an easel on which to paint his superb set-pieces. Originally shown as a 3-hour-plus film at the London Film Festival some years ago, now cut (by Visconti) down to 2¼ hours but still seeming very long. Cast: *Helmut Berger, Romy Schneider, Trevor Howard, Silvana Mangano, Gert Fröbe, Helmut Griem, Isabella Telezynska, Umberto Orsini, John Moulder Brown, Sonia Petrova, Folker Bohnet, Heinz Moog, Adriana Asti, Marc Porel, Nora Ricci, Mark Burns, Maurizio Bonuglia, Alexander Allerson, Bert Bloch, Manfred Furst, Kurt Grosskurt, Anna Maria Hanschke, Gerhard Herter, Jan Linhart, Carla Mancini, Gernot Mohner, Clara Moustawcesky, Alain Naya, Alessandro Perrella, Karl Heinz Peters, Wolfram Schaerf, Henning Schluter, Helmut Stern, Eva Tavazzi, Louise Vincent, Gunnar Warner, Karl Heinz Windhorst, Rayka Yurit.* Dir: Luchino Visconti. Pro: Ugo Santalucia. Story & Screenplay: Visconti & Enrico Medioli; with collaboration of Suso Cecchi D'Amico. Ex Pro: Robert Gordon Edwards. Ph: Armando Nannuzzi. Art: Mario Chiari & Mario SScisi. M: Schumann, Weagner & Offenbach. (MGM–Supreme) Rel: Floating ; first shown London, October 1978. 135 mins. Cert A.

Madame Rosa
Schmaltzy little French–Jewish film with a marvellously gripping performance by *Simone Signoret,* playing the old, ex-prostitute who now tends the children of younger whores while they go about their business. Full of increasingly crippling disease, she is finally confined to her room where one of her small charges, an Arab boy long ago placed with her and apparently forgotten, comforts and tends her until and after her death. And though her appearance is distressing and her performance moving, the film is not all pain and sorrow, having a slim vein of quiet, chuckly comedy and some pithy, witty comments about Jews and Arabs. Delightful performances by *Samy Ben Youb* as the boy and *Claude Dauphin* as the old doctor. Rest of cast: *Gabriel Jarbour, Michal Bat Adam, Costa Gavras, Stella Anicette.* Dir: Moshe

Mizrahi. Pro: Ralph Baum. Screenplay: Moshe Mizrahi; based on the book *Momo* by Emile Ajar. Ph: Nestor Almendros. Ed: Sophie Coussein. Art: Bernard Evein. M: Philippe Sarde. (Lira Films, Paris–Secroft-International.) Rel: Floating; first shown London, April 1979. 105 mins. Cert AA.

Magic
Thriller about a ventriloquist's doll ('Fats') which takes over the performer's personality and twists him from a gentle, modest creature into a ruthless killer. Not particularly strong in conviction but powerful and subtle in other ways. Cast: *Anthony Hopkins, Ann-Margret, Burgess Meredith, Ed Lauter, E. J. Landre, Jerry Houser, David Ogden Stiers, Lillian Randolph, Joe Lowry, Beverley Sanders, I. W. Klein, Stephen Hart, Patrick McCullough, Bob Hackman, Mary Munday, Scott Garrett, Brad Beesley, Michael Harte.* Dir: Richard Attenborough. Pro: Joseph & Richard P. Levine. Ex Pro: C. O. Erickson. Screenplay: William Goldman; based on his own novel. Ph: Victor J. Kemper. Ed: John Bloom. Pro Des: Terence Marsh. M: Jerry Goldsmith. Pro Man: Alex Hapsas. (Joseph E. Levine–Fox.) Rel: 18 March. 107 mins. Cert X.

The Main Actor—Der Hauptdarsteller
Brilliantly subtle German film which tells the largely true story of the young lad chosen by director Reinhard Hauff as the star of his previous movie (*Pepe's Life*). At the end of the film the youngster expects to be taken care of by the director, who does indeed allow him to stay in his flat, but when the lad refuses to take a job and creates constant trouble the director packs him off home, whereupon the star embarks on a series of crimes and is finally jailed. Beautifully ironic in its observation and comments on the business of movie-making. Cast: *Vadim Glowna, Michael Schweiger, Mario Adorf, Hans Brenner, Rolf Zacher, Akim Ahrens, Carola Wittmann, Doris Dorrie, Eberhard Hauff.* Dir: Reinhard Hauff. Pro: Eberhard Junkersdorf. Pro Man: Herbert Kerz. Screenplay: Christel Buschmann & Reinhard Hauff. Ph: Frank Brühne. Ed: Stefanie Wilke. Art: Winifried Hennig. M: Klaus Doldinger. (Bioskop Film, Munich–WDR Köln–Scala.) Rel: Floating; first shown London, July 1978. 88 mins. Cert X.

The Manitou
Weird little thriller from the late William Girdler (who died at the age of thirty while he was preparing his next movie) about a witch-doctor who emerges from a tumour in unfortunate *Susan Strasberg's* neck and starts to go on the rampage. Rest of Cast: *Tony Curtis, Michael Ansara, Stella Stevens, Jon Cedar, Ann Sothern, Burgess Meredith, Paul Mantee, Jeanette Nolan, Lurene Tuttle, Hugh Corcoran, Ann Newman-Mantee, Jan Heininger, Michael Laren, Cindy Stanford, Tenaya, Beverly Kushida, Charles Kissinger, Michael Andreas, Nick Dyrenforth, Loren Elaine, Felix Silla, Joe Gieb.* Dir & Pro: William Girdler. Ex

Pro: Melvin G. Gordy. Assoc Pro: Jon Cedar & Gilles A. DeTurenne. Screenplay: William Girdler, Jon Cedar & Thomas Pope; based on the novel by Graham Masterton. Ph: Michel Hugo. Ed: Bub Asman. Sup Ed: Gene Ruggiero. Pro Des: Walter Scott Herndon. M: Lalo Schifrin. (Manitou Productions–Enterprise–Avco Embassy.) Rel: 13 May. 105 mins. Cert X.

*The Medusa Touch
Glossy, expensive, well made and progressively taut thriller based on the Peter Van Greenaway novel about a man with a malevolent mind who finds that he only has to wish for disaster for it to happen! He starts by wishing the deaths of his parents, wife, schoolmaster and the judge who irritates him, then goes on to bigger things such as failing an American moonshot and collapsing a cathedral, and carries on even when his body is dead! Cast: *Richard Burton, Lino Ventura, Lee Remick, Harry Andrews, Marie-Christine Barrault, Michael Hordern, Gordon Jackson, Derek Jacobi, Michael Bryne, Jeremy Brett, Robert Lang.* Dir: Jack Gold. Pro: Jack Gold & Anne V. Coates. Screenplay: John Briley; based on the book by Peter Van Greenaway. Assoc Pro: Dennis Holt. Ph: Arthur Ibbetson. Pro Sup: Colin Brewer. Ed: Anne V. Coates. Art: Peter Mullins. M: Michael J. Lewis. (Lew Grade in assoc. with Arnon Milchan & Elliott Kastner–Coates/Gold Film–ITC Film Distributors Ltd.) Rel: 25 June 1978. 109 mins. Cert A.

Memories Within Miss Aggie
Somewhat indifferent (to put it kindly!), loosely and ill-constructed 1974 piece of celluloid porn from the so-called king of it, Gerard (*Deep Throat*) Damiano: a series of sexual encounters which with or without the censor's attention stop at—well, very little. Cast: *Deborah Ashira, Patrick L. Farrelly, Kim Pope, Mary Stuart, Darby Lloyd Rains, Eric Edwards, Harry Reems, Leo Zorba, Ralph Herman, Christopher Kersen, Rolf Beck.* Dir: Gerard Damiano. Screenplay: Ron Wertheim & Gerard Damiano. Ph: Harry Flecks. Ed: St Marks Place. Set Dec: David Beames. M: Rupert Holmes. (Inish Kae–Oppidan.) Rel: Floating; first shown Lond, July 1978. Cert X. 60 mins.

Midnight Express
Grim, brutal and harrowing film, based on a true story, about a young American caught trying to smuggle dope out of Turkey and sentenced first to four years, and later to thirty more, in a jail which is pictured as a horrifyingly depraved place where inmates are beaten into insanity or killed or otherwise rot away. Well produced and well acted and something of an odd piece of 'I Accuse'-type propaganda. Cast: *Brad Davis, Randy Quaid, Bo Hopkins, John Hurt, Paul Smith, Mike Kellin, Norbert Weisser, Irene Miracle, Paolo Bonacelli,*

Michael Ensign, Franco Diogene, Kevork Malikyan, Mihalis Yannatos, Gigi Ballista, Tony Boyd, Peter Jeffrey, Ahmed El Shenawi, Zanninos Zanninou, Dimos Starenios. Dir: Alan Parker. Pro: David Puttnam & Alan Marshall. Screenplay: Oliver Stone; based on the book by Billy Hayes & William Hoffer. Ex Pro: Peter Guber. Ph: Michael Seresin. Ed: Gerry Hambling. Art: Evan Hercules. Pro Des: Geoffrey Kirkland. M: Giorgio Moroder. (Casablanca Filmworks–Columbia.) Rel: 10 September. 120 mins. Cert X.

Montreal Main
The waxing, and waning, of a friendship between a 13-year-old street boy and a 28-year-old artist, seen against the teeming background of the Canadian city's East Side. Described with some insight as 'a cross between Warhol and Cassavetes' in style! Dir: Frank Vitale, Allan Bozo Moyle & Maxine McGillivray. Assoc Pro: Kirwan Cox. Screenplay: Frank Vitale, Allan Bozo Moyle, John, Dave & Ann Sutherland, Jackie Holden, Peter Brawley, Pam Marchant & Steve Lack. Ph: Erich Bloch & Chris Anstead. Ed: Frank Vitale, Roman Soleki & Jon Michaelson. No Art credit. M: Beverly Glenn-Copelann. (President Films–Canadian Film Development Corp–Harris Films.) Rel: Floating; first shown London, September 1978. No cert.

The Music Machine
Minor league British disco movie. Cast: *Gerry Sundquist, Patti Boulaye, David Easter, Michael Feast, Ferdy Mayne, Clarke Peters, Richard Parmentier, Billy McColl, Chrissy Wickham, Frances Lowe, Johnny Wade, Mandy Perryment, Garry Shail, Brenda Fricher, Thomas Baptiste, John Gorman, Cathy Lewis, John Fowler, Ian Lindsay, Tony Pierce, John Blundell, Mark Wingett, Sebastian Smedley-Aston, Esther Rantzen.* Dir: Ian Sharp. Pro: Brian Smedley-Aston. Ex Pro: James Kenelm Clarke. Assoc Pro: Vic Caira. Screenplay: James Kenelm Clarke. Ph: Phil Meheux. Ed: Alan Pattilo & Brian Smedley-Aston. Art: Roger King. M: Aaron Harry & The Music Machine. Ex M Sup: Robin Phillips. (Norfolk International Pictures/Daycastle–Target.) Rel: June 17. 90 mins. Cert. A.

Music in Progress
The story of composer/band leader Mike Westbrook and his small- and large-band jazz music. Dir & Screenplay: Charles Mapleston. Ph: Ian Wilson. Ed: Hugh Newsam. (Malachite Ltd–Arts Council of GB.) Rel: Floating. 44 mins. No cert.

National Lampoon's Animal House
Bitterly satirical—and terrifying!—look at American college life about which *Time* magazine said it was the first film to tackle the subject with realism. The master teaches his pupils to smoke pot and sleeps with the girls in his class; the pupils get drunk, wilfully destroy, fornicate, violently assault the citizens and otherwise live up to the nickname of their 'House'. The scene is set in 1962 and, as the publicity has it: 'When you've stopped laughing consider this: these boys are men, now. And they're running America.' Cast: *John Belushi, Tim Matheson, John Vernon, Verna Bloom, Thomas Hulce, Cesare Danova, Peter Riegert, Mary Louise Weller, Stephen Furst, James Daughton, Bruce McGill, Mark Metcalf, DeWayne Jessie, Karen Allen, James Widdoes, Martha Smith, Sarah Holcomb, Lisa Baur, Kevin Bacon, Donald Sutherland, Douglas Kenney, Christian Miller, Bruce Bonnheim, Joshua Daniel, 'Junior', Sunny Johnson, Stacy Grooman, Stephen Bishop, Eliza Garrett, Aseneth Jurgenson, Katherine Denning, Raymone Robinson, Robert Elliott, Reginald H. Farmer, Jebidiah R. Dumas, Priscilla Lauris, Rick Eby, John Freeman, Sean McCartin, Helen Vick, Rick Greenough, Gary McLarty, Albert M. Mauro, Karen Werner, Fred Hice, Bill Hooker, Clifford Happy, Pam Bebermeyer, Dud Ekins, Jim Halty, R. A. Rondell, Walter Wyatt, Gilbert Combs.* Dir: John Landis. Pro: Matty Simmons & Ivan Reitman. Screenplay: Harold Ramis, Douglas Kenney & Chris Miller. Ph: Charles Correll. Ed: George Folsey Jun. Art: John J. Lloyd. M: Elmer Bernstein. (Universal–CIC.) Rel: 4 March. 109 mins. Cert AA.

Nest of Vipers
Polished Italian film about a young man, training to be a professional pianist, who becomes involved first with the mother of his friend and then with the daughter of a rich family. And apart from this polish the film is lifted by the lush, late-1930s, *dolce vita* background of Venice and the irony which gives the climax a memorable quality; it gives, too, an extra dimension to the melodramatic story of passion, jealousy and murder. Cast: *Ornella Muti, Senta Berger, Capucine, Christian Borromeo, Stefano Patrizi, Mattia Sbragia, Giuliana Calandra, Paolo Bonacelli, Maria Monti, Eros Pagni, Giancarlo Sbragia.* Dir: Tonino Cervi. Pro: Piero La Mantia. Screenplay: Tonino Cervi & Cesare Frugoni, in collaboration with Goffredo Parise; from a story by Roger Peyrefitte. Ph: Armando Nannuzzi. Ed: Nino Baragli. Art: Luigi Scaccianoce. General Organisation & Dir of Pro: Michele Marsala. M: Vincenzo Tempera. (Mars–CIC.) Rel: Floating; first shown London, March 1979. 105 mins. Cert X.

Newsfront
Technically and otherwise brilliant Australian film which—with smoothly edited sequences of old newsreels, reconstructions of history and a warmly human and wholly credible central story of an honest and dedicated newsreel cameraman—tells something of the history of Australia from 1948 to the present day, covering the rabbit plague, the immigrant influx, floods, fire and the remarkable seventeen-year political reign of Robert Menzies, as well as touching on the great Redex cross-country car rally, the referendum about Communism, President Nixon's visit, the 1956 Olympics and the advent and encroachment of television on the territory of the newsreel. Superbly well acted by *Bill Hunter* as the newsreel reporter and the entire cast: *Gerard Kennedy, Wendy Hughes, Angela Punch, Chris Haywood, John Ewart, Don Crosby, John Dease, John Clayton, Bryan Brown, Tony Barry, Drew Forsythe, Lorna Lesley, Brian Anderson, Alexander Archdale, Brian Blain, Bunney Brooke, Peter Carroll, Slim de Grey, Gerry Duggan, John Flaus, Les Foxcroft, Anne Haddy, Johnny Quicksilver, Bruce Spence, Kit Taylor, Sue Walker, Mark Holden, Paul Jones, Jude Kuring, Bill Lyle, Tessa Mallos, Ray Marshall, Ray Meagher, Robyn Moase, Chad Morgan, Alan Penney, Don Philps, Rob Steele, Franco Valentino, Joan Winchester.* Dir: Phillip Noyce. Pro: David Elfick. Screenplay: Phillip Noyce from an original screenplay by Bob Ellis and a concept by David Elfick. Assoc Pro: Richard Brennan. Ph: Vincent Monton (Cam Op: Louis Irving). Ed: John Scott. Art: Larry Eastwood. Pro Des: Lissa Coote. (Mainline.) Rel: Floating; first shown London, November 1978. 110 mins. Cert A.

Nighthawks
British. The rather dreary life of a homosexual school-teacher who appears to have little control over his passions or his pupils. Cast: *Ken Robertson and supporting amateur players.* Dir, Pro & Screenplay: Ron Peck & Paul Hallam. Pro Co-Ord: Patsy Nightingale. Ph: Joanna Davis, Patrick Duval, Sebastian Dewsbery, Ian Owles & Steve Shaw. Ed: Richard Taylor, Mary Pat Leece, Debra Daley & Tim Horrocks. Art: Jan Sender, Frank Biggs, Andreas Dimitriou, Bill Hayes & Rhys Thomas. M: David Graham Ellis. (Nashburgh/Four Corner Films–Cinegate.) Rel: Floating; first shown London, March 1979. 113 mins. Cert X.

No Longer Alone
The true life-story of British girl *Joan Winmill Brown* who after finding success as a stage, TV and film actress in the 1950s still found herself unfulfilled, until a friend took her along to one of Billy Graham's London rallies—an experience which changed her completely. Also starring: *James Fox, Simon Williams, Belinda Carroll.* Dir: Nicholas Webster. (World Wide Pictures—the film division of the Billy Graham Organisation.) Rel: Floating; first shown London, February 1979. 100 mins. Cert AA.

No 1 of the Secret Service
Minor British James Bond spoof about a mad toy-maker millionaire who with the aid of KRASH (an almost equally crazy professional group of killers) sets out to eliminate arms-making profiteers. Violent, fast-paced, familiar. Cast: *Nicky Henson, Richard Todd, Aimi Macdonald, Geoffrey Keen, Dudley Sutton, Sue Lloyd, Jon Pertwee, Milton Reid, The Baker Twins, Fiona Curzon, Jenny Till, Katya Wyeth, Roberta Gibbs, Oliver MacGreevy, Elizabeth*

Releases of the Year in Detail

Tyrrell, *Allen Ambridge, Dave Carter*. Dir: Lindsay Shonteff. Pro: Elizabeth Gray. Assoc Pro: Lewis Force. Screenplay: Howard Craig. Ph: Ivan Strasburg. Ed: John Luton. M: Leonard Young. (Lindsay Shonteff Films–Hemdale.) Rel: Floating. 93 mins. Cert AA.

Nosferatu the Vampyre
Werner Herzog's version of the old Dracula story in which he ignores all modern sophistication of the tale to get back to basics. The blood-sucking Count, a macabre, bald, ashen-faced, light-fearing figure, seduced by the pure-minded, self-sacrificing beauty in order to save her husband, a vain sacrifice as it turns out to be. All starkly black-and-white (in colour, of course); true German gothic horror, owing something to the original old Murnau silent of the same title and also to *Caligari*. A remarkable performance by *Klaus Kinski* as the Count whose greatest cross is his inability to die. Rest of cast: *Isabelle Adjani, Bruno Ganz, Roland Topor, Walter Ladengast, Dan Van Husen, Jan Groth, Carsten Bodinus, Martje Grohmann, Ryk de Gooyer, Clemens Scheitz, Lo Van Hensbergen, Lohn Leddy, Margiet van Hartingsveld, Tim Beekman, Jacques Dufilho*. Dir, Pro & Screenplay: Werner Herzog. Ex Pro: Walter Saxer. Ph: Jörg Schmidt-Reitwein. Ed: Beate Mainka-Jellinghaus. M: Popol Vuh/Florian Fricke (& Wagner's 'Rheingold' & Gounod's 'Santus', etc.). (Fox.) Rel: Floating; first shown London, May 1979. 107 mins. Cert. AA.

The Odd Job
British film which veers—sometimes unsteadily but quite often amusingly—between black, crazy and farcical comedy as it re-tells the old story about the man who, wanting but not having the courage to commit suicide, employs someone to kill him and then, when circumstances alter and he wants to live, finds himself in constant deadly danger. Broad performance by *Graham Chapman* as the employer and *David Jason* as the odd-job man employed. Rest of cast: *Diana Quick, Simon Williams, Edward Hardwicke, Bill Paterson, Michael Elphick, Stewart Harwood, Carolyn Seymour, Joe Melia, George Innes, James Bree, Zulema Dene, Richard O'Brien, Carl Andrews, Dave Atkins, John Judd, Nick Edmett, Toby Salaman, Tiny Keeling, David Hatton, Anthony Milner, Mark Penfold*. Dir: Peter Medak. Pro: Mark Forstater & Graham Chapman. Ex Pro: Tony Stratton Smith & Steve O'Rourke. Screenplay: Bernard McKenna & Graham Chapman; based on the former's play. Ph: Ken Hodges. Ed: Barrie Vince. Art: Tony Curtis. M: Howard Blake. (Columbia.) Rel: 8 October. 86 mins. Cert A.

The One and Only
Occasionally mildly amusing comedy about a completely untalented egotist who tells himself, and everyone else, what a great actor he is but ends up as a rather pathetic show-off in the wrestling ring, where he plays a transvestite! Cast: *Henry Winkler,*

Kim Darby, Gene Saks, William Daniels, Harold Gould, Polly Holliday, Hervé Villechaize, Bill Baldwin, Anthony Battaglia, Ed Begley Jun, Peter Brocco, Brandon Cruz, Lucy Lee Flippin, Charles Frank, Chavo Guerrero, H. B. Haggerty, Dennis James, Richard Karron, Jean LeBouvier, Ralph Manza, Ken Olfson, Jack Scalici, Will Seltzer, Amzie Strickland, Mary Woronov. Dir: Carl Reiner. Pro: Steve Gordon & David V. Picker. Screenplay: Steve Gordon. Ex Pro: Robert Halmi. Ph: Victor J. Kemper. Ed: Bud Molin. Pro Des: Edward Carfagno. M: Patrick Williams. (First Artists–Paramount–CIC.) Rel: 13 August. 98 mins. Cert A.

One Sings, The Other Doesn't—L'Une Chante L'Autre Pas
Beautifully achieved, minor-key Agnès Varda film about two women, over a period of fourteen years. Friends with varying class backgrounds, they keep in touch throughout their divergent sexual and marital experiences and meet ten years later at a demonstration for the rights of legalised abortion. A really unusual and thoughtful, and certainly restrained, 'woman's picture'. Delightfully acted. Cast: *Valérie Mairesse, Thérèse Liotard, Robert Dadiès, Ali Affi, Jean-Pierre Pellegrin, François Wertheimer*. Dir & Screenplay: Agnès Varda. Pro: no credit. Ph: Charlie Van Damm. Ed: Joelle Van Effenterre. Art: no credit. M: François Wertheimer. (Cine Tamaris–Gaumont–Cinegate.) Rel: Floating; first shown London, September 1978. 105 mins. Cert AA.

On the Line
Very politically-conscious American film made in 1976, the intention of which is to urge militant workers to take action against the slump that is seen to be inevitable. Narrated by *Rip Torn*. Dir & Pro: Barbara Margolis. (The Other Cinema.) Rel: Floating; first shown London, January 1979. 54 mins. No cert.

Outrageous
Strange, certainly original, Canadian film about an odd relationship which develops into undemanding love between a girl who's slightly off her trolley and a homosexual hairdresser who becomes a star female impersonator. Starring *Craig Russell* who is in fact such an international star and whose witty and wicked impressions of Bette Davis, Barbra Streisand, Judy Garland and others give the film some of its best moments. Lots of sentiment, love and devotion and a clever skating over of the less pleasant homosexual angles. Rest of cast: *Hollis McLaren* (quite outstanding as the girl), *Richard Easley, Allan Moyle, David McIlwraith, Gerry Salzberg, Andrée Pelletier, Helen Shaver, Martha Gibson, Helen Hughes, Jonah Royston, Richard Moffatt, David Woito, Rusty Ryan, Trevor Bryan, Jackie Loren, Michael Daniels, Mike Ironside, Rene Forier, Maxine Miller, Michel*. Songs sung by *Brenda Hoffert &*

Cecille Frennette. Dir & Screenplay: Richard Benner; based on a story from *Butterfly Ward* by Margaret Gibson. Pro: William Marshall. Assoc Pro: Peter O'Brian. Ph: James B. Kelly. Ed: George Appleby. Art: Karen Bromley. Original lyrics: Brenda Hoffert. M: Paul Hoffert. (John Nasht Productions–Film Consortium of Canada–Miracle.) Rel: Floating; first shown London, September 1978. 96 mins. Cert X.

Paradise Alley
Third film from writer–director–star (and, in this case, theme-song singer too!) *Sylvester Stallone*, whose first effort *Rocky* was an Oscar-winner. Not much likelihood of awards, however, for this cliché-ridden, confused story of three brothers living in the 'Hell's Kitchen' district of New York (*circa* late 1940s) and their changing relationship as two of them promote the bone-crunching rise of the third, a gentle-giant wrestler. Rest of cast: *Lee Canalito, Armand Assante, Frank McRae, Anne Archer, Kevin Conway, Terry Funk, Joyce Ingalls, Joe Spinell, Aimee Eccles, Tom Waits, Chick Casey, James J. Casino, Fredi O. Gordon, Lydia Goya, Michael Jeffers, Max Leavitt, Paul Mace, Polli Magaro, Pamela Miller, John Monks Jun, Leo Nanas, Frank Pesce, Stuart K. Robinson, Ray Sharkey, Maria Smith-Caffey, Patricia Spann, Frank Stallone Jun, Jeff Wald*. Dir & Screenplay: Sylvester Stallone. Pro: John F. Roach & Ronald A. Suppa. Ex Pro: Edward Pressman. Assoc Pro: Arthur Chobanian. Ph: Laslo Kovacs. Ed: Eve Newman. Pro Des: John W. Corso. Art: Deborah Beaudet. M: Bill Conti. Song 'Too Close to Paradise' sung by *Sylvester Stallone*. (Force Ten Productions/A Moonblood Film–Universal–CIC.) Rel: 4 February. 109 mins. Cert A.

Pardon Mon Affaire, Too—Nous Irons Tous À Paradis
A still hilarious, though less so and less comically inventive, follow-up to one of the best comedy films of the French year (*Pardon Mon Affaire*), following the adventures of four great pals, with one buying a 'bargain' house (bought during an airport strike and then discovered to be just at the end of the local aerodrome take-off area), another losing his mother, and Etienne (*Jean Rochefort*, as superb as ever) suspecting his wife of taking a lover. All lightly fluffy fun. Rest of cast: *Victor Lanoux, Guy Bedos, Claude Brasseur, Danièle Delorme, Marthe Villalonga, Jenny Arasse, Josiane Bolasko, Anne-Marie Blot, Elizabeth Margoni, Pascale Reynaud, Maia Simon, Catherine Velor, Christophe Bruce, Jean-Pierre Castali, Vania Vilers, Daniel Gélin, Gaby Sylvia, Jean Anneron, Monique Brum-Chambord, Christophe Cauchoux, Philippe Chemin, Paul Descouiveves, Mary Françoise, Carole Jacquinot, André Lambert, Claude Legros, Jean-Pierre Leroux, Elisabeth Rambert, Yves Renaud*. Dir: Yves Robert. Pro: Yves Robert & Alain Poire. Assoc Pro: Daniel Deschamps. Screenplay: Jean-Loup Dabadie; from a story by Yves Robert. Ph: René Mathelin. Ed: Pierre Gillette. Art: Jean-Pierre

Kohut-Svelko. M: Vladimir Cosma. (Les Productions de la Gueville/Gaumont International–Enterprise Pictures.) Rel: Floating; first shown London, October 1978. 112 mins. Cert AA.

The Passage
Chase theme with *James Mason*, the American professor with valuable atomic knowledge, being smuggled with his family out of occupied France across the mountains to safety in Spain; a journey fraught with thrills, death and bloodshed as the struggling fugitives are led by a tough Basque shepherd–guide (*Anthony Quinn*) and relentlessly pursued by a young, sadistic Nazi whose revolting crimes are dwelt upon excessively and include the burning alive of a gypsy and the drawn-out cutting off of the fingers of one of the French Underground members he catches. With Mason's and Quinn's underplaying, *Malcom McDowell*'s overplaying of the role of the Nazi stands out all the more. Rest of cast: *Patricia Neal, Kay Lenz, Christopher Lee, Michael Lonsdale, Marcel Bozzuffi, Paul Clemens, Rose Alba, Neville Jason, Robert Rhys, Peter Arne, Robert Brown, James Broadbent, Terence York, Terence Maidment*. Dir: J. Lee Thompson. Pro: John Quested. Ex Pro: John Daly & Derek Dawson. Co Pro: Lester Goldsmith & Maurice Binder. Screenplay: Bruce Nicolaysen; based on his own novel *The Perilous Journey*. Assoc Pro: Geoffrey Helman. Ph: Michael Reed. Ed: Alan Strachan. Art: Jean Forestier. M: Michael J. Lewis. (General Film Co–Passage Films Inc–Hemdale.) Rel: 29 April. 98 mins. Cert X.

Pete's Dragon
Delightful Disney musical comedy with a cast of humans plus one gentle and quite endearing—animated—green dragon, whose good deed is safely to install his little, ill-used orphan pal Pete in a good and loving home. Simple humour, tuneful melodies, nice performances adding up to outstanding family screen fun. Cast: *Helen Reddy, Jim Dale, Mickey Rooney, Red Buttons, Shelley Winters, Sean Marshall* (Pete), *Gary Morgan, Jane Kean, Jeff Conaway, Jim Backus, Cal Bartlett, Charles Tyner, Charlie Callas* (the voice of Elliott, the dragon), *Walter Barnes, Robert Easton, Al Checco, Roger Price, Henry Slate, Robert Foulk, Jack Collins, Ben Wrigley, Joe Ross*. Dir: Don Chaffey. Pro: Ron Miller & Jerome Courtland. Screenplay: Malcolm Marmorstein; based on a story by Seton I. Miller & S. S. Field. Ph: Frank Phillips. Ed: Gordon D. Brenner. Music & Lyrics: Al Kasha & Joel Hirschhorn. Elliott created by Ken Anderson (also Animation Art Dir). Animation Dir: Don Bluth. (Walt Disney.) Rel: 17 December. 106 mins. Cert U.

Piranha
Horror-thriller about the accidental escape of some specially-bred shoals of the killer fish of the title (originally intended as a Vietnam war secret weapon!) and their flesh-eating way down-river where they cause bloody havoc at a holiday-camp bathing gala before being polluted to death (well, so 'tis hoped by brave polluter *Bradford Dillman*). To be taken with salt—lots of it. Rest of cast: *Heather Menzies, Kevin McCarthy, Keenan Wynn, Dick Miller, Barbara Steele, Belinda Balaski, Melody Thomas, Bruce Gordon, Barry Brown, Paul Bartel, Shannon Collins, Shawn Nelson, Richard Deacon, Janie Squire, Roger Richman, Bill Smillie, Guich Koock, Jack Pauleson, Eric Henshaw, Robert Vinson, Virginia Dunnam, Hill Farnsworth, Bruce Barbour, Robyn Ray, Mike Sullivan, Jack Cardwell, Roger Creed, Nick Palminsano, Bobby Sargent*. Dir: Joe Dante. Pro: Jon Davison. Screenplay: John Sayles; from a story by Richard Robinson & John Sayles. Ex Pro: Roger Corman & Jeff Schechtman. Co Pro: Chako Van Leeuwen. Ph: Jamie Anderson. Ed: Mark Goldblatt & Joe Dante. (Roger Corman/Van Leeuwen–UA.) Rel: 26 November. 94 mins. Cert X.

The Playbirds
British, murder most foul, with the gorgeous girls who pose for the centre-spread each month of a 'sexplicit' magazine as the victims. And how the pretty woman cop who is persuaded to become a decoy eventually learns who committed the murders, and how and why. Cast: *Mary Millington, Glynn Edwards, Gavin Campbell, Alan Lake, Windsor Davies, Derren Nesbitt, Kenny Lynch, Suzy Mandel, Peggy Spencer, Sandra Dorne, Dudley Sutton, Alex Mango*. Dir & Pro: Willy Roe. Ex Pro: David Sullivan. Screenplay: Bud Tobin & Robin O'Connor. Ph: Douglas Hill. Ed: Jim Connock. M: David Whitaker. (Roldvale Productions–Tigon Film Dist.) Rel: 24 September. 94 mins. Cert X.

The Point is to Change It—Es kommt drauf an, Sie zu verändern
German documentary made by feminist Claudia Aleman seeking to show how far off is real equality of the sexes. Made in 1973, with this new English version prepared by Linda Dove and Fran MacLean. (The Other Cinema.) Rel: Floating; first shown London, January 1979. 55 mins. Black-and-white.

Power Play
Dubious politics, dangerous plots, double-crossing and an unfortunate country finding itself exchanging one corrupt police-state regime for another. Cast: *Peter O'Toole, David Hemmings, Donald Pleasence, Barry Morse, Jon Granik, Marcella Saint-Amant, George Touliatos, Chuck Shamata, Gary Reineke, Harvey Atkin, August Schellenberg, Eli Rill, Dick Cavett, David Calderisi, Alberta Waston*. Dir & Screenplay: Martyn Burke. Pro: Christopher Dalton. Ex Pro: Robert M. Cooper & Ronald I. Cohen. Assoc Pro: John M. Eckert. UK Co-Pro: David Hemmings. Ph: Ousama Rawi. Pro Des: Karen Bromley. M: Ken Thorne. (Magnum International Productions Inc of Toronto/Cowry Film Productions, London–Rank.) Rel: Floating. 103 mins. Cert AA.

Prisoner of Passion—La Orca
Uneasy Italian mix of sex and crime, about a young girl kidnapped by a gang who begin to disintegrate when their demands for ransom are refused. The girl ends up by killing the captor who has fallen in love with her. Cast: *Michele Placido, Rena Niehaus, Flavio Bucci, Bruno Corazzari, Adriano Amedei Migliano, Anna Canzi, Livia Cerini, Vittorio Mezzogiorno*. Dir: Eriprando Visconti. Pro: Marcello D'Amico. Screenplay: Lisa Morpurgo & E. Visconti. Ph: Blasco Giurato. Ed: Franco Arcalli. Art: Francesco Vanorio. M: Federico Monti Arduini. (Serena Films '75–Intercontinental.) Rel: Floating. 98 mins. Cert X.

Punk in London
A German look at our punk-rock scene, with interviews with musicians, fans and managers: what it is and how it works. Cast: *The Sex Pistols, The Stranglers, X-Ray Spex, The Lurkers, The Electric Chairs*, etc. Dir: Wolfgang Buld. (Essential.) Rel: Floating; first shown London, July 1978. 106 mins. No cert.

Race for Your Life, Charlie Brown
Another—the third—cartoon feature for 'Peanuts' fans, in which Charlie and his gang experience a series of minor adventures while at their summer camp in the country, climaxing with an exciting river race. Dir: Bill Melendez. Pro: Lee Mendelson & Bill Melendez. Co Dir: Phil Roman. Screenplay: Charles M. Schulz, based on his strip cartoon characters. Ed: Chuck McCann & Roger Donley. Camera: Dickson/Vasu. M: Ed Bogas. Animation: Don Lusk, Bob Matz, Hank Smith, Rod Scribner, Ken O'Brien, Al Pabian, Joe Roman, Jeff Hall, Sam Jaimes, Bob Bachman, George Singer, Bill Littlejohn, Bob Carlson, Patricia Joy, Terry Lennon, Larry Leichliter. Voices: Duncan Watson, Greg Felton, Stuart Brotman, Gail Davis, Liam Martin, Kirk Jue, Jordan Warren, Jimmy Ahrens, Melanie Kohn, Tom Muller, Bill Melendez, Fred Van Amburg. (Paramount–CIC.) Rel: 13 August. 75 mins. Cert U.

The Rain People
1969 Francis Ford Coppola film only now being released in GB. Interesting treatment of a story about a pregnant wife who, feeling she is unsatisfactory as a woman and a wife—and will make an equally unsatisfactory mother—gets up one morning and takes off in the family car on an aimless drive towards California, soon picking up an ex-college football player with a metal plate in his head and who behaves like a child. Forced by her conscience into a sense of responsibility she gives up trying to get rid of him and eventually causes his death at the hands of the child whose father she has decided will satisfy

153

her sexual need. Cast: *Shirley Knight, James Caan, Robert Duvall, Marya Zimmet, Tom Aldredge, Laurie Crews, Andrew Duncan, Margaret Fairchild, Sally Gracie.* Dir & Screenplay: Francis Ford Coppola. Pro: Bart Patton & Ronald Colby. Ph: Wilmer Butler. Ed: Blackie Malkin. Art: Leon Ericksen. M: Ronald Stein. (Warner.) Rel: Floating; first shown London, December 1978. 102 mins. Cert AA.

Rape
American documentary which takes three victims of this kind of assault and records their discussion about their experiences and the implications for all their 'sisters.' Dir: Jo Ann Elam. (The Other Cinema.) Rel: Floating; first shown London, January 1979. 35 mins. Black-and-white. No cert.

Rapunzel, Let Down Your Hair
The first British feature film to be made entirely by women—a combined live action and animated telling and re-telling of the Brothers Grimm's fairy-tale, each telling bringing out a new angle on it, the symbolism and ideology from the feminist point of view. Dir: Susan Shapiro, Esther Ronay & Francine Winham. (BFI.) Rel: Floating; first shown London, October 1978. 80 mins. Cert AA.

Remember My Name
Having professed the ambition of making an 'old-fashioned' movie 'updating the classic woman's melodramas of the Bette Davis, Barbara Stanwyck, Joan Crawford era,' Robert Altman protégé, director Alan Rudolph, following his directorial début with *Welcome to L.A.*, made this story of the involvement of a man with his ex-wife and present wife and how it worked out for each of them. Cast: *Geraldine Chaplin, Anthony Perkins, Moses Gunn, Berry Berenson, Jeff Goldblum, Timothy Thomerson, Alfred Woodard, Marilyn Coleman, Jeffrey S. Perry, Carlos Brown, Dennis Franz, Terry Wills, Ina Gould, Jette Seear, Belita Moreno, Barbara Dodd, Jim Thalman, Tom Oberhaus, Diana Daves, Maysie Hoy, Herb Kerns, Steve Mendillo, Richard Wahl, George Walsh.* Dir & Screenplay: Alan Rudolph. Pro: Robert Altman. Ex in charge of Pro: Tommy Thompson. Assoc Pro: Robert Eggenweiler & Scott Bushnell. Ph: Tak Fujimoto. Ed: Thomas Walls & William A. Sawyer. Art: no credit. M Ed: Ted Whitfield; songs written and sung by *Alberta Hunter*. (Lion's Gate Films–Columbia.) Rel: Floating 94 mins. Cert AA.

Renaldo and Clara
Bob Dylan, at considerable length, attempting to reveal the real Bob Dylan! He wrote, directed, produced and even co-edited this collection of concert and other footage in an effort to provide a composite picture of the man and his work. Cast: *Bob & Sara Dylan, Joan Baez, Ronnie Hawkins, Ronee Blakley, Jack Elliott, Harry Dean Stanton, Bob Neuwirth, Mel Howard, Allen Ginsberg, David Mansfield, Jack Baran, Helena Kallianiotes, Rubin*

'Hurricane' Carter, Scarlet Rivera, Mamma Maria Frasca, Mad Bear, Roger McGuinn, David Blue & Joni Mitchell, Rob Stoner, Ruth Tyrangiel, Steven Soles, Mick Ronson, Anne Waldman, Denise Mercedes & Linda Thomases, T-Bone Burnett, Shelia Shotton, Kevin Crossley, Larry Sloman, Hal Frazier, M. Will, Sam Shepard, Howie Wyeth & Luther Rix, Andre Bernard Tremblay, Dominic Paulo, Arlo Guthrie. Dir, Pro & Screenplay: Bob Dylan. Assoc Pro: Mel Howard. Ph: David Myers, Paul Goldsmith & Howard Alk. Ed: Bob Dylan & Howard Alk. Art: No credits. M: various composers. (Lombard Street Films–Artificial Eye.) Rel: Floating; first shown London, August 1978. 235 or 112 mins (alternative editings). Cert AA.

Return from Witch Mountain
Amusing and entertaining sequel to the *Escape to Witch Mountain* movie about the two children with supernatural powers. This time they are held by a wicked scientist who, after witnessing their powers, decides to use them in his experiments to develop a mind-control system which will turn the world into a land of human robots completely under his control. Grand Disney family fun. Cast: *Kim Richards, Ike Eisemann, Bette Davis, Christopher Lee, Jack Soo, Anthony James, Dick Bakalyan, Ward Costello, Christian Juttner, Brad Savage, Poindexter, Jeffrey Jacquet, Denver Pyle.* Dir: John Hough. Pro: Ron Miller & Jerome Courtland. Screenplay: Malcolm Marmorstein (from characters created by Alexander Key). Ph: Frank Phillips. Ed: Bob Bring. Art: John B. Mansbridge & Jack Senter. Spec Eff: Eustace Lycett, Art Cruickshank & Danny Lee. M: Lalo Schifrin. Assoc Proc: Kevin Corcoran. (Disney.) Rel: 15 April. 93 mins. Cert U.

Revenge of the Dead
Another minor 'Exorcist' spin-off, set in Los Angeles and all about the demon summoned by the assaulted professor (left for dead along with his murdered wife and family by some of his students) who sets the creature off on a revenge assignment! Cast: *Christopher Lee, Larry Justin, J. Arthur Craig, James Habif, Robert Clark, Doug Senior, Bob Meed, Alisa Beaton, Pat Nagel, Woody Wise, Paul Kelleher, Undine Hampton, Lisey Kramer, Doug Ely, Natasha, Carol Silverman, Dawn Walden, John De Rose, Charles Woodard, Lyle Steven, Ellen Nicklous, Guerdon Trueblood, Dorian Crane, Phil Meyer, Miklos Gyulai, Drew Michaels, Don Ling, Steve Singer, Olie West, Ken Horne, George Selin, Ed Wood, Marge Kazan, Jim Bagdonas, Carol Wood, Toni Telo.* Dir: Evan Lee. Pro: Ray Atherton. Ex Pro: Julie Ellen Fine. Pro Ex: Steve Singer. Screenplay: Keith Burns & Ray Atherton. (Add Material: Miklos Gyulai & Steve Singer). Ph: Guerdon Trueblood. Ed: Miklos Gyulai. No Art credit. M: Joe Azarello, Ed Scannel, Gary Ray, Steve Singer & Jay Stewart. (Forest Film Productions–Brent Walker.) Rel: Floating. 87 mins. Cert X.

The Revenge of the Pink Panther
A further very funny episode in the career of the bumbling, ineffective, but tremendously lucky (now Chief) Inspector Clouseau, as he returns from the (nearly) dead to break up, defeat and otherwise smash (literally) The French—Mafia—Connection. All by now familiar, but highly effective and very funny, with Blake Edwards's neat and pacey direction jelling beautifully with *Peter Seller's* outrageously farcical performance. Rest of cast: *Herbert Lom, Dyan Cannon, Robert Webber, Burt Zwouk, Paul Stewart, Robert Loggia, Graham Stark, Andre Maranne, Sue Lloyd, Tony Beckley, Valerie Leon.* Dir & Pro: Blake Edwards. Ex Pro: Tony Adams. Screenplay: Frank Waldman, Ron Clark & Blake Edwards; from the story by Blake Edwards. Assoc Pro: Derek Kavanagh & Ken Wales. 2nd Unit Dir: Anthony Squire. Ph: Ernie Day. Ed: Alan Jones. Art: John Siddall. M: Henry Mancini. Animation Sequences: DePatie-Freleng. (UA.) Rel: 27 August. 100 mins. Cert A.

The Riddle of the Sands
Commendably straightforward, modest-budgeted (costing less than £1 million) British adaptation of the famous Erskine Childers pre-1914 German spy story, set against the beautifully airy backgrounds of sea, mud-flats and islands along the north-west coast of Germany, where amateur yachtsman *Simon MacCorkindale* and Foreign Office pal *Michael York* stumble on and thwart a German plot to invade England via The Wash. Rest of cast: *Jenny Agutter, Alan Badel, Jurgen Andersen, Olga Lowe, Hans Meyer, Michael Sheard, Wolf Kahler, Ronald Markham.* Dir: Tony Maylam. Pro: Drummond Challis. Screenplay: Tony Maylam & John Bailey; from the Erskine Childers novel. Ph: Christopher Challis. Ed: Peter Hollowth. Art: Terry Pritchard. M: Howard Blake. (Rank.) Rel: Floating. 102 mins. Cert U.

Roots, Rock & Reggae
Documentary with *Bob Marley, Jimmy Cliff, Mighty Diamond, Inner Circle* etc. Dir: Jeremy Marre. (Independent Production–Osiris Films.) Rel: Floating; first shown London, December 1978. 55 mins. Cert U.

Ruby
Minor thriller about a ghost who won't credit the lady's love for him; a spin-off of *The Exorcist* and other like movies. Cast: *Piper Laurie, Stuart Whitman, Roger Davis, Janet Baldwin, Crystin Sinclaire, Paul Kent, Len Lesser, Jack Perkins, Edward Donno, Sal Vecchio, Fred Kohler, Rory Stevens, Raymond Kark, Jan Burrell, Kip Gillespie, Tamar Cooper, Patricia Allison, Stu Olson, Mary Robinson, Michael Alldredge, Allison Hayes.* Dir: Curtis Harrington. Pro: George Edwards. Ex Pro: Steve Krantz. Ph: William Mendenhall. Ed: Bill George Edwards & Barry Schneider; from a story by

Steve Krantz. Ph: William Mendenhall. Ed: Bill Magee. Art: Tom Rasmussen. M: Don Ellis. (Steve Krantz Productions–Brent Walker.) Rel: 19 November. 85 mins. Cert X.

Same Time, Next Year
Straightforward screen version of the play by Bernard Slade about a couple—both happily married—who meet in a hotel dining room, take coffee together and end up in bed, both feeling guilty because for both it is their first marital cheating. But not guilty enough to stop them from repeating the stolen weekend every year! A highly unlikely supposition which is spun out to far too great a length but which has some amusing moments, quite a few laughable lines, and very polished performances by *Ellen Burstyn* and *Alan Alda*. Rest of cast: *Ivan Bonar, Bernie Kuby, Cosmo Sardi, David Northcutt, William Cantrell*. Dir: Robert Mulligan. Pro: Walter Mirisch & Morton Gottlieb. Screenplay: Bernard Slade; based on his own stage play. Ph: Robert Surtees. Ed: Sheldon Kahn. Pro Des: Henry Bumstead. M: Marvin Hamlisch (the theme song 'The Last Time I Felt Like This' sung by *Johnny Mathis & Jane Olivor*). (Universal–CIC.) Rel: 11 March. 120 mins. Cert AA.

Satan's Slave
1976 British witchcraft thriller about an unfortunate young lady who, going to her uncle's mansion with her parents for the weekend, is pitchforked into some horrible experiences while going up the driveway, ending with her being frustrated from escaping from all the horror by her dad in his full satanic regalia! Cast: *Michael Gough, Martin Potter, Candace Glenning, Barbara Kellerman, Michael Craze, Gloria Walker, James Bree, Celia Hewitt, David McGillivray, Moira Young, Andrzj Jasiewicz, Walter Zerlin Jun, Monika Ringwald, Carolyn Withington, Paula Patterson*. Dir: Norman J. Warren. Pro: Les Young and Richard Crafter. Assoc Pro: Moira Young. Screenplay: David McGillivray. Ph: Len Young. Ed: No credit. Art: Hayden Pearce. M: John Scott. (Monumental Pictures–Brent Walker.) Rel: 19 November. 86 mins. Cert X.

The Savage—Le Sauvage
Generally amusing and sometimes very funny Franco-Italian farce-comedy about a lovely French girl—trying to escape from her jilted, very violent Italian husband-to-be—who settles on an island-owner, fruit-and-vegetable grower and expert perfume originator as most likely saviour. Her decision leads to a lot of wild action, destruction of property and eventual romance between the two. Not always easy to follow but very easy to enjoy. A remarkably lively performance by the incomparable *Catherine Deneuve*, a smoothly apt comedy one by *Yves Montand*. Rest of cast: *Luigi Vannucchi, Tony Roberts, Dana Wynter, Bobo Lewis, Luis Gerardo Tovar, Vernon Dobtcheff, Gabriel Cattand, Jeffrey

Carey, Peggy Romero, Rina Franchetti, Gustavo Blanco, Jean-Michel Lacor, Toni Maestri. Dir: Jean-Paul Rappeneau. Pro: Raymond Danon. Ex Pro: Ralph Baum. Screenplay: Jean-Paul Rappeneau, Jean-Loup Dabadie & Elizabeth Rappeneau. Ph: Pierre Lhomme. M: Michel Legrand. (Curzon.) Rel: Floating; first shown London, September 1978. 107 mins. Cert A.

Sawrana—Our Revolution
Documentary made by the Eritrean People's Liberation Front about their seventeen-year struggle to gain independence from Ethiopia. Dir: Christian Sabatier. (Workers Film Assoc–Scala.) Rel: Floating; first shown London, February 1979. 60 mins. No cert.

The Scenic Route
Odd, obviously shoe-string budgeted little movie which with considerable ambiguity attempts, according to its writer–director–producer Mark Rappaport, to say something about the difference between what we say and what we feel, and what we say and what we mean; saying it through the story of a very uncommunicative and dreary man and the two sisters he seduces and then lives with—sisters whose love for each other always seems to be on the verge of lesbianism. And it's all pretty heavy going. With *Randy Danson* as the story-telling sister the most exciting ingredient. Rest of cast: *Marilyn Jones, Kavin Wade, Grant Stewart, Claudia Weill, Arthur Ginsberg, Milton Ginsberg, Eric Mitchell, Marion Greenstone, Bill Karnovsky, Judith Sobol, Margot Breier, Joe Keller*. Dir, Pro & Screenplay: Mark Rappaport. (BFI.) Rel: Floating; first shown London, January 1979. 76 mins. No cert.

Second Chance—Si C'Etait à Refaire
Quietly effective Claude Lelouch film which, carefully avoiding dramatic climax and tight directorial or writing patterns, tells the story of a woman with courage who, coming out of prison after fifteen years (spent there for assisting her lover in the unpremeditated murder of her boss–ravisher), faces up to all the problems that her re-entry into life poses—problems accentuated by the fact that her 15-year-old son is initially unaware of his relationship to her. With typical Lelouch touches, like the sudden silencing of dialogue in some of the more lyrical sequences, the abrupt switching of period, and, of course, that catchy little theme tune (by Francis Lai) which keeps popping up right through the movie. Cast: *Catherine Deneuve, Anouk Aimée, Charles Denner, Francis Huster, Niels Arestrup, Colette Baudot, Jean-Jacques Briot, Manuella Papatakis, Jean-François Remy, Bernard Donnadieu, Jacques Villeret, Jean-Pierre Kalfon, Zoe Chauveau*. Dir, Screenplay & Pro: Claude Lelouch. Ph: Jacques Lefrançois. Ed: Georges Klotz. Art: Eric Moulard. M: Francis Lai. (Les Films 13–UA.) Rel: Floating; first shown London, October 1978. 99 mins. Cert AA.

Sergeant Pepper's Lonely Hearts Club Band
Lavish, £6,000,000 modern musical based on the old Beatles album and starring new top-popper *Peter Frampton* (a blond, tousle-haired young man with no clearly observable reasons for his fame), the *Bee Gees*, lots of top-line pop stars, *Frankie Howerd, Donald Pleasence*, and the film's greatest asset, veteran comic *George Burns*, chewing on his cigar and trying to explain an often pretty surrealistic story about the band, their rise to fame and the temptations it brings in the Big City, and their final return to their now threatened Heartland to put everything and everyone right. A film definitely for 'selected audiences' as the trade film-critic had it! Rest of cast: *Paul Nicholas, Barry, Robin & Maurice Gibb (the Bee Gees), Sandy Farina, Dianne Steinberg, Steve Martin, Aerosmith, Alice Cooper, Earth, Wind & Fire, Billy Preston, Stargard, Carel Struycken, Patti Jerome, Max Showalter, John Wheeler, Jay W. MacIntosh, Eleanor Zee, Scott Manners, Stanley Coles, Stanley Sheldon, Bob Mayo, Woodrow Chambliss, Hank Worden, Morgan Farley, Delos V. Smith, Pat Cranshaw, Teri Lynn Wood, Tracy Justrich, Anna Rodzianko, Rose Aragon*. Dir: Michael Schultz. Pro: Robert Stigwood. Ex Pro: Dee Anthony. Screenplay: Henry Edwards. Ex in charge of Pro: Roger M. Rothstein. Assoc Pro: Bill Oates. Ph: Owen Roizman. Ed: Christopher Holmes. Pro Des: Brian Eatwell. M Dir: George Martin. Music and lyrics by the Beatles. (Geria Productions/RSO Films–Paramount–CIC.) Rel: 18 February. 111 mins. Cert U.

The Serpent's Egg
Ingmar Bergman's first (German) film since he fled Sweden, and became (temporarily) a tax exile, is powerful and in part brilliant (certainly visually so) but ultimately well below his best work for the screen. A story of the distant threatening rumblings in Germany in the 1920s (the time of hyper-inflation) and of the dark menace of the 1930s. Fine performances by several of the cast including *Liv Ullmann* and *Gert Froebe* but a superficial and unhappy one by *David Carradine* as the American Jewish circus performer stranded in Berlin and, often, in a drunken stupor. Rest of the cast: *Heinz Bennent, James Whitmore, Glynn Turman, Georg Hartmann, Edith Heerdegen, Kyra Mladek, Fritz Strassner, Hans Quest, Paul Burks*. Dir & Screenplay: Ingmar Bergman. Ex Pro: Horst Wendlandt. Ph: Sven Nykvist. Ed: Not credited. Art: Rolf Zehetbauer. M: Rolf Wilhelm. (Dino de Laurentiis–Enterprise Pictures.) Rel: Floating; first shown London, October 1978.

Seven
Comedy against Hawaiian backgrounds. Cast: *William Smith, Chick Koock, Barbara Leigh*. Dir & Pro: Andy Sidaris. Screenplay: William Driskill & Robert Baird; from a story by Andy Sidaris. (Barber Dann Films.) Rel: June 24. No further credits available at press time.

Releases of the Year in Detail

Shark's Cave—La Fossa Maledetta
Italo-Spanish melodramatic Bermuda Triangle story, a spin-off from *Orca*, out of *The Deep* plus *Jaws*! Lots of above- and under-water villainy, lots of suspicious sharks and a bloody climax when they decide it is dinner-time. And one can't just take it too seriously. Cast: *Andrés García, Janet Agren, Arthur Kennedy, Pino Colizzi, Máximo Valverde, Cinzia Monreale, Adriana Falco, Sergio Doria, Oscar Alvárez, Angelo Calligaris, Sergio Sinceri*. Dir: Anthony Richmond. Pro: Nino Segurini. Screenplay: Fernando Galiana, Manrico Melchiorre & Teodoro Ricci; from a story by the first-named. Dir of underwater sequences: Mario Morales. Ph: Juan Jurado. Ed: Angelo Curi. Art: No credit. M: Stelvio Cipriani. (Koala Cinematografica, Rome/Amaneer Films, Madrid–Entertainment.) Rel: 11 March. 90 Mins. Cert AA.

Shipwreck!
Simple, pleasing 'Swiss Family Robinson'-type film from the same star–director–producer team, and much along the same lines as their previous success, *The Adventures of the Wilderness Family*. About a young man who with a young girl, a stowaway and his family sets out to sail around the world but is shipwrecked and marooned on a remote island in wildest Alaska, where they have to face up to nature more or less in the raw. Cast: *Robert Logan, Mikki-Jamison Olsen, Heather Rattray, Cjon Damitri Patterson, Shannon Saylor*. Dir & Screenplay: Stewart Raffill. Pro: Joseph C. Raffill. Ex Pro: Peter R. Simpson. Ph: Thomas McHugh. Ed: Dan Greer, R. Hansel Brown & Art Stafford. M: Fred Steiner, with add mus by Lyn Murray & Jeff Alexander. Assoc Pro, 2nd Unit Dir & Ph: Gerard Alcan. Pro Sup: Hal Schwartz. (Raffill–Warner.) Rel: 15 October. 102 mins. Cert U.

The Silent Flute
Quite extraordinary mixture of poetic image, pretentious dialogue and kung-fu fighting in the story of an ambitious young martial arts disciple (*Jeff Cooper*) and his Holy-Grail-type pilgrimage through various testing situations towards a monastery where is kept The Book, which, when he finally gets to looking into it, is just pages of mirrors reflecting his own image! And along the chequered way towards illumination the young man is both helped and hindered by *David Carradine* in all sorts of weird disguises. Most odd! But often lovely to look at, sometimes repellently violent and in sum total all pretty silly. Rest of cast: *Roddy McDowall, Eli Wallach, Erica Creer, Christopher Lee, Anthony de Longis, Earl Maynard, Heinz Bernard, Ziporra Peled, Jeremy Kaplan, Kam Yuen, Elizabeth Motzkin, Bobby Ne'eman, Dov Friedman, Ronen Nabah, Michal Nedivi, Nissim Zohar, Donnie Williams, Tom Ascensio, Wil Chang,* *Robert Gardner, Michel Vendrell, Janet Watson, Leo Whangs*. Dir: Richard Moore. Pro: Sandy Howard & Paul Maslansky. Ex Pro: Richard St. Johns. Pro Ex: Derek Gibson. Assoc Pro: Ziv Spielmann. Pro Sup: Terence A. Clegg. Pro Co-Ord: Carmela Spencer. Screenplay: Stirling Silliphant & Stanley Mann; based on a story by Bruce Lee, James Coburn & Silliphant. Ph: Ronnie Taylor. Ed: Ernie Walter. Pro Des: Johannes Larsen. M: Bruce Smeaton. (Rank.) Rel: 10 December. 95 mins. Cert AA.

The Silent Partner
Straightforward screen adaptation of the highly ingenious Anders Bodelson story about a young bank clerk who sees an aborted hold-up at his 'window' (and suspects the crook will try again, as he does not know he has given himself away) as the opportunity for his own stealing of a fortune without the possibility of being suspected of the crime. And when he does in fact pull it off he manages finally to outwit the outraged villain when he is threatened with violence and exposure if he does hand over the money. All amusing enough but with stronger direction and performances—especially from *Elliott Gould*—this could have been one of the best crime comedy-thrillers in years. Rest of cast: *Christopher Plummer, Celine Lomez, Michael Kirby, Sean Sullivan, Ken Pogue, John Candy, Gail Dahms, Movchale Donaghue, Jack Duffy, Nancy Simmonds, Nulala Fitzgerald, Guy Sanvido, Charlotte Blunt, Aino Pirskanen, Michele Rosen. Ben Williams, Sandy Crawley, Jan Campbell, Jimmy Davidson, Eve Norman, John Kerr, Sue Lumsden, Reverend Harry Amey, Candace O'Connor, Stephen Levy*. Dir: Daryl Duke. Pro: Joel B. Michaels & Stephen Young. Ex Pro: Garth H. Drabinsky. Pro Co-Ord: Alice Ferrier. Screenplay: Curtis Hanson; based on the novel *Think of a Woman* by Anders Bodelson. Ph: Billy Williams. Ed: George Appleby. Pro Des: Trevor Williams. M: Oscar Peterson. (Enterprise Pictures.) Rel: 10 September. 105 mins. Cert X.

Slavers
A number of top-class players involved in a minor West German melodrama about African slaves, Arab slavers and others who suffer in one way or another from the trade. Cast: *Trevor Howard, Ron Ely, Britt Ekland, Jürgen Goslar, Ray Milland, Don Jack Rousseau, Helen Morgan, Ken Gampu, Cameron Mitchell, Larry Taylor, Brian O'Shaughnessy, Erica Schramm, Art Brauss, Eric Schumann, Vera Jesse, Rinaldo Talamonti, Judy Goldman, Peter Elliott, Ekard Block, Herbert Mahlaba, Sam Williams, Octavia Thengeni, Caroline Perry, Isabel Goslar, Wolf Goldan, Konrad Georg*. Dir & Pro: Jürgen Goslar, Ex Pro: Barrie Saint Clair. Assoc Pro: Stefan Abendroth. Screenplay: Henry Morrisson, Nathaniel Kohn & Marcia McDonald. Ph: Igor Luther. 2nd Unit Ph: Keith Dunkley. Ed: Fred Serp. Art: John Rosewarne & Peter Schoener. M: Eberhard Schoener. (Lord Film Produktion–Eagle.) Rel: 15 October. 102 mins. Cert X.

Somebody Killed Her Husband
This is a film with a pleasing difference because it starts out deceptively as a familiarly foolish romantic comedy and takes a rapid turn for the better by switching to good crazy comedy. This takes place with the advent of the first corpse and the ludicrous decision of the murdered man's wife and her lover to push the body into the fridge and delay telling the cops until they've found out why he was killed and who killed him—a decision even more ridiculously adhered to when several bodies later they discover that their own names are high on the murderer's list! But once you forget all thoughts of credibility it becomes good fun as director Lamont Johnson pushes the story along at frenetic pace. And stars *Jeff Bridges* and (TV's 'Charlie's Angel') *Farrah Fawcett-Majors* (starring debut) do their entertaining best to keep up with the director's pretty exhausting demands made on them. Rest of cast: *John Wood, Tammy Grimes, John Glover, Patricia Elliott, Mary McCarty, Lawrence Guittard, Vincent Robert Santa Lucia, Breeson Carroll, Eddie Lawrence, Arthur Rhytis, Jean-Pierre Stewart, Terri DuHaime, Sands Hall, Joseph Culliton, Dave Johnson, Melissa Ferris, Jeremiah Sullivan, Sloan Shelton, Mary Alan Hokanson, John Corcoran, Marck Haber*. Dir: Lamont Johnson. Pro: Martin Poll. Screenplay: Reginald Rose. Ph: Andrew Laszlo. Ed: Barry Malkin. Pro Des: Ted Haworth. Art: David Chapman. M: Alex North (Song 'Love Keeps Getting Stronger Every Day' by and sung by Neil Sedaka). (Melvin Simon/Martin Poll–Trident Barber Dist.) Rel: Floating. 96 mins. Cert A.

Space Cruiser
Japanese science-fiction 'disaster' feature-cartoon about the raising of a Japanese battleship and re-equipping it as a space cruiser which, on its maiden voyage, is able to deflect an earth-smashing bomb aimed by the horrid inhabitants of the planet Gorgon! Dir & Pro: Yoshinobu Nishizaki. Assoc Pro: Masaharu Nagashima, Kazushi Namura, Takayuki Tsutsumi. Screenplay: Yoshinobu Nishizaki, Keisuke Fujikawa & Eiichi Yamamoto. Animation Dir: Noboru Ishiguru. M: Yasushi Miyagawa. (Academy–Enterprise Pictures.) Rel: Floating. 101 mins. Cert U.

Speedtrap
Hired by the insurance companies to catch 'The Roadrunner'—an expert electronics thief who defies all the efforts of the cops as he steals cars on a vast scale—private-eye Pete Novick soon finds himself involved in drugs, gangsters, girls and gun battles. Cast: *Joe Don Baker, Tyne Daly, Richard Jaeckel, Robert Loggia, Morgan Woodward, Dianne Marchal, James Griffith, Timothy Agoglia Carey, Lana Wood, Phil*

Adams, Bimmy Bakewell, Carver Barnes, Roberta Collins, Larry Dunn, John Furlong, Janet Heil, Bill Heywood, Burke Rhind, Jim Sanick, Earl Smith, Joanne Smith, Donald Starr, Steve Williams, Allen Wood. Dir: Earl Bellamy. Pro: Howard Pine. Co-Pro: Fred Mintz. Pro Co-Ord: Bridget Murphy. Screenplay: Walter M. Spear & Stuart A. Segal; from a story by Fred Mintz & Henry C. Parke. Ph: Dennis Dalzell. Ed: Michael Vejar. Art: Fred Hope. M: Anthony Harris. (First Artists Productions/Intertamar–Hemdale.) Rel: 3 December. 101 mins. Cert A.

Spider Man Strikes Back

Light-hearted thriller about a student who becomes bitten by a radioactive spider which injects into him superhuman powers—useful when he becomes suspected of stealing plutonium from the local atomic-power plant and is pursued by the cops, the FBI and pretty newspaper columnist *JoAnna Cameron* who, seeking an interview, gets *him!* Rest of cast: *Nicholas Hammond, Robert F. Simon, Michael Pataki, Chip Fields, Robert Alda, Randy Powell, Sid Clute, Herbert Braha, Emil Farkas, Dick Kyker, Leigh Kavanaugh, David Somerville, Walt Davis, Gino Audito, Kerrie Cullen, Steve Goodwins, Bonnie Johns, George Barrows, Orin Kennedy, Barry Roberts.* Dir: Ron Satlof. Pro: Robert Janes & Ron Satlof. Ex Pro: Charles Fries & Daniel Goodman. Screenplay: Robert Janes; script consultant, Stan Lee. Ph: Jack Whitman. Ed: David H. Newhouse & Erwin Dumbrille. Art: Bill McAllister. M: Stu Phillips. (Charles Fries Productions Inc/Dan Goodman Productions Inc–Columbia.) Rel: 8 April. 93 mins. Cert U.

The Stepford Wives

Bryan Forbes's 1974 American film, only now seen in Britain; a quiet and played-down thriller about a small community in New York's commuter belt where the men, thanks to an ex-Disneyland mechanic–magician, replace their wives with robot 'doubles'. Obviously a film which takes flight from all credibility, but it is most ably directed and full of creepy atmosphere. A lovely minor-key comedy performance by *Paula Prentiss*. Rest of cast: *Katharine Ross, Peter Masterson, Patrick O'Neal, Carol Rossen, Paula Trueman, Carole Mallory, Nanette Newman, Josepf Somer, Tina Louise, Franklin Cover, William Prince, George Coe, Toni Reid.* Dir: Bryan Forbes. Pro: Edgar J. Scherick. Screenplay: William Goldman; based on the novel by Ira Levin. Ph: Owen Roizman. Ed: Timothy Gee. M: Michael Small. (Contemporary Films.) Rel: Floating; first shown June 1978. 115 mins. Cert AA.

Stevie

An adaptation of the Hugh Whitemore play, which ran for a while at London's Vaudeville Theatre in 1977, which in turn was based on the uneventful life, cocooned in a small terrace house in Palmers Green with a beloved aunt, of poetess Stevie Smith, who shied away from her only marriage proposal, wrote her simple poems, enjoyed the housework and won the Queen's Prize. A chamberwork movie with a brilliant performance in the title role by *Glenda Jackson* (repeating her stage success) and a matching one by *Mona Washbourne* as auntie. *Trevor Howard* as the friend; *Alec McCowen* as the suitor. Dir & Pro: Robert Enders. Screenplay: Hugh Whitemore. Ph: Freddie Young. Art: Robert Jones. M: Patrick Gowers. (First Artists/Grand Metropolitan–Enterprise Pictures.) Rel: Floating; first shown London, November 1978. 102 mins. Cert AA.

Straight Time

Grim and depressingly convincing story (apparently based on a true case) about a flawed character who has been a crook since childhood and who, when let out on parole after several years 'inside' for armed robbery, tries desultorily to go straight but when let down by a moronic parole officer drifts back into crime, going from small and brutal one-man shop robbery to team bank and jewellery store hold-ups, coming unstuck by greed and misjudgement of character, committing callous murder and ending up on the run . . . with a footnote to say that it wasn't for long and the character is now doing a life sentence. A quite interesting and convincing examination of a born crook's character, well directed and ably acted. Cast: *Dustin Hoffman, Theresa Russell, Harry Dean Stanton, Gary Busey, M. Emmet Walsh, Sandy Baron, Kathy Bates, Edward Bunker, Stuart I. Berton, Barry Cahill, Corey Rand, James Ray, Fran Ryan, Rita Taggart.* Dir: Ulu Grosbard. Pro: Stanley Beck & Tim Zinnemann. Screenplay: Alvin Sargent, Edward Bunker & Jeffrey Boam; based on the novel *No Beast So Fierce* by Edward Bunker. Ph: Owen Roizman. Ed: Sam O'Steen and Randy Roberts. Pro Des: Stephen Grimes. M: David Shire. (Sweetwall Productions–First Artists–Warner.) Rel: 16 July. 114 mins. Cert X.

Summer Paradise

(Formerly called *Paradise Place*.) 1977 Swedish film with a message: behind the story of a summer vacation of four generations of lady doctor (Wilki's family, which ends in suicide and disaster, is a plea by actress-turned-director Gunnel Lindblom, that her native country should stop and think about the dangers of the way in which the State takes over from the individual, producing free-living women and independent children and an increasingly cold and materialistic society. A favourite Ingmar Bergman actress, Miss Lindblom worked with him as her producer and one senses him peering over her shoulder as the movie progresses. A thoughtful, finely-acted movie. Cast: *Birgitta Valberg, Agneta Ekmanner, Margaretta Byström, Holger Löwenadler, Dagny Lind, Maria Blomqvist, Anna Borg, Pontus Gustafson, Sif Ruud, Göran Stangertz, Per Myrberg,* *Solveig Ternström, Toni Magnusson, Inga Landre, Oskar Ljung.* Dir: Gunnel Lindblom. Pro: Ingmar Bergman. Screenplay: Ulla Isaksson & Gunnel Lindblom; from the former's novel. Ph: Tony Forsberg. Ed: Siv Lungren. M: George Riedel. No art credit. (Cinematograph AB–Swedish Film Institute–Svensk Filmindustri–Contemporary Films.) Rel: Floating; first shown London, November 1978. 113 mins. Cert AA.

Superman—The Movie

A generally lavish, sometimes stunning, always delightfully tongue-in-cheek film about the famous comic-strip character whose immense, other-world powers include the ability to fly like a bird, abort earthquakes, push back cracking dams and generally act as a phenomenal do-gooder. Vast and spectacular, the film is something of a mixture of *Close Encounters of the Third Kind, Earthquake, The Perils of Pauline* and *Batman*. A really super movie and super screen fun. A nice performance as the dual personality hero (shy reporter and superman) by *Christopher Reeve*, an attractive one by *Margot Kidder* and a nice villainous contribution by *Gene Hackman*. Rest of main cast: *Marlon Brando, Ned Beatty, Jackie Cooper, Glenn Ford, Trevor Howard, Jack O'Halloran, Valerie Perrine, Maria Schell, Terence Stamp, Phyllis Thaxter, Susannah York, Jeff East, Marc McClure, Sarah Douglas, Harry Andrews. And: Vass Anderson, John Hollis, James Garbutt, Michael Gover, David Neal, William Russell, Penelope Lee, John Stuart, Alan Cullen, Lee Quigley, Aaron Sholinski, Diane Sherry, Jeff Atcheson, Brad Flock, David Petrou, Billy J. Mitchell, Robert Henderson, Larry Lamb, James Brockington, John Cassady, John F. Parker, Antony Scott, Ray Evans, Su Shifrin, Miquel Brown, Vincent Marzello, Benjamin Feitelson, Lise Hilboldt, Leueen Willoughby, Jill Ingham, Pieter Stuyck, Rex Reed, Weston Davin, Stephen Kahan, Ray Hassett, Randy Jurgenson, Matt Russo, Collins Skeaping, Bo Rucker, Paul Avery, David Baxt, George Harris II, Michael Harrigan, John Cording, Raymond Thompson, Oz Clarke, Rex Everhardt, Jayne Tottman, Frank Lazarus, Brian Protheroe, Lawrence Trimble, Robert Whelan, David Calder, Norwick Duff, Keith Alexander, Michael Ensign, Larry Hagman, Paul Tuerpe, Graham McPherson, David Yorston, Robert O'Neill, Robert MacLeod, John Ratzenberger, Alan Tilvern, Phil Brown, Bill Bailey, Burnell Tucker, Chief Tug Smith, Norman Warwick, Chuck Julian, Colin Etheringdon, Mark Wynter, Roy Stevens.* Dir: Richard Donner. Ex Pro: Ilya Salkind. Pro: Pierre Spengler. Assoc Pro: Charles F. Greenlaw. Screenplay: Mario Puzo, David Newman, Leslie Newman & Robert Benton; from a story by Mario Puzo. Ph: Geoffrey Unsworth. Ed: Stuart Baird. Pro Des: John Barry. M: John Williams. Superman created by Jerry Siegel & Joe Shuster. Creative Consultant: Tom Mankiewicz. (Dovemead Ltd.–Alexander Salkind–Warner.) Rel: 10 December. 143 mins. Cert A.

Releases of the Year in Detail

Sven Klang's Combo
Something of a minor classic from Sweden about the impact on a small and happy-go-lucky dance band in the fifties of a dedicated and highly talented saxophonist, an impact which finally leads to the break-up of the group. Based on fact, completely authentic in the music and style and beautifully acted and, musically, played. Cast: *Anders Granström, Henric Holmberg, Eva Remaeus, Jan Liddell, Christer Boustedt, Bo Gunnar Andersson, Ingmar Andersoon, Reinhold Andersson, Olle Blegel, Peter Bromgren, Birgit Eggers, Steffean Holmgren, Catrin Parment, Einar Persson, Ulla Rodhe, Lou Rossling, Michael Segerström, Mona Mellegard, Ninne Ollson, Olle Westholm, Per Eggers.* Dir: Stellan Olsson. Pro: Per Berglun. Pro Sup: Olle Westholm. Pro Man: Hans Iveberg. Screenplay: Ninne Olsson, Henric Holmberg & Stellan Olsson; based on the play by Musikteatergruppen Oktober. Ph: Kent Persson & Bengt Franzen. Ed: Roger Sellberg. Art: Elisabeth Carlström. M: Christer Boustedt. (Svenska Filminstutet–Stockholm Film–Europa Films–Folkets Husforeningarnas Riksorganisation–Sveriges Radio TV2–Musikteatergruppen Oktober–Essential.) Rel: Floating; first shown August 1978. 100 mins. Cert AA.

The Swarm
Science-fiction movie about a swarm of African killer bees which emigrate to America and, starting by picking off a picnicking family, end up by decimating whole towns as they close in on Houston. Meanwhile unlikely entomologist *Michael Caine,* crippled immunologist *Henry Fonda* and Air Force General *Richard Widmark* try to find an answer to the venomous clouds. A wonderful cast of old-timers like *Fred MacMurray, Olivia de Havilland* and *Slim Pickens* fight a good fight against their often awful lines! Rest of cast: *Katharine Ross, Richard Chamberlain, Ben Johnson, Lee Grant, Jose Ferrer, Patty Duke Astin, Bradford Dillman.* Dir & Pro: Irwin Allen. Screenplay: Stirling Silliphant; based on the novel by Arthur Herzog. Ph: Fred J. Koenekamp. Ed: Harold F. Kress. Pro Des: Stan Jolly. M: Jerry Goldsmith. (Irwin Allen–Warner.) Rel: 30 July. 116 mins. Cert A.

Swedish Confessions
Art, gangsters, blackmail, sex, and final tragedy as the heroine shoots dead her lover's mistress—revealed as her own teenager daughter!—and commits suicide. Cast includes: *Barbra Scott, Jack Frank* and *Anne Von Lindberger.* Dir & Pro: Andrew Whyte. (Rebel Films–Watchgrove.) Rel: Floating. 90 mins. Cert X.

Sweet Hunters
1969 film (made in France, with American cast and English dialogue) which, shown at the London Film Festival of that year and since shown at several other Festivals with critical acclaim, now gets its first public run in GB. A strange, haunting story set on a Bergmanesque off-shore island, almost constantly wreathed in drifting fog, where a gaunt ornithologist waits with his nets for the birds that never come, his wife wanders the island looking for the escaped convict said to be in the vicinity, and her young sister considers with doubt her future marriage. And when the killer does turn up, to die, the holiday and the film quietly ends. A collector's piece. Cast: *Sterling Hayden, Susan Strasberg, Maureen McNally, Andrew Hayden, Stuart Whitman.* Dir: Ruy Guerra. Pro: Claude Giroux. Screenplay: Philippe Dumarcay, Gerard Zingg & Ruy Guerra. Ph: Ricardo Aronovich. Ed: Kenout Peltier. Art: Bernard Evein. M: Carl Orff, Tadeusz & Edu Lobo (General–Monarch Films.) Rel: Floating; first shown London, November 1978. 100 mins. No cert.

Tarka the Otter
Simple, charming adaptation of the Henry Williamson classic about the life of an otter in the quiet, lovely countryside, estuary and rushing streams along the Devon-Somerset borders. Cast: *Spade, Osla* and *Boatman* (the otters); *Peter Bennett, Edward Underdown, Brenda Cavendish, John Leeson, Reg Lye, George Waring, Stanley Lebor, Max Faulkner, Kendal & Dist Hunt, the inhabitants of Torrington, and the Appledore lifeboat crew.* Dir & Pro: David Cobham. Screenplay: Gerald Durrell & David Cobham; based on the book by Henry Williamson, as related by Peter Ustinov. Assoc Pro: Janet Cobham & Frank Powis. Ph: John McCallum (underwater ph by Slim Macdonnell; wildlife ph by Terry Channell; additional wildlife ph by John Buxton). Ed: Charles Davis. M: David Fanshawe. (Tor Films–Rank) Rel: Floating. 91 mins. Cert A.

The Terror of Dr Chaney
1975 American minor horror thriller about a crazy surgeon who, when his daughter loses her sight, starts to remove the eyes from sundry citizens he captures—and keeps locked in the basement—to try to replace her sightless eyes, always without success. Cast: *Richard Basehart, Trish Stewart, Gloria Grahame, Lance Henriksen, Al Ferrara, JoJo D'Amore, Libbie Chase, Katharine Fitzpatrick, Vic Tayback, Arthur Spave.* Dir: Michael Pataki. Pro: Charles Band. Screenplay: Frank Ray Perilli. Ph: Andrew Davis. Ed: Harry Keramidas. Art: Roger Pancake. M: Robert O. Ragland. (Charles Band Assoc–Brent Walker.) Rel: Floating. 89 mins. Cert X.

Thank God It's Friday
One of the best of at least the early wave of 1978 'discotheque' musicals, which while making a prolonged and severe assault on both the optic and aural nerves does it with considerable good humour, youthful charm and a good, old-fashioned happy-ever-after series of stories. The background to the noisy action is a Hollywood night-spot called The Zoo (which was surely named with tongue in cheek?), where the wolfish owner nearly seduces the nice lady (whose husband just survives an attack by a be-wigged, tablet-dispensing weirdie); a couple of chicks get their dance contest-winning wish; lovely coloured singer Donna Summer gets her breakthrough chance, and others get their hearts' desires while disc jockey Speed (no relative, truly!) plays, bellows and directs the action. Cast: *Valerie Landsburg, Terri Nunn, Chick Vennera, Donna Summer, Ray Vitte, Mark Lonow, Andrea Howard, Jeff Goldblum, Robin Menken, Debra Winger, John Friedrich, Paul Jabara, Marya Small, Chuck Sacci, Hilary Beane, DeWayne Jessie, The Commodores;* with *Phil Adams, Judith Brown, Marianne Bunch, Tony Cacciotti, Jacqueline Carlin, Linda Creamans, Gregory V. Karliss, Wade Collings, Cosie Costa, Chris DeLisle, MacIntyre Dixon, Michael Durrell, Al Fann, Harry Gold, Heidi Gold, Nanci Hammond, Steven Hartley, Howard Itzkowitz, Osko Karaghosian, Solomon Karriem, Sheila MacKenzie, J. W. Bear Martin, Shelley Parsons, Sherry Peterson, Nicholas Shields, Vaya Warren, Richard Weinberg, Sandra Will, Jonathan Wynne, Bill Couch, Bud Davis, Gary Davis, Don Pulford, Rock A. Walker, Ernie Robinson, Bob Masino, Terry Nichols, Benji Bancroft, Benny Moore, Dick Ziker.* Dir: Robert Klane. Pro: Rob Cohen. Ex Pro: Neil Bogart. Screenplay: Barry Armyan Bernsten. Co Pro & Unit Pro Man: Phillip Goldfarb. Ph: James Crabe. Ed: Richard Halsey. Pro Des: Tom H. John. Assoc Pro: Tony Masters & Lauren Shuler. M Ed: Erma E. Levin. (Warner.) Rel: 16 July. 89 mins. Cert A.

Theatre Girls
Documentary film about and made in a hostel for homeless women in Soho which won the first prize at a Festival at Mannheim. Made by Kim Longinotto & Claire Pollack and produced by the National Film School. In black-and-white. 75 mins. No cert.

The Thief of Baghdad
Fourth filming (previous: 1924, 1940 and 1960) of this Arabian Nights fairy tale with *Kabir Bedi* now the Prince who outwits his rival (*Terence Stamp*) to gain the hand of Caliph *Peter Ustinov's* lovely daughter *Pavla Ustinov.* All good U-certificated film fun. Rest of cast: *Roddy McDowall, Frank Finlay, Marina Vlady, Daniel Emilfork, Ian Holm, Neil McCarthy, Ahmed El-Shenawi, Kenji Takaki, Vincent Wong, Leon Greene, Bruce Montague, Raymond Llewellyn, Arnold Diamond, Geoffrey Cheshire, Gabor Vernon, Kevork Malikyan, Michael Chesoon, Ahmed Khail, Yashar Adem, George Little.* Dir: Clive Donner. Pro: Aida Young. Ex Pro: Thomas M. C. Johnston. Screenplay: A. J. Carothers. Adaptation: Andrew Birkin. Ph: Denis Lewiston. Ed: Peter Tanner. Art: Edward Marshall. M: John Cameron. Pro Sup: Christopher Sutton. (British/French co-production: Palm Films Ltd–Victorine Studios SA–Columbia.) Rel: 8 April. 102 mins. Cert U.

The 39 Steps

Third filming (previous versions by Hitchcock in 1935 with Robert Donat and Madeleine Carroll, and by Ralph Thomas in 1959 with Kenneth More and Tania Elg) of the classic John Buchan spy thriller about the innocent hero Hannay, becoming involved, through MI5's Colonel Scudder, in a plot to kill off an eminent visitor while he's speaking to the House of Commons and so trigger off the war the German agents are assigned to set in motion. One long, eventful chase that leads from London up to the Scottish Highlands and back to the face of Big Ben, where the breathlessly exciting climax takes place. Good, thrilling fun. Cast: *Robert Powell, David Warner, Eric Porter, Karen Dotrice, John Mills, George Baker, Ronald Pickup, Donald Pickering, Timothy West, Miles Anderson, Andrew Keir, Robert Flemyng, William Squire, Paul McDowell, David Colings, John Normington, John Welsh, Edward de Souza, Tony Steedman, John Grieve, Andrew Downie, Donald Bisset, Derek Anders, Oliver Maquire, Joan Henley, Prentis Hancock, Leo Dolan, James Garbutt, Artro Morris, Robert Gillespie, Raymond Young, Paul Jerricho, Michael Bilton.* Dir: Don Sharp. Pro: Greg Smith. Ex Pro: James Kenelm-Clarke. Screenplay: Michael Robson; based on the book by John Buchan. Assoc Pro: Frank Bevis. Ph: John Coquillion. Ed: Eric Boyd-Perkins. Pro Des: Harry Pottle. M: Ed Welch. (Norfolk International–Rank Film Dist.) Rel: 11 February. 102 mins. Cert A.

Three the Hard Way

Minor 1974 American thriller about mad scientist who develops a serum to kill the black races and intends to use it to purify the planet! Well, they don't let him get away with that, in spite of his collection of enthusiastic Nazi storm-trooper sympathisers. Cast: *Jim Brown, Fred Williamson, Jim Kelly, Sheila Frazier, Jay Robinson, Charles McGregor, Howard Platt, Richard Angarola, David Chow, Marian Collier, Junero Jennings, Alex Rocco, Corbin Bernsen, Renie Radish, Janice Carroll, Angelyn Chester, Norman Evans, Pamela Serpe, Marie O'Henry, Irene Tsu, Robert Cleaves, Roberta Collins, Lance Taylor, Jeanie Bell, Victor Brandt, Maria Roccuzzo, Don Gazzaniga.* Dir: Gordon Parks Jun. Pro: Harry Bernsen. Assoc Pro: Leon Chooluck. Screenplay: Eric Bercovici & Jerry Ludwig. Ph: Lucien Ballard. Ed: Robert Swink. M: Richard Tufo. (E. L. Wolf/Allied Artists–EMI.) Rel: Floating. 92 mins. Cert X.

Thunder and Lightning

Comedy about the Florida Everglades moonshiners (illicit alcohol brewers) in which spectacular boat-chases are substituted for the usual motor-car mayhem! With *David Carradine* and 'Charlie's Angel' *Kate Jackson* mainly involved. Rest of cast: *Roger C. Carmel, Sterling Holloway, Ed Barth, Ron Feinberg, George Murdock, Pat Cranshaw, Charles Napier, Hope Pomerance, Malcolm Jones, Charles Willeford, Christopher Raynolds, Claude Jones, Emilio Rivera.*

Dir: Corey Allen. Pro: Roger Corman. Screenplay: William Hjortsberg. Ph: James Pergola. Ed: Anthony Redman. Art: no credit. M: Andy Stein. (Fox.) Rel: 21 January. 93 mins. Cert A.

Tilt

Brooke Shields, the child star of the controversial (and as yet in Britain banned) 'Pretty Baby' film, pairs as the genius of the pin-ball boards. The film follows her travelling adventures across the States with partner and rock singer *Ken Marshall*. Rest of cast: *Charles Durning, Harvey Lewis, Bob Berger, John Crawford, Geoffrey Lewis, Karen Lamm, Gregory Walcott, Lester Fletcher, Lorenzo Lamas, Gary Mule Deer, George Jacobs, Don Stark, Fred Ward, Helen Boll, Gary Laszwitz, Buffy Queen, Frank Pesce, Kathryn Gresham-Lancaster, Paul Berlin, Charlie Lehman, Jim Galante, Bruce Mackey, Teck Murdock, Morgan Stoddard.* Dir, Pro and Screenplay: Rudy Durand. Ex Pro: Ron Joy. Assoc Pro: Dale Cline. Ph: Richard Kline. Ed: Bob Wyman. Pro. Exec; John Thiele. Pro Des: Ned Parsons. M: Lee Holdridge. (Melvin Simons–Barber Dann Films.) Rel: June 3.

Too Many Chefs

Uneasy comedy–thriller, about a series of murders of some of Europe's top chefs, more or less held together by *Robert Morley*'s very expansive playing of the epicurean publisher with a large waistline, a delight in the goodies which are medically forbidden him, and a wicked wit. And there's some pretty outrageous solving of the whodunnit question. Rest of cast: *Jacqueline Bisset, George Segal, Jean-Pierre Cassel, Philippe Noiret, Jean Rochefort, Luigi Proietti, Stefano Satta Flores.* Dir: Ted Kotcheff. Pro: William Aldrich. Screenplay: Peter Stone; from the novel by Nan & Ivan Lyons. Ex Pro: Merv Adelson & Lee Rich. Assoc Pro: Lynn Guthrie. Ph: John Alcott. Pro Des: Rolf Zehetbauer. Ed: Thom Noble. M: Henry Mancini. (Geria Bavaria Productions–Lorimer–Aldrich–GTO Films.) Rel: 25 February. 112 mins. Cert A.

The Turning Point

Brilliantly-acted women's-magazine-type story about feminine conflict between marriage and career, illustrated by the story of Deedee (*Shirley MacLaine*) who gives up her career as a ballet dancer for marriage and motherhood, passing across a star-making role to her friend Emma (*Anne Bancroft*), who stays it with both feet and goes on to become the company's principal ballerina. Years later, on the night that Deedee's daughter is making a great success in the same company, the two old friends recriminate each other in a bar and finally brawl before coming to terms with their respective, not entirely happy, situations. Superb ballet sequences, fine music, outstanding acting and consistent good taste and artistry. Rest of cast: *Mikhail Baryshnikov, Leslie Browne, Tom Skerritt, Martha Scott, Antoinette Sibley, Alexander Danilova, Starr Danias, Marshall*

Thompson, James Mitchell, Scott Douglas, Daniel Levans, Jurgen Schneider, Anthony Zerbe, Phillip Saunders, Lisa Lucas, Saax Bradbury, Hilda Morales, Donald Petrie, James Crittenden, David Byrd, Alexander Minz, Dennis Nahat, Enrique Martinez, Anne Barlow, Howard Barr, Martha Johnson. Special guest stars: *Lucette Aldous, Fernando Bujones, Richard Cragun, Suzanne Farrell, Marcia Haydee, Peter Martins, Clark Tippet, Marianna Tcherkassky, Martine Van Hamel, Charles Ward.* Dir: Herbert Ross. Pro: Herbert Ross & Arthur Laurents. Screenplay: Arthur Laurents. Ex Pro: Nora Kaye. Assoc Pro: Roger M. Rothstein. Assoc to the Producers: Howard Jeffrey. Ph: Robert Surtees. Ed: William Reynolds. Pro Des: Albert Brenner. M: John Lanchbery. (Fox.) Rel: 9 July. 119 mins. Cert A.

The Tree of Wooden Clogs

Ermanno Olmi's painstakingly detailed saga of life as it was for the peasant and small-tenancy farmer near Bergamo towards the end of the last century; revealing it as a constant drudgery lit only by such occasional joys as the travelling fair and a wedding— the latter providing one of the finest and most moving sequences in three often long-seeming hours which also include the less pleasant butchering of a pig! Acted remarkably well by a non-professional cast, against visually poetic backgrounds of the misty, muddy and bleak Po Valley flatlands. Dir & Screenplay: Ermanno Olmi. Pro Sup: Giulio Mandelli. General Organiser: Alessandro Calosci. Pro Inspector: Domenico Di Parigi. Ph: Carlo Petriocioli. Ed Assistant: Emma Rigioni. Set Designer: Franco Gambarana. Art: Enrico Tovaglieri. Music by J. S. Bach; played on the organ by Fernando Germani. (CPC Gruppe Produzione Cinema, Milano–RAI Radiotelevisione Italiana–Italnoleggio Cinematografico SpA–Curzon Films.) Rel: Floating; first shown London, April 1979. 186 mins. Cert A.

Turtle on its Back—La Tortue sur le Dos

Highly individual, and in some respects experimental, French film, the first feature-direction effort by Luc Béraud, whose intention it is to show a writer at work, by a series of short scenes and quick cuts of him at his desk, in the street, looking out of the window, quarrelling with his girl-friend (who keeps him), visiting the cinema, picking up girls and tearing up his unsatisfactory manuscript pages. It adds up to generate a somewhat surprising interest in the short, undistinguished hero. Latterly more incident creeps in as he starts on some experiences which inspire him to complete his second novel—and return to his girl-friend, where the story seems likely to repeat itself. Cast: *Jean-François Stévenin, Bernadette Lafont, Claude Miller, Virginie Thévenet, Véronique Silver.* Dir: Luc Béraud. Pro: Hubert Niogret. Screenplay: Luc Béraud & Claude Miller. Ph: Bruno Nuytten. Ed: Joele van Effenterre. (Filmoblic–Connoisseur.) Rel: Floating; first shown London, March 1978. 105 mins. Cert X.

Releases of the Year in Detail

The Uncanny

Combination of three short stories (and films) centred on the menace of cats, who play a big part in the action. (A) In London in 1912 they kill the murderess of their mistress; (B) in Quebec in 1975 a cat's small mistress, with the cat's help, removes a nasty little tormentress; and (C) in Hollywood in 1936 an unkillable feline writes finish for the man who tries to kill it! Cast A: *Susan Penhaligon, Joan Greenwood, Simon Williams, Roland Culver.* Cast B: *Alexandra Stewart, Chloe Franks, Katrina Holden, Donald Pilon, Renée Giraud.* Cast C: *Donald Pleasence, Samantha Eggar, John Vernon, Sean McCann, Jean Leclerc, Catherine Bégin.* Dir: Denis Héroux. Pro: Claude Héroux & René Dupont. Ex Pro: Harold Greenberg, Richard R. St Johns & Robert A. Kantor. Pro Sup: Claude Léger. Screenplay: Michel Parry. Ph: Harry Waxman & James Bawden. Ed: Peter Weatherley, Keith Palmer & Michel Guay. Pro Des: Wolf Kroeger & Harry Pottle. M: Wilfred Josephs. M Dir: Philip Martell. (Cinevideo, Quebec–Tor Productions, Pinewood–a Milton Subotsky film–Rank.) Rel: Floating. 85 mins. Cert X.

An Unmarried Woman

An essentially American examinaton of the situation of a wife of many years who, thinking her marriage is cosily and completely established, is suddenly told by her husband he is leaving her for a younger woman with whom he has 'fallen in love'. Glossy, not entirely satisfactory beneath the sophisticated surface, but with wit, a certain shrewdness and with some fine performances, notably from *Jill Clayburgh*, who won the Best Actress award at the 1978 Cannes Film Festival with her playing of the title role. Rest of cast: *Alan Bates, Michael Murphy, Cliff Gorman, Pat Quinn, Kelly Bishop, Lisa Lucas, Linda Miller, Andrew Duncan, Daniel Seltzer, Matthew Arkin, Penelope Russianoff.* Dir & Screenplay: Paul Mazursky. Pro: Paul Mazursky & Tony Ray. Ph: Arthur Ornitz. Pro Des: Pato Guzman. Ed: Stuart H. Pappe. M: Bill Conti. (Fox.) Rel: 13 August. 124 mins. Cert X.

Violette and François—Violette et François

Wryly amusing, essentially Gallic, film about a young, ill-matched couple living in Paris. She is lively, competent and the bread-winner; he is weak, lazy and a compulsive shoplifter. They live together, have a child and marry; she is persuaded to team up with him in crime but is caught and shocked back to honesty. He goes on with his thieving and is caught; gets away with it, but not with her, and they part. Cast: *Isabelle Adjani, Jacques Dutronc, Serge Reggiani, Lea Massari, Françoise Arnoul, Sophie Daumier, Catherine Lachens.* Dir: Jacques Rouffio. Pro: Jacques-Eric Strauss. Assoc Pro: Alain Sarde. Screenplay: Jean-Loup Dabadie. Ph: Andréas Winding. Ed: Geneviève Winding. Art: Jean André. M: Phillipe Sarde. (President Films–FR–Gala.) Rel: Floating; first shown London, October 1978. 99 mins. Cert X.

Violette Nozière

Claude Chabrol's reconstruction of the story of the crime of a young French girl who, in Paris in 1933, poisoned her parents, was accused, condemned and finally pardoned. A flesh-creeping portrait by the director and his remarkable young star *Isabelle Huppert* of a teenager who steals (from her parents), lies (she accuses her father, falsely, of incest in order to explain her motive), becomes an amateur whore, and when found out remains stolidly unmoved and unrepentant. Chabrol presents all this in a strangely detached manner as if trying to find in the film some explanation for the girl's utterly anti-social outlook. Isabella Huppert's acting is one of the major performances of the year. Rest of cast: *Isabelle Huppert, Stephanie Audran, Jean Carmet, Jean-Francois Garreaud, Lisa Langlois, Philippe Procot, Bernadette Lafont, Francois Maistre, Dora Doll, Bernard Alane, Gregory Germain, Henri-Jacques Huet, Fabrice Luchini, Jean Paredes, Maurice Vaudaux, Guy Hoffmann, Jean Dalmain, Jeanne Herviale, Priscilla Saillard, Suzanne Berthois, Zoe Chauveau, Mario David, Jacqueline Parreux, Bruno Rozenker,* Dir: Claude Chabrol. Ex Pro: Eugène Lépicier & Dennis Heroux. Screenplay: Odile Barski, Hervé Bromberger & Frédéric Grendel ('Script' credit: Aurore Paquiss. 'Adaptation & Dialogue' credit: Odile Barski). Pro Dir: Roger Morand. Ph: Jean Rabier. Art: No credit. M: Pierre Jansen. (Curzon Films.) Rel: Floating; first shown London, February 1979. 120 mins. Cert X.

Visages—Michael Cacoyannis

Half-hour 1976 Greek documentary: the work and thoughts of Greek director Cacoyannis with scenes from both his *Iphigenia* and *Trojan Women* movies. Dir: Huguette Imbert-Vier. Ph: François About. Ed: Chantal Piquet. M. Mihalis Christodoulides. (Contemporary.) Rel: Floating; first shown London, November 1978. 28 mins. Cert U.

Warlords of Atlantis

A well-made portion of good old Hollywood hokum, with under sea explorer *Peter (Onedin Line* captain) *Gilmore* and naval inventor *Doug McClure* finding plenty of excitement when their diving-bell takes them down to the sunken city of Atlantis. Lots of clever model work, highly incredible escapes and, in spite of all the travail that besets them, a sense of enjoyment as the heroes and villains battle their way in and out of the Lost Continent. Rest of cast: *Shane Rimmer, Lea Brodie, Michael Gothard, Hal Galili, John Ratzenberger, Derry Power, Donald Bisset, Ashley Knight, Robert Brown, Cyd Charisse, Daniel Massey.* Dir: Kevin Connor. Pro: John Dark. Screenplay: Brian Hayles. Ph: Alan Hume. Ed: Bill Blunden. Pro Des: Elliot Scott. M: Mike Vickers. Monster sequences by Roger Dicken. Art: Jack Maxsted. (John Dark/Kevin Connor–EMI.) Rel: 23 July. 97 mins. Cert A.

The Warriors

This film earned considerable notoriety in the United States by being credited with at least three youthful killings, and so much trouble in the cinemas that extra staff were often employed to keep order! The almost nebulous story concerns the New York street gang of the title (who are suspected of the murder of the leader of a gang 'get-together' which they have attended) making their hazardous way to their own Coney Island 'territory'. Routinely acted, repetitious in incident, basic in language but with a remarkable atmosphere of de-populated streets by night, subways and trains. Cast: *Michael Beck, James Memar, Thomas Waites, Dorsey Wright, Brian Tyler, David Harris, Tom McKitterick, Macelino Sanchez, Terry Michos, Deborah van Valkenburgh, Roger Hill, David Patrick Kelly, Lynn Thigpen, Ginny Ortiz, Edward Sewer, Ron Ferrell, Fernando Castillo, Hubert Edwards, Larry Sears, Mike James, Gregory Cleghorne, George Lee Miles, Stanley Timms, John Maurice, Jamie Perry, Winston Yarde, Joel Weiss, Harold Miller, Dan Bonnell, Dan Battles, Tom Jarus, Michael Garfield, Chris Harley, Mark Baltzar, J. W. Smith, Cal St. John, Joe Zimmardi, Carotte William Williams, Marvin Foster, John Barnes, Ken Thret, Michael Jeffrey, Paul Greco, Apache Ramos, Tony Michael Pann, Neal Gold, James Margolin, Chuck Mason, Andy Engels, Ian Cohen, Charles Serrano, Charles Doolan, Jerry Hewitt, Bob Ryder, Joseph Bergman, Richard Ciotti, Tony Latham, Eugene Bicknell, T. J. McNamara, Steven James, Lane Ruoff, Harry Madsen, Billy Anagnos, John Gibson, Lisa Maurer, Kate Klugman, Dee Dee Benrey, Jordan Cae Harrell, Donna Ritchie, Doran Clark, Patty Brown, Iris Alahanti, Victoria Vanderkloot, Laura De Lano, Suki Rothchild, Heidi Lynch, Craig Baxley, A. J. Bakanus, Cary Baxley, Konrad Sheehan, Eddie Earl Hatch, Tom Huff, Leon Delaney, Irwin Keyes, Larry Silvestri, Sonny Landham, Frank Ferrara, Pat Flannery, Leo Ciani, Charlie McCarthy.* Dir: Walter Hill. Pro: Lawrence Gordon. Ex Pro: Frank Marshall. Screenplay: David Shaber & Walter Hill, based on the novel by Sol Yurick. Ph: Andrew Laszlo. Ed: David Holden. Art: Don Swanagan & Bob Wightman. M: Barry de Vorzon. Assoc. Pro: Joel Silver. (Paramount–CIC.) Rel: May 13. 94 mins. Cert. X.

The Water Babies

Lionel Jeffries's winning adaptation of the Charles Kingsley classic fairy story, with a central animated sequence (of Tom's underwater adventures) sandwiched between two live-action sequences in which the ill-treated sweep's boy meets the lovely little Ellie and through her rises to a life above stairs. The cartoon heart of the movie was made in Poland and has a lot of the charm and humour (and melody) of the earlier Disney work; the live sections contain some fine performances by *James Mason* as Grimes the villainous sweep, *Billie Whitelaw* as the mysterious fairy figure, *Joan Greenwood, Bernard Cribbins, David Tomlinson, Paul Luty, Tommy Pender* (as Tom) and *Samantha Gates* (as Ellie). Dir: Lionel Jeffries. Pro: Peter Shaw. Screenplay: Michael Robson; from the book by Charles Kingsley. In charge of UK Pro: Ben Arbeid. Pro Sup: Bruce Sharman. Ph: Ted Scaife. Ed: Peter Weatherley. Art: Herbert Westbrook. M: Bill Martin & Phil Coulter. (Pethurst International: animation by Tony Cuthbert Cartoons Ltd, and Films Polski, Warsaw.) Rel: 15 April. 92 mins. Cert U.

Watership Down
British animated feature based on the Richard Adams story about some human problems in a rabbit warren, with a very clever rabbit (apparently with extra-sensory perception!) who, foretelling disaster to the warren (and it comes in the shape of estate builders with their bulldozers), leads a few bold stalwarts into the unknown to seek happier territory and to establish a new warren, but finding lots of snags—including cats, dogs and dictator rabbits—along the way. The voices: *John Hurt, Richard Briers, Michael Graham-Cox, John Bennett, Simon Cadell, Roy Kinnear, Richard O'Callaghan, Terence Rigby, Ralph Richardson, Denholm Elliott, Zero Mostel, Mary Maddox, Hannah Gordon, Lyn Farleigh, Harry Andrews, Nigel Hawthorne, Clifton Jones, Michael Hordern, Joss Ackland, Michelle Price.* Dir, Pro & Screenplay: Martin Rosen. Animation Dir: Tony Guy. Animation Sup: Philip Duncan. Ed: Terry Rawlings. M: Angela Morley & Malcolm Williamson (song 'Bright Eyes' sung by Art Garfunkel). (Martin Rosen–Nepenthe Productions–CIC.) Rel: 12 November. 92 mins. Cert U.

A Wedding
Richly- and ironically-observed Robert Altman film about a classy American wedding which gradually reveals, during the ceremony and the reception that follows, all sorts of skeletons in all manner of cupboards; including the fact that the bride's sister has been made pregnant by the groom; the ostracism of the groom's mother on account of a long-ago marriage to an Italian waiter, and her need for the 'fixes' given by the drunken family doctor; the planning by the bride's mother to spend an illicit week with a ridiculous relative who professes instant love for her—and so on. Delightfully witty dialogue, universally first-class performances and a smart pace make one almost forgive the sudden lurch to apparent tragedy (and the subsequent, outrageous doubling back) and the reluctance to bring the whole thing to a quick and tidy end. Cast: *Carol Burnett, Paul Dooley, Amy Stryker, Mia Farrow, Dennis Christopher, Gerald Busby, Peggy Ann Garner, Lillian Gish, Nina Van Pallandt, Vittorio Gassman, Desi Arnaz Jun, Belita Moreno, Dina Merrill, Pat McCormick, Virginia Vestoff, Howard Duff, Ruth Nelson, Geraldine Chaplin, John Considine, Lauren Hutton, Allan Nicholls, Maysie Hoy, Viveca Lindfors, John Cromwell.*

Dir & Pro: Robert Altman. Ex Pro: Tommy Thompson. Screenplay: John Considine, Patricia Resnick, Allan Nicholls & Robert Altman; from a story by Robert Altman. Assoc Pro: Robert Eggenweiler & Scott Bushnell. Ph: Charles Rosher. Ed: Tony Lombardo. Art: No credit. M: Tom Walls. (Lion's Gate Films Inc–Fox.) Rel: 31 December. 125 mins. Cert AA.

Why Shoot the Teacher?
Pleasant little Canadian film about the experiences of a young man in his first teaching job at a remote Saskatchewan school in the Depression year of 1935. Quiet, credible and quite magnificently atmospheric. Cast: *Bud Cort, John Friesen, Samantha Eggar, Chris Wiggins, Joanne McNeal, Norma West, Gary Reineke, Dale McGowan, Michael J. Reynolds, Kenneth Griffith.* Dir: Silvio Narizzano. Pro: Lawrence Hertzog. Screenplay: James Defelice; based on the novel by Max Braithwaite. Ph: Marc Champion. Ed: Stan Cole & Max Benedict. Art: Karen Bromley. M: Ricky Hyslop. (Contemporary.) Floating; first shown London, September 1978. 99 mins. Cert A.

Wifemistress
Italian film sometimes reminiscent, in its visual lushness and tasteful presentation of occasional explicit sexual scenes, of the late Visconti; but with a confected, ironic story about a rich, travelling wine-merchant who neglects his lovely wife for his mistress, but when after a political indiscretion he has to hide and pretend to be dead he becomes increasingly lustful for her as he watches her take over his business and blossom into delicious maturity. And it is perhaps just by chance that *Laura Antonelli*, the star of Visconti's last film, should have been chosen to play opposite *Marcello Mastroianni!* Rest of cast: *Leonard Mann, William Berger, Annie Belle, Olga Karlatos, Stefano Patrizi, Armando Brancia, Maria Monti, Elsa Vazzoler, Gastone Moschin.* Dir: Marco Vicario. Pro: Franco Cristaldi. Ex Pro: Alberto Pugliese. Screenplay: Rodolfo Sonego & Marco Vicario. Ph: Ennio Guarnieri. Ed: Nino Baragli. Art: Mario Garbuglia. M: Armando Trovaioli. (Vides Cinematografica SPA Rome–Warner.) Rel: Floating; first shown London, April 1979. Floating. 106 mins. Cert X.

The Wild Geese
Large, handsome, bloody and very professionally polished, if in large part familiar, battle piece about a brilliantly planned and executed commando raid by a band of British mercenaries whose assignment is to rescue and bring out of captivity one of Africa's more able Presidents. But at the last minute the backer double-crosses rescued and rescuers alike and makes a bargain with the enemy, and the mission finds itself isolated in enemy country with only a slim hope of ever getting out by battling their way to an old airplane standing on a jungle airstrip. Cast: *Richard Burton, Roger Moore, Richard Harris, Hardy Kruger,*

Stewart Granger, Jack Watson, Winston Ntshona, John Kani, Kenneth Griffith, Frank Finlay, Barry Foster, Jeff Corey, Ronald Fraser, Ian Yule, Brook Williams, Percy Herbert, Patrick Allen, Glyn Baker, Rosalind Lloyd, Jane Hylton, David Ladd, Paul Spurrier. Dir: Andrew V. McLaglen. Pro: Euan Lloyd. Screenplay: Reginald Rose; based on the novel by Daniel Carney. Assoc Pro: Chris Chrisafis. Ph: Jack Hildyard. Ed (and 2nd Unit Dir): John Glen. Pro Des: Syd Cain. M: Roy Budd (song 'Flight of the Wild Geese' written & performed by Joan Armatrading). (Euan Lloyd–Richmond Film Productions (West) Ltd for Varius Entertainment Trading Co, SA–Rank Film Dist.) Rel: 17 September. 134 mins. Cert AA.

With Babies and Banners
Documentary (USA 1976) about the General Motors strike of that year which led to other strikes and unrest in support of the movement for a closed shop in a number of key American industries. Dir: Lorraine Grey. (Women's Labour History Film Project–The Other Cinema.) Rel: Floating; first shown London, January 1979. 46 mins. No cert.

Word is Out
American feature-length documentary about homosexuality, with some twenty-six interviews with men and women of different ages and backgrounds. Dir by the Mariposa Film Group (Nancy Adair, Peter Adair, Andrew Brown, Robert Epstein, Lucy Massie, Phenix Silver). (Scala.) Rel: Floating; first shown London, October 1978. 128 mins. Cert AA.

The World Is Full Of Married Men
Adaptation of Jackie Collins' novel: it's paradoxically old-fashioned—in terms of moral—here the wages of sin are death! The story of a modern with-it group of high-livers. The hero neglects his pretty young wife and children for the sake of a loose-moralled, ambitious young 'actress' which leads to the latter going off with a pop singer and the distraught hubbie's murder of that man. Cast: *Anthony Franciosa, Carroll Baker, Gareth Hunt, Georgina Hale, Anthony Steel, Sherrie Lee Cronn, Paul Nicholas, Hot Gossip (Group).* Dir: Robert Young. Pro: Oscar Lermanx & Malcolm Fancey. Ex Pro: Adrienne Fancey. Screenplay: Jackie Collins. No other credits to hand at press time. (New Realm.) Rel: June 10. 97 mins. Cert X.

Young Bedmates—Schulmädchen Report 10
Minor 1976 West German sex film in which the nubile lasses of a girls' school recount incidents calling for a great deal of undressing! Cast: *Astrid Bohner, Yvonne Kerstin.* No others named. Dir: Walter Boos. Pro: W. C. Hartwig. Ex Pro: Ludwig Spitaler. Screenplay: Günther Heller. Ph: Werner Kurz. Ed: Herbert Taschner. Art: Georg Stielhe. M: K. A. Dielz. (Rapdi–Eagle.) Rel: Floating. 79 mins. Cert X.

IN MEMORIAM

Though primarily a cabaret, vaudeville and stage performer, EDGAR BERGEN—who, aged 75, was found dead in his bed by his wife on 30 September 1978—appeared in a considerable number of films including *The Goldwyn Follies*, *Stage Door Canteen*, *I Remember Mama* and *Charlie McCarthy, Detective*. The last mentioned was the name of his famous dummy, with which Bergen reached the peak of the art of ventriloquism. He died in Las Vegas, where he had gone to appear in a show at Caesar's Palace.

One of the most polished and professional players ever to grace the screen, CHARLES BOYER died from a deliberately self-administered drug overdose at his Paradise Valley, Arizona, home on 26 August 1978, just two days after the death of his wife of 44 years and two days prior to reaching his 79th birthday. Born at Figeac in the south of France, Boyer started acting in school plays at the age of seven. After considerable amateur experience he turned professional after finalising his studies at Toulouse University and the Paris Sorbonne. His first appearance in films was made in 1920 and his Hollywood screen début was nearly ten years later, in the French version of *The Big House* (1930), followed by that of *The Trial of Mary Dugan*. Thereafter came a long succession of French and American films, with Boyer playing opposite many of the great feminine stars of that era, including Danielle Darrieux

Charles Boyer, as the Baron (with Anny Duperey) in Alain Resnais's *Stavisky*—one of his last film roles.

in Anatole Litvak's *Mayerling*, Garbo in *Marie Walewska*, Dietrich in *The Garden of Allah*, Bergman in *Arch of Triumph* and Michèle Morgan in *Maxime*; the list is long. He started the 1960s with *Fanny* and ended them with a role in Bryan Forbes's sadly under-rated *The Madwoman of Chaillot*. One of his last performances was that of the penniless French aristocrat in *Stavisky*. Though he will undoubtedly be remembered as the romantic French lover, he played many other very diverse roles with equal skill and intelligence. He, wisely, never lost his charming accent, nor his quietly assured, aristocratic presence. His only child, son Michael, committed suicide in 1965.

PETER BUTTERWORTH, who died while appearing in a children's stage show at Coventry on 16 January 1979 aged 59, after a heart attack, was a popular comedian with a special appeal to children. Making his screen début in 1950, he appeared in several of the famous 'Carry On' films and similar British comedies. He also did a lot of TV work.

DOLORES COSTELLO (daughter of the early silent-screen star Maurice), who died in February 1979 aged 73, was regarded by her contemporaries as one of the most beautiful actresses ever to grace the screen. She made her first big film, *Lawful Larceny*, in 1923 and three years later co-starred with John Barrymore in *The Sea Beast*, subsequently marrying him in 1928 and divorcing him in 1935. Among her best performances was one of her last as the widow in the Orson Welles classic *The Magnificent Ambersons*.

DAN DAILEY, who died in Hollywood on 16 October 1978 at the age of 62, was born in New York and brought up in a Long Island theatrical colony, appearing in local shows there while still a child. As a young man he became a dancer in vaudeville and cabaret—and also, when such work was scarce, became in turn grocery-store assistant, waiter, golf caddie and shoe-shop assistant! In the stage show of *Babes in Arms*, he was subsequently given the juvenile lead role in the touring

Dan Dailey

production of *I Married An Angel* and it was while he was appearing in this in Hollywood that he was seen by a talent scout and offered a role in *The Mortal Storm* (1940), his first film of many, including *The Ziegfeld Girl*, *Lady Be Good* and *Mother Wore Tights*.

CLAUDE DAUPHIN, who died in Paris on 16 November 1978, was a French actor who appeared in many American and French films. Born in Corbeil 75 years ago last August and educated in Paris, Dauphin had great charm, accentuated in later years by his silver hair, and the talent to take him to stardom on the stage on both sides of the Atlantic. He made his first Hollywood film, *Deported*, in 1950, and among the many others were *Casque d'Or*, *April in Paris*, *Phantom of the Rue Morgue* and *The Madwoman of Chaillot*. He served in the French and Allied Armies from 1940 to 1945.

Found dead in her hotel bedroom in February 1979, 51-year-old JANE HYLTON, who was appearing at a Glasgow theatre at the time, was a product of RADA and the Rank Charm School. She made her professional début in 1945 at the Worthing Repertory Theatre. She started her film career under her own name, Gwen Clark, in *Daybreak* in 1946, and it was after her next movie, *The Upturned Glass*, that she

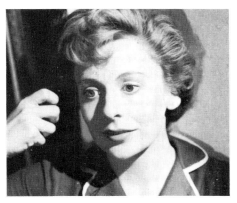

changed it to Jane Hylton. Under this name she made appearances in *It Always Rains on Sunday, My Brother's Keeper, Passport to Pimlico, The Weak and the Wicked, Circus of Horrors* and many more. She also appeared regularly on TV and in 1977 joined the National Theatre Company.

I. STANFORD JOLLEY, who died in California's Woodland Hills Hospital on 7 December, 1978 at the age of 78, was a very familiar figure in Western films in which, including serials and television Westerns, he appeared in no less than 475! His successful screen début as a baddie was in *Silver Spurs* in 1940. He appeared with William Boyd in many of the Hopalong Cassidy episodes and also in many Roy Rogers and Gene Autry movies. Later he appeared in a number of the TV *Gunsmoke* segments on TV.

VINCENT KORDA, youngest of the three Hungarian Korda brothers, who died in January 1979, was a well-known artist when his brother, Alexander, brought him into his London Films Productions when it was formed in 1932. As Art Director-in-Chief of the company, he was responsible for the art direction of such films as *The Private Life of Henry VIII, The Ghost Goes West, Things to Come* and *Rembrandt*. The last film on which he worked was *The Fallen Idol* in 1948.

164

BEN LYON, who died while acting as entertainer during a cruise of the *Queen Elizabeth 2* in late March 1979, was 78 and had been in show business for 60 of those years. Born in Atlanta, Georgia, on 6 February 1901, he was educated in Baltimore. His first film, as a result of signing a long-term contract with First National, was *The Heart of Maryland* in 1922. Another of his early films was *No Greater Love*, but his great success came in *Hell's Angels*, co-starring with Jean Harlow. He married Bebe Daniels in 1930 and their marriage became something of a Hollywood legend. In England when World War II broke out, they stayed on through the blitz and took their radio shows, Hi Gang and Life With the Lyons, to the top of the polls and earned the love of the British public. They made films of both *Hi Gang* (in 1940) and *Life With the Lyons* (1954). Bebe Daniels died in 1971 and Ben subsequently married Marian Nixon. Latterly he was a talent scout and casting director for Fox and as such gave opportunities to many young players.

As much writer as actress, YVONNE MITCHELL was actually working on a book about the Redgrave family when cancer killed her on 22 March at the age of 53. She made her film début in 1949 in *Queen of Spades* and subsequently appeared in a number of movies including *The Trials of Oscar Wilde, The Main Attraction, The Divided Heart* and *Woman in a*

Dressing Gown, the last two both bringing her awards. She appeared in the BBC TV serial based on Colette's *Chéri* and subsequently toured in a one-woman stage show about the French authoress; she also wrote a well-received biography of her. She appeared in both the Old Vic and Stratford companies; she wrote a play which won an Arts Council Competition; she directed writer–husband Derek Monsey's play when it was staged at the Arts Theatre, and she had some dozen novels and children's books to her credit, too.

ANDRÉ MORELL, who died in late November 1978 at the age of 69, was born in London with the name of Mesritz. Starting in amateur theatricals he succeeded in getting parts in various repertory theatres and came to London (as understudy to Owen Nares in *Call It a Day*) in 1936. He was with the Old Vic

André Morell

Company both before and after World War II (from which he emerged in 1946 as a major in the army) and appeared in a large number of films including *Clouded Yellow, His Majesty O'Keefe, The Baby and the Battleship, The Man Who Never Was, Seven Days to Noon, Bridge on the River Kwai* and *10 Rillington Place*. His last film was *The Message*.

An extended note about the death of *Mary Pickford*—'the world's Sweetheart'—will appear in next year's annual. She died of a heart-attack on 29 May 1979 at the age of 82. Mary, whose real name was Gladys Mary Smith, was born in Toronto, Canada, on 8 April 1893 and began her stage career at the age of 5. Her film career commenced in 1909 as a bit player, and seven years later she signed a two-year contract for more than half a million pounds. Along with Chaplin and husband Fairbanks she was the founder of United Artists (1919), but in recent years she had become a recluse.

On 20 June 1978, just a few days after completing the direction of *Avalanche Express* (starring, among others, Robert Shaw who also died before the film could be shown) 64-year-old MARK ROBSON died after a heart-attack. Born in Montreal, Canada, Robson started his film career as a 'props' man for 20th Century–Fox. Later he became a film editor and then assistant to director Robert Wise. Subsequently he served

director Val Lewton similarly over a long period before branching out on his own account with some small horror films such as *Seventh Victim* in 1943 and *Isle of the Dead* two years later. In 1945 Robson made *Champion*, the film which really launched Kirk Douglas into major stardom. For Stanley Kramer he directed *Home of the Brave* before moving to Goldwyn for *My Foolish Heart* in 1949. Other Mark Robson successes included *The Bridges at Toko-Ri, The Harder They Fall, The Inn of the Sixth Happiness, Nine Hours to Rama, Peyton Place, Lisa (The Inspector), Von Ryan's Express* and *Valley of the Dolls*.

LOUIS DE ROCHEMONT, who died on 23 December 1978 at the age of 79, will always be best remembered as the producer of the *March of Time* documentaries, for which he was responsible over a period of nine years, but in fact he produced many first-class feature films, such as *The House on 92nd Street, Windjammer* and *Animal Farm*. He fell in love with photography while serving in the US Navy and when he was demobilised became an Associate Editor with Pathe News.

ROBERT SHAW, who died from a sudden heart-attack at the early age of 51 while out for a car ride near his Co. Mayo, Eire, home on 28 August 1978, was both a writer and an actor of quality. His novel *The Sun Doctor* won him the Hawthorden literary prize. Another of his novels, *The*

Robert Shaw

Man in the Glass Booth, was adapted as a play which was staged in London (not with any great success) and he was following his other books, *The Flag* and *A Card from Morocco*, with a sixth novel, *Ice Floes*, which remained uncompleted at his death. The son of a doctor, born in the Orkney Islands and educated in Cornwall, he won a prize at RADA and went from there to appear at Stratford-upon-Avon, where he was seen by Alec Guinness and invited to appear in the latter's West End production of *Hamlet* in 1951. Subsequently he toured with the Old Vic company but he had a pretty thin time prior to his screen début in *The Dam Busters* in 1957. Thereafter followed a number of fine film performances, notable in Pinter's *The Caretaker* and *Birthday Party*, Losey's (remarkably under-valued) *Figures in a Landscape, A Man for All Seasons* (as the young King Henry VIII) and *The Royal Hunt of the Sun*. Recently he appeared in a number of big film spectaculars including *Jaws, The Deep, Black Sunday* and *The Sting*. At the time of his death he had two films still to be screened: *Force 10 from Navarone* and *Avalanche Express*. He leaves a wife and a family of ten children.

SUSAN SHAW, who died in a London hospital on 27 November 1978, was a graduate from the Rank Charm School of the late 1940s. Her real name was Patsy Sloots. She appeared in a number of films including *Holiday Camp, The Intruder, The Good Die Young* and *Carry on Nurse* but gave up acting in 1963, when she took various jobs such as barmaid, office girl and night-club hostess. She was 49.

The best, most widely known and acclaimed of Argentinian film directors, LEOPOLDO TORRE NILSSON, died from cancer on 8 September 1978 at the age of 54 in a Buenos Aires hospital. Making his first film in 1953, he became internationally praised for his mid-fifties movies such as *La Casa del Angel* and *La Caida*.

One of the last of the old pioneers, JACK L. WARNER died at his Los Angeles home in August 1978 at the age of 86. The youngest of four brothers, sons of a Polish cobbler who had emigrated to Canada, Jack

was born in Ontario on 2 August 1892. Educated in Ohio, Jack started his career at the age of 13 singing in minstrel shows and operettas. Then he joined brothers Harry and Albert in their bicycle shop venture and with them was involved in the running of their first cinema in Newcastle, Pennsylvania singing accompaniment to slides and choosing the films to be shown. But the venture failed and Jack went off to Hollywood where, with brother Sam, he laid the foundations of their future success with the production of *My Four Years in Germany* in 1917. In 1918 he took charge of the Warner Sunset Studios but by 1925, in spite of the fillip provided by his discovery and exploitation of dog star Rin Tin Tin, the brothers' fortunes were at a low ebb and it was then that they took the great gamble of going into sound. *The Jazz Singer*'s success and all that followed is familiar history. Under Jack's supervision the studios gained a reputation for fast-moving gangster and social-problem movies such as *Little Caesar, Scarface, I Am a Fugitive From a Chain Gang* and *They Won't Forget*; also a series of spectacular and memorable musicals such as *42nd Street*, and *The Gold-diggers* series. Jack, who survived his brothers, and the contraction of the film industry, continued to make a few big personally supervised movies, such as *My Fair Lady* (bought for something less than £3,000,000 and costing another £9,000,000 to make, but earning many times that total)

and *Camelot*. One of the last of the old-style movie dictators, Jack Warner may not have been universally loved but he was certainly admired and respected for his achievements.

CHILL WILLS, who died from cancer at his Californian home on 15 December 1978 at the age of 76, was born in Seagoville, Texas, and was in medicine, minstrel and circus shows before he graduated to burlesque, vaudeville, cabaret and, finally, theatre. It was when he was giving his act in a Hollywood night-club that he was seen by a talent scout and lured to the film studios, where he became one of the most reliable of all the old Western supporting stars. His enormous number of screen appearances included the Hopalong Cassidy series and the George O'Brien Westerns. His films include: *The Westerner, Western Union, Belle Starr, Billy the Kid, Thunder in the Dust, The Alamo, The Yearling, Meet*

Me in St Louis and the 'Francis the Mule' series, in which he played the voice of the talking mule. His last performance was in a recent TV film, *Stubby Pringle's Christmas*.

Though GIG YOUNG, who committed suicide on 19 October 1978, will probably be best remembered for his lighter roles, he was in fact a very versatile actor capable of expertly filling any kind of part. Born as Byron Barr in St Cloud, Minnesota, on 4 November 1917, he became a car salesman while appearing in local amateur stage productions in the evenings. Then he gained a Pasadena Playhouse scholarship while working as garage hand and car-park attendant to raise enough money for his drama studies. His first professional stage appearance was in a Los Angeles production of *Abie's Irish Rose,* in which he was seen by a Hollywood casting director and offered a screen test. His first appearance before the movie cameras was in a short, *Here Comes the Cavalry*, in 1941, but he quickly graduated to feature films. He earned Oscar nominations with his performances in *Come Fill the Cup* (1951) and *Teacher's Pet* (1958) and finally won a Best Supporting Actor award for his performance as the cynical MC in *They Shoot Horses, Don't They?* in 1970. Some of his other films were *Wake of the Red Witch, Holiday for Sinners, Young at Heart* and *One Touch of Mink*. During the war he served (1943–6) in the US Navy.

Other deaths during the period include those of:

LINDA CARSTENS, the German actress who gave such a wonderful performance as the old lady in *Lina Braake* (September 1978).

LEE GARMES. Outstanding Hollywood photographer whose credits included *Gone With the Wind* (September 1978).

GEOFFREY UNSWORTH. Brilliant British photographer whose films included *Superman* (October 1978).

JOSETTE DAY. French actress and star of many films including Cocteau's *La Belle et la Bête* in which she played Beauty (June 1978).

CARLETON HOBBS. Veteran British actor with many stage and screen credits (July 1978).

CLIFFORD McLAGLEN. One of the first screen Tarzans, if not actually *the* first (September 1978).

O. E. HASSE. German actor of note who went to Hollywood and made a number of movies including *I Confess* (September 1978).

The two faces of Gig Young—in comedy and in drama.

Soundtrack!—
The Year in Film Music

by Derek Elley

It would be an impertinence to start this year's review with any name other than that of Nino Rota, the Italian composer, whose death in a Rome clinic on 10 April, 1979 (of a blood clot) robbed film music of one of its greatest figures. Rota's first film score was in 1933; his last merely a few months before his death. In between stretched a string of legendary creations, the most famous in the dance-hall style developed for his Fellini films and the larger symphonic canvases for such works as Visconti's *The Leopard,* King Vidor's *War and Peace,* Zeffirelli's *The Taming of the Shrew* and *Romeo and Juliet,* and (one of his very greatest scores, which has not appeared on disc so far) Anthony Harvey's *The Abdication.*
Rota's meticulous scoring, his gift for life-enhancing melody and almost diffident application of his skills (concert compositions occupying his time between film assignments) will be sorely missed. His best work dates from the 1950s and 60s; later scores such as *The Godfather* and the recent *Death on the Nile* (EMI EMC 3256) evinced less substance, the latter score sporting a particularly inappropriate Wagnerian main theme, despite considerable musical invention elsewhere. At the time of his death his scores to Jan Troell's *Hurricane* and Fellini's *Orchestra Rehearsal* still await general release. On the American scene the two flourishing figures of John Williams and Jerry Goldsmith have continued to dominate; Williams following

through on the promise of *Close Encounters of the Third Kind* and Goldsmith drawing level with perhaps the richest year in his entire career. Williams's *Jaws 2* (MCA MCF 2847) was his most completely satisfying score of the year, not only due to its exciting transformation of material written for the original but also because it showed to perfection the new compositional phase Williams has entered since his writing for *Close Encounters.* The exploration of texture and colour has now assumed prime importance; so subtle was the integration of some of the first film's thematic material— amid, incidentally, totally new 'interludes' like the catamaran race— that *Jaws 2* not only qualified as a fresh work in its own right (unlike the film) but also entered that select pantheon in which the sequel outpassed the original. Williams' post-*Close Encounters* stature was already apparent in *The Fury* (Arista SPART 1056), a more monothematic score but with astonishingly versatile exploitation of its five-note leading motif often looming up on heavy brass with appropriate menace. The clearest demonstration, however, of Williams' new authority came with the much-awaited *Superman* (Warner K66084), preserved on a double album of less-than-excellent quality. Like the film, the score had a schizophrenic personality, being heroic, epic and romantic by turn— and certainly of less overall invention than *Jaws 2*—but it contained some dazzling orchestral tapestries (e.g. the flying sequence's use of the love theme) which exhumed the ghost of such late-and-great Hollywood master-orchestrators as Conrad Salinger.

Jerry Goldsmith also faced a sequel with aplomb (rather than have the studio re-edit the original's tracks or hire someone to copy his style, he confided): *Damien Omen II* significantly developed and expanded the Orffian choral writing of *The Omen* to more unifying effect. It was an extraordinarily rich year for Goldsmith: *Capricorn One* added bite and a sense of omniscient danger to an uneven film but it was very much in Goldsmith's regular, safe, adventure mould; and hints of a new phase in his development came in *The Swarm* (Warner K56541), a much-underrated score of considerable complexity beneath its trilling effects. Goldsmith himself recognises a new maturity in his style, brought about by the jettisoning of the easy solutions of percussive and ostinati effects, and a greater concentration on symphonic line. Both *The Boys from Brazil* (A & M AMLH 64731) and *MacArthur* (MCA MCF 2828) showed evidence of this; these less-than-subtle films were given depth and some stature by music which had an interior logic of its own. *MacArthur* contained much glorious string writing which probed the general's character, while *The Boys from Brazil* had a frightening juxtaposition of Viennese and German waltz traditions re-expressed in Goldsmith's own

language. Similarly, the decision to use almost exclusively a string orchestra for *Magic*, punctuated by unnerving interjections by a harmonica suggesting the dummy's presence, produced an effect of *multum in parvo*. Perhaps his most successful score of the year—certainly his most joyous—was for Michael Crichton's *The First Great Train Robbery*, a period caper film suffused with melodic transformation, effortless tunefulness and a symphonic unity which seemed to grow from the very essence of the picture. Goldsmith's relationship with Crichton (which earlier had produced the atonal *Coma* MGM Super 2315 398) could well become as productive as that with Franklin Schaffner.

There are, certainly, strong signs (and not just from majors like Goldsmith and Williams) that the symphonic tradition, after almost two decades of decline, is making itself felt again in film scoring. The increase in escapist, entertainment fare is partly the reason—composers are bound to be swayed by what they are given rather than blindly follow their own inclinations—but other factors are a general awareness of past traditions and the interest aroused. The concentration on re-recording classic scores has showed signs of waning during the past twelve months and no major record company has any undertaking at the moment [May 1979] on the scale of a couple of years ago: Decca have dropped their Historical Rózsa series

and Warners have pulled out their support from Elmer Bernstein's Film Music Collection (which appears to have wound up, with *Madame Bovary* and a pair of Tiomkin albums as its final releases). The spotlight in this field has shifted back to the minor labels on which it began: Entr'acte are doing a splendid job re-issuing Waxman's *Sayonara* (ERS 6513–ST) in presentable sound, plus his *Crime in the Streets* suite and a couple of jazz compositions (ERM 6001), while Citadel has continued to be extraordinarily productive in locating original tracks and tapes and putting them out as 'non-commercial' limited editions (with special commitment to Rózsa, namely, *Blood on the Sun* (CT–6031), and *Sodom and Gomorrah* extracts plus *The Power* (CT–MR–1)) or undertaking subsidised specials like 'Four Film Suites by Jerry Fielding', a superbly-engineered double album with twenty-odd minutes each from *The Mechanic*, *Chato's Land*, *Lawman* and *Straw Dogs* (CT/JF-2/3). Elmer Bernstein's label also issued, for the first time, the original tracks to the over-rated Fielding's *Scorpio* (FMC–11).

As if in recognition of the brightening film-music scene, veteran Miklós Rózsa also returned to the fray, following *Providence* (EMI Pathe–Marconi 2 C 066–14406) and *The Private Files of J. Edgar Hoover* of 1977 with *Last Embrace* in the autumn of 1978 and *Time after Time* in the spring of 1979. Elmer

Bernstein himself, long immersed in TV work, has now returned to features with a vengeance; *Animal House* (MCA MCF 2868), though pathetically represented on the LP, neatly underscored its ironic subject (Bernstein has just written the follow-up also), but it was his towering music to *Zulu Dawn* that reaffirmed his stature as a film composer.

Of newer names, Bill Conti has shown consistent promise from feature to feature: *F*I*S*T* (UAS 30181) triumphantly built on the heroic propensity of the earlier *Rocky* to produce Conti's best score to date. His popular/jazz origins are still evident but a symphonic mind is there to be nurtured. In Britain, Ed Welch's *The Thirty-Nine Steps* (UAG 30208) also announced a talent of similar origins and expectations, if only half-realised at present. The main problem for British composers is a regular supply of production along the lines of their Hollywood counterparts, but it shows no signs of being solved. All the big projects, whether made in Europe or America, are invariably given to American composers (witness the time spent in London each year by West Coast names) while the works requiring delicate crafting are farmed out locally. This often produces some very fine scores—Patrick Gower's strings-and-guitar one for *Stevie* (CBS 70165) or Angela Morley's splendid *Watership Down* (CBS 70161), the latter hastily given to her after Malcolm Williamson found he

could not complete on time—but it does nothing to shift the balance eastwards.

In addition there is little increased awareness of European composers. The nomination of Ennio Morricone's score to *Days of Heaven* for an Oscar in 1979 was sufficiently surprising in itself; no one ever expected him really to win it. But Morricone, like other European composers, can well do without the cosmetic decoration of the Academy Awards—especially after the farce of *Midnight Express*'s mindless wallpaper music finally winning, against deserving opposition from the much-thwarted Goldsmith and already-honoured Williams. Morricone's reputation is assured within Europe, even to the extent that Beat Records, a Rome-based film company much interested in his more recent scores (*Holocaust 2000, Il prefetto di ferro*), have reached back into the sixties for his few works which remain unreleased on disc. A thoroughly laudable 'Serie blue' series, devoted to classic Italian scores, began with Morricone's *Il grande silenzio,* an icy accompaniment to a little-known Sergio Corbucci Western of 1968. (Details from Rare Records, Manchester 2.)

This, however, like most European soundtracks, was a specialist import to British markets—one of many which achieve limited sale among collectors but make no impression on the general market. And even those American scores issued by majors like Warner or United Artists or

Arista still have a limited sale when compared with the mass appeal of song-albums like *Grease, American Hot Wax, The Wiz* and the like. Even companies who entered the historical market a few years ago found to their cost that the large expenses involved in re-recording vintage scores—even using London orchestras, who are considerably cheaper than their American or European counterparts—are diffcult to recoup from what is still (despite isolated phenomena like *Star Wars*) a limited, if devoted, buff market. The tens of thousands who flocked to buy the *Star Wars* double LP, and its disco off-shoots, did not, significantly, patronise Williams' *The Fury* or *Jaws 2*. Film music is, and will remain, a quiet backwater of the record market, as it is of film appreciation, and it is developments like the present raising of compositional standards among living composers that one should welcome rather than breakthroughs in the haphazard world of vinyl.

The Film Books of the Year

Reviewed by Ivan Butler

For the first time since this book-review section was started, there has been an appreciable decrease in the number of books on the cinema, most notably in the 'show-biz biography' section. This is, perhaps, not altogether surprising, as it has sometimes seemed lately that every conceivable aspect, and every single personality, of the film world had been covered—and covered again. Among the absences to be regretted are those of The Film Classics Library, edited by Richard J. Anobile, each volume covering a single film, with all the dialogue and between one and two thousand frame blow-ups, together with a brief introductory note. Some eight issues appeared and then the series apparently lapsed; certainly they have not appeared in Britain. This is a pity, because a collection of, say, one hundred classic films preserved in this fashion would have provided not only a feast of nostalgia but also a chance to study in detail and at leisure the techniques and approaches of the various directors, editors, etc., concerned. A casualty, perhaps, of the world economic situation. However, the year's offerings, if curtailed, still contain a generous proportion of valuable publications, as a glance through the following pages will show.

The usual, slightly arbitrary classification system has been adopted. My thanks, once more, to those publishers who have kept me in touch with their film titles.

BIOGRAPHY, MEMOIRS

The Actor's Life: Charlton Heston; Allen Lane, £6.95/Dutton, $12.95.

In 1956 Charlton Heston started to keep a comprehensive working journal. This nicely-produced volume, of 482 pages, consists of entries from that journal until 1976, edited by the experienced Hollis Alpert. Interspersed among the entries are comments by the author on how he views them from today's standpoint. He also contributes a brief introductory chapter. Literate, intelligent, informative, frank and sensitive, this is a fascinating record of a distinguished artist at work; things that came off, things that did not, plans that carried or miscarried, pertinent comments on smaller events which may well have been lost to memory had they not been swiftly jotted down and views expressed in the heat—or coldness—of the moment are all included. It is a refreshingly different (and inevitably rare) form of 'show-biz autobiography'. Among the films he worked on, or was connected with, during the period are *Touch of Evil, Ben Hur, The Greatest Story Ever Told, El Cid, Khartoum* and *Planet of the Apes.* Theatrical ventures are also included, such as *Macbeth* with Vanessa Redgrave.

Dozens of fellow-artists appear, and a good section of photographs illustrates an enviably happy personal life.

It is only surprising that, in a volume produced so handsomely, there is no index. The yearly section headings make reference to film titles comparatively easy, but an index of personal names should surely have been regarded as essential.

Bardot—an Intimate Biography: Willi Frischauer; Michael Joseph, £5.75.

As indicated by the sub-title, this is a personal rather than a professional account, though the films receive such prominence as their mainly ephemeral qualities warrant. The number of these, over the twenty-one years covered by B.B.'s career, may surprise some people—but many of them are eminently unmemorable. They are listed here in a brief filmography which, in line with the general approach of the book, gives a brief synopsis of each story but no other details whatever. What we have is a pleasantly written, warm but frank and often perceptive study of a personality and a phenomenon which belong most exactly to their period—a period which today seems strangely set in a long-since-changed (for better or worse) world. The illustrations—vital, surely, in any book on Bardot—are generous and quite well reproduced as well as being gratifyingly unfamiliar.

Charles Bronson—Superstar: Steven Whitney; Robert Hale, £5.25/Dell (1975), pb. $1.50.

As indicated by the title, extremely high claims are made for the subject of this lively and very 'readable' biography. It will presumably need no recommendation to the 'countless millions all over the world' (see blurb) who 'throng to see him'—the 'men who envy him' and the 'women who want him'. But it should also interest many other filmgoers whose enthusiasm is perhaps slightly below white heat but who are nevertheless appreciative of skilled film acting. The films themselves are treated interestingly and perceptively (e.g. the controversial *Death Wish*), and the filmography is magnificent, taking up sixty pages and a model of what this reference section should be. Obviously the result of long and painstaking research, it covers, as fully as possible, Bronson's entire career from his early years as extra and bit-player (as Charles Buchinski), with detailed technical information, and the most complete cast-lists I have seen—even in books which set out to be primarily reference works. There follows a brief but adequate list of TV appearances. Strangely, after a reference section that could hardly be bettered, there is no index.

Charlie Chaplin: John McCabe; Robson Books, £5.25/ Doubleday, $10.00.
Mr McCabe will be remembered for his books on Laurel and Hardy, notably the delightful double biography *Mr Laurel and Mr Hardy*. In his Introduction to the present volume he remarks: 'When my publisher suggested a Chaplin biography I reacted as I think most film historians would: enough. . . . It must all have been done.' Even if that were true (and it probably never will be) there will always be room for so warm, moving and often amusing a biography as this. The author has delved deep—one need only glance at the positively formidable *Select* Bibliography to realise this—and has obviously gone to immense trouble to sift as much truth as possible from the vast mass of often contradictory (contradictory, at times, from Chaplin himself) material available. In this task he acknowledges the great help he received from Stan Laurel, who knew and loved Chaplin so well.
Mr McCabe's own admiration and affection are everywhere apparent, but are not allowed to gloss over either failings or misfortunes. In addition to biographical details he provides a full synopsis of all the main films, perhaps the least *essential* part of the book but obviously included for the sake of completeness; and Denis Gifford adds a really magnificent filmography, a boon to any researcher. The off-screen are interesting, but the stills are unremarkable—moderately good reproductions of very familiar friends.
Highly recommended—not least for its easy, readable style.

The Complete Crosby: Charles Thompson; W. H. Allen, £5.95.
This is a chatty, affectionate, and obviously well-informed biography (the author also wrote a fourteen-hour broadcast series on Bing); but to call it the 'complete' Crosby is surely stretching things a little. The book has no filmography, no discography, not even an index—in fact no reference sections whatever. The approach is adulatory, and the writing style casual. A Postscript consists of a number of brief,

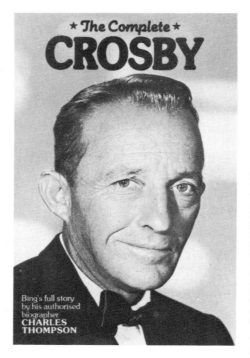

unsurprising eulogistic comments from fellow artistes and other well-known people (including President Carter). However, discount expectations aroused by the word 'Complete', and this is a pleasant enough 'read', with some very good illustrations.

The Cinema of Orson Welles: Peter Cowie; Tantivy, £3.75/Barnes, $6.95.
This is the paperback version of the admirable book on Welles (and, indeed, on Shakespeare in part) noted in an earlier *Film Review*. Full analyses, plenty of good stills, script extracts from *Citizen Kane* and *The Magnificent Ambersons*, and several reference appendices. Stoutly bound, and excellent value.

Errol Flynn: Michael Freedland; Arthur Barker, £5.95/Morrow, $9.95.
Biographers of film stars must surely be conscious of an immense debt to television. How many copies would be sold of the lives of, say, Milton Sills or Richard Dix—big stars in their day—but that day just too early for their films to be chosen (or available) for revival on the sitting-room screen? Errol Flynn's memory, on the other hand, will

doubtless be kept alive for some time to come, and Mr Freedland's chatty, entertaining and 'readable' book is very recommendable to any old-movie fanatic.
Probably nobody could make Errol Flynn a particularly admirable character, but under the author's scrutiny he becomes, at least to those people who are intrigued by the mysterious vagaries of box-office besottedness, an interesting phenomenon. No filmography is given, but these are available elsewhere and the approach of the book does not really require one; but an index might have been provided.

The Films of Hedy Lamarr: Christopher Young; Citadel, dist. by LSP Books, £11.50/Citadel Press, $14.95.
Pride of place in this rather fulsome volume is given to the illustrations—lavish and magnificent—which is undoubtedly wise, because the films themselves are on the whole a fairly unmemorable lot. Indeed, this luxurious book, which is exceptionally strong also in its reference sections, does Miss Lamarr more than proud. In addition to the films, television appearances are covered with stills, casts and brief synopses. Of especial interest to the film buff is the space given to the five early films from Austria, Germany and Czechoslovakia (including the famous *Ekstase*), details of which are not easy to find elsewhere. A twenty-page section of photographs, unsullied by printed matter, is introduced by a verse from Byron; he little knew the posthumous honour to come to him!

Fred Astaire: Storyline: Benny Green; Hamlyn, £5.95.
In this very attractive tribute to Fred Astaire on his 80th birthday, the author provides a brief but adequate text to accompany a large number of excellent pictures. In particular the many early photographs, covering in the main his stage career with the enchanting Adele, are to be treasured. A filmography, discography and stage career reference section (how long before we will have to suffer 'stageography'?) are included, together with an index. Fred Astaire has been handsomely represented in books recently, but this warm-hearted birthday greeting is a very welcome addition to the shelf.

Good Morning Boys—Will Hay: Ray Seaton & Roy Martin; Barrie & Jenkins, £5.95.
It is extraordinary that no full account of Will Hay's life and career has appeared before this; but in their concise yet informative book the authors here have made handsome amends. Hay was a complex character. His interests in flying, astronomy and mechanical inventiveness considerably outweighed those in stage or screen. This is not, however, to say that he was in any way content to give less than his best to his performances, or to rest ultimately on his laurels. On the contrary he was a hard task-master and a ruthless perfectionist. He does not appear in these

pages as a particularly lovable—not even always a likeable—character, treating neither his family nor his professional associates with undue generosity. But he was certainly a man of integrity where his work was concerned, and without any doubt one of the brightest lights—both in the music hall and on the screen—of the British comedy scene of the thirties and early forties.

The authors provide a full biography, and a filmography which contains sharply observant notes. Here is a book which should stand on the shelves of anyone interested in either screen comedy or the British cinema. It also, one must add, deserves an index.

'Hello, I Must Be Going'—Groucho and His Friends: Charlotte Chandler; Robson Books, £6.95/ Doubleday, $10.95; Penguin, $2.95.
From wherever he regards the world today, Groucho can surely have little to grumble at in respect of the posthumous literature which continues to appear about him. This fat (570 pages), handsome and pleasant-to-handle book is a worthy addition to the pile. It is a miscellaneous collection of reminiscences, interviews, comments and—in particular—conversations in dialogue form, garnered over a period by a friend of several years. The large and varied 'cast list' includes Jack Nicholson, Henri Langlois, Jack Benny, George Burns, Julius Epstein and, especially, Erin Fleming. The pages often sparkle with humour, and sometimes glow with warmth. There is a useful chronology, but no index. The illustrations are rare, and in many cases old and fading, which must excuse their occasional smudginess. A book, obviously, for the Groucho enthusiast—which may not include everyone—but for the many in that category it is an essential, both to read and to possess.

Hitch: John Russell Taylor; Faber & Faber, £6.50/ Pantheon, $10.00.
In many ways this—described as the 'authorised biography'—is the best book yet on the much-written-about Alfred Hitchcock. Mr Taylor has been brought further into his subject's confidence than any writer hitherto, and the result is absorbing reading, packed with fascinating personal details, working methods and incidental comments. (There is, for instance, a devasting example of an exhibition of boorish bad manners by Paul Newman.) The author's comparatively brief summaries of the films are illuminating and penetrating, and mercifully free from the pomposities and puerilities of so much of the 'higher criticism' on film. In particular, Mr Taylor gives a welcome prominence to the important British period of Hitch's career, and even the minor and less successful movies receive due attention.

Regrettably it has to be said that the author's style is not always of the happiest; he is at different times slangy, clumsy or plain careless. To take just one small example, a misuse of the word 'anticipate' quite destroys the sense of a comment on *Frenzy*. There are

also some incidental errors: e.g. Clare Greet was a British actress, not an 'American star'; O'Casey's Hyde Park play was entitled *Within the Gates*, and Sidney Gilliat's name is mis-spelt throughout, as is Jack Sheppard's, the 18th-century villain. However, the author's subject-matter is sufficiently engrossing to permit the reader to put up with occasional infelicities of manner. The illustrations, too, are excellent, wisely-chosen production and personal photographs rather than the old, too-familar film stills. The index is full and useful. Taken together with the famous Truffaut/Hitchcock interview book and Robin Wood's fine analyses of the films, this completes as full a portrait of the 'master of suspense' as we may hope to see, at any rate in the foreseeable future.

In Search of Butch Cassidy: Larry Pointer; University of Oklahoma Press, dist. Bailey Bros & Swinfen, £8.45/UOP $9.95.
In three separate fields this fascinating account will grip the reader: as a mystery story, as a Western, and as a corrective to film fantasy. Worshippers of the Newman/Redford romance are in for a few shocks—a mere glimpse at the illustrations will be all that is

necessary for that. And just what *did* happen after that famous end-of-film freeze? A strong case is made out here that Cassidy in fact lived on most quietly and respectably—as Mr E. T. Phillips—until 1937. Despite *The Man Who Shot Liberty Valance*, the truth is always more satisfying than the myth, and here a most painstaking attempt has been made to uncover the truth behind a famous legend. Well written, impressive in argument but never turgid, splendidly illustrated, this is the sort of book which should be compulsorily displayed in the lobby of every movie-house showing a supposedly 'real-life' film!

Joan Crawford: Bob Thomas; Weidenfeld & Nicolson, £6.95/Simon & Schuster, $10.95; Bantam, $2.75.
A good deal has been appearing recently about Miss Crawford—not a little of it sensational. Mr Thomas has, as might be expected from so experienced a hand, turned out a good, sound, professional job of biography, omitting none of the sensations but setting them in the context of, and in due proportion with, her professional career; and she was, surely, the *Professional* star *par excellence*. There are many

interesting episodes of her public life (e.g. the filming of *Whatever Happened to Baby Jane?*) and the private storms, conflicts and tragedies are recounted with sympathy and frankness. The book is well illustrated, soundly documented, and excellently indexed.

Lauren Bacall by Myself: Lauren Bacall; Jonathan Cape, £5.95/Knopf, $10.95.
This long (370 pages), solid (in the best sense), well-written and thoroughly entertaining book comes high up among the most important of the year's show-business autobiographies. Miss Bacall wastes little time on her early years, and by p. 21 we have already been brought to the American Academy of Dramatic Art. From there on we accompany her on a busy and varied professional life in theatre and cinema. Vivid accounts of film-making and stage productions, and lively portraits of the dozens of well-known personalities with whom she has been associated fill her generous pages. 'Bogie', obviously, has pride of place—a full and at times moving personal portrait. Aside from the purely professional activities, episodes such as the famous, or notorious, HUAC investigations are described in some detail.
A warm, often amusing, sometimes wise book, handsomely produced and well illustrated. But why—*why*—has it been deprived of an index?

Life is a Banquet: Rosalind Russell and Chris Chase; W. H. Allen, £5.95.
In his warm and moving Preface Frederick Brisson—Rosalind Russell's husband and Carl Brisson's son—says that she was still editing her autobiography until a few days before her death. In her introduction Rosalind Russell herself says: 'Now I've written this book.' What, then, was Miss Chase's contribution? A posthumous editing, perhaps, but it again points up the unsatisfactory vague 'autobiography with . . .' situation.
That said, this is a most lively, brave and interesting story of a courageous, witty and intelligent woman—a leading personality of both stage and screen. It is full of good stories, both professional and personal, embellished with comments that are sharp but never malicious. The result is a most likeable and thoroughly entertaining book. In addition to an adequate index and a list of screen appearances there are two generous sections of unusually well reproduced illustrations.

Love Scene, the Story of Laurence Olivier and Vivien Leigh: Jesse Lasky Jr & Pat Silver; Angus & Robertson, £9.95/T.Y. Crowell, $10.95.
Yet another account of 'Olivier and Leigh', and with such a title? This might cause some apprehension in the mind of a prospective reader—another 'great romance of the theatre' perhaps? In fact, it is a frank, engrossing and often moving account of a vital period in the life of the most illustrious actor of our time and one of the most beautiful actresses. It is, indeed, far more than its somewhat unworthy title implies, being a full-scale picture of the theatrical and cinematic world of the period. None of the pain and

tragedy is omitted, and, equally, none of the exhilaration and triumph. The personal relationship, though the core and central subject, is set firmly in its place in the wider events among which it developed.
The book is exceptionally well illustrated with many rare stills and personal photographs. There is a full bibliography, and an index. Finally, we are assured, none of the dialogue is invented. This is commendably honest, because if Miss Leigh was beautiful to look at, she evidently was often far from beautiful to listen to; and there are probably many people who will not altogether relish the four-letter words so tediously reported as proceeding from her lips.

Mary Pickford and Douglas Fairbanks: Booton Herndon; W. H. Allen, £6.95/Norton, $9.95.
Devotees of either star cannot complain of lack of reading material about their idols, but this study must surely rank among the best. After fairly brief, but adequate, accounts of their separate early lives it concentrates on their marriage—happy at first, but ill-starred—concluding with a brief epilogue after the parting of the ways. Important films are discussed, and a vivid picture of the unfailingly fascinating Hollywood scene during the high-summer period is painted. There are many illustrations, including some very old friends but also many fresh ones. Authoritative, thoroughly researched and well documented (and indexed) this joint biography can be unreservedly recommended.

Mommie Dearest: Christina Crawford; Granada Publishing, £5.95/Morrow, $9.95.
If you have illusions, prepare to shed them now. The author was legally adopted as a baby by Joan Crawford in May 1940. The life she led (or, rather, endured) is the subject of her book—and a horrifying story it is. 'Devastating exposé' is a cliché, but it is difficult to imagine two more suitable words to describe the revelation of the tyrannical, coarse, brutal, almost maniacal woman behind the glamorous superstar image, which is presented here. It says much for Miss Crawford's strength of character, tolerance and magnanimity that she can write about her horrendous upbringing with sympathy and compassion. She has a dreadful story to tell, and tells it without shrinking.
Her style is at times a little lurid, but then she has a pretty lurid subject, so on the whole it is well suited—though she should avoid using the word 'fortuitous' when she means, apparently, 'fortunate'. Perhaps the most repulsive pages in this whole appalling but engrossing story are those covering a verbatim transcript of a radio programme on a 'Hollywood family Christmas' at the Crawford home. Was anyone ever really taken in by such nauseating mush?

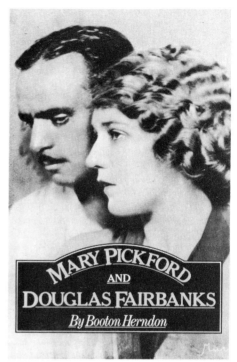

No Bed of Roses: Joan Fontaine; W. H. Allen, £5.95/ Morrow, $9.95.
Not the least wickedly witty thing about this barbed book is its charmingly rose-decorated appearance; for beneath the roses are plenty of thorns—sharp but thoroughly entertaining. Miss Fontaine's accounts of personal relationships (with her mother, her first husband, Brian Aherne, and her sister, Olivia de Havilland), and her stories of professional encounters (with the Oliviers, the 'British Colony' of the forties and the columnist Hedda Hopper), are equally at times devastatingly frank—typed, one might say, with ribbons of vitriol. But, however unsparing, she is never ungenerous, mean or spiteful; and when she likes or admires (Boyer, Milland), she is at pains to express the fact. A tough, hard-hitting book, well illustrated and indexed, compulsively 'readable'.

Nostalgia Isn't What It Used To Be: Simone Signoret; Weidenfeld & Nicolson, £6.95/Harper & Row, $12.95; Penguin, $12.95.
It may be that the ardent filmgoer will feel that Simone Signoret devotes too much space to political activities (distinctly left inclined) and not enough to the

important subject of her career in this lengthy, lively and sometimes hard-hitting book. Admittedly the glimpses of a notable actress at work are tantalisingly brief; even so, there are plenty of compensations. There is a very enjoyable picture of her life in Hollywood (including a splendidly scathing passage on Hedda Hopper of 'hat' notoriety). There are interesting 'snippets'—such as the fact that Carole Lombard's 'bangs' hid an ugly scar, and that it was Simone Signoret who was largely responsible for leading Katharine Ross to *The Graduate* and stardom after they had appeared together in a not particularly elevating picture, *Games*. There are short but sharp accounts of the making of, among others, *Room at the Top*, *Les Diaboliques* (of which she unkindly betrays the secret, but perhaps it is common knowledge now), *The Seagull* (which she ardently loved) and, of course, *Casque d'Or*. (The jacket blurb also refers to *Term of Trial*, but neither I nor, apparently, the indexer could find it.) There is much about her husband, Yves Montand, and a certain amount about Marilyn Monroe—the stories which circulated about them being dealt with succinctly. No reference section and no illustrations—but a good, clear index.

Paul Newman—Superstar: Lionel Godfrey; Robert Hale, £4.80/St Martins Press, $8.95.
In his modest and courteous Introduction Mr Godfrey states that Paul Newman declined to co-operate in any way with his projected book. This has not, however, hindered the author from producing a first-rate, concise account of his subject's life and career—among the best of the year's film biographies. He deals with the films perceptively and with refreshing independence (though giving undue attention to the comments of Pauline Kael)—see his trenchant comments on the over-rated *Butch Cassidy* and *The Sting* and his good word for the under-rated *What A Way To Go*. He gives as much space to the star's political activities and opinions as most readers will find necessary, and deals sensitively and sympathetically with his private life— in particular, of course, his marriage to Joanne Woodward. Her comments on the dreariness of present-day film-making, incidentally, make sad if convincing reading.
There are interesting sections of illustrations, a concise but adequate filmography (Newman as star and director), a list of Joanne Woodward's films, and a good index.

Peter Finch: Trader Faulkner; Angus & Robertson, £6.95
This is a good, sound biography of one of the more interesting figures of stage and screen, told by a fellow-actor who knew him well (in fact, he trained under Finch at the Mercury Theatre) for many years. Peter Finch was a complex and often troubled man— in some ways, perhaps, one is reminded of Montgomery Clift—and could not have been an easy subject for dissection on the biographical table. The author, however, most sympathetically and clear-sightedly portrays all the facets: the drunkenness and

NO BED OF ROSES
an autobiography
Joan Fontaine

boorishness as well as the undoubted charm and brilliance. His book is vivid and full, well researched and containing a wealth of fascinating details both professional and personal. Particularly interesting are the accounts of the lesser-known but important years in Australia before Finch became a star of world-wide repute.

There are adequate appendices, a good index, and generous sections of illustrations.

Queen of the Ritz: Samuel Marx; W. H. Allen, £5.95
Though not to be described as a 'film book', this fascinating and often exciting account of the famous Paris hotel from the 1920s to the German Occupation—ending in a double shooting tragedy—contains brief glimpses of a number of famous film personalities, e.g. Olive Thomas (who died mysteriously in the hotel) and, in particular, Pearl White.

The Red Raven: Lilli Palmer; W. H. Allen, £4.95/ Macmillan, N.Y., $8.95.
A borderline case, perhaps, for inclusion here, but Miss Palmer's autobiographical novel is not only enjoyable (a love story, warm, witty and touching) in its own right, but it will present the film enthusiast with a pleasing puzzle in estimating how much fact is embedded in the fiction. Readers of her previous book, *Change Lobsters and Dance,* will not need even this recommendation.

Sophia—Living and Loving: A. E. Hotchner; Michael Joseph, £5.95/Morrow, $9.95.
This is another 'as-told-to' 'auto'-biography—a form never wholly satisfying, as the writing in the first person and the knowledge that the 'writer' is not in fact the writer make for a general uncertainty as to who is saying what, and which personality is dominant. However, at least the 'ghost' is acknowledged and named, which makes things a bit more honest. The subtitle of the book fairly denotes its general trend: not much serious film coverage, but a 'human' story, and as such it serves well enough. The narrative is broken up by comments from friends and family (notably, of course, Carlo Ponti), which serves to fill in the portrait. There are generous sections of illustrations. There is also a nicely set-out filmography (but no index), and an appendix on clothes, make-up, hair, cooking and other fringe benefits.

With Those Eyes: Michèle Morgan; W. H. Allen, £7.50
Perhaps the most interesting part of this chatty (indeed, at times somewhat gushy) but readable 'collaborated' autobiography is the view of Hollywood through the eyes of a disenchanted visitor; and who can blame her for her disenchantment, on the evidence of that 'pin-up' embarrassment facing p. 168! However, Miss Morgan—a fine screen actress by any standards—has more than this to relate. Her life has had its full share of peaks and valleys and, if one can

accept its style, the book has much to offer. Her close association with Jean Gabin is given appropriate prominence, as are her marital troubles and her anxieties over the fortunes and problems of the war in her homeland. The star of such films as *Quai des Brumes, Symphonie Pastorale* and *The Fallen Idol* might, perhaps, have warranted a deeper study, but the present book fills a gap on the over-flowing shelves of show-business personalities. There are some pleasant illustrations, but at £7.50 the book is pricey enough to deserve an index.

HISTORY, CRITICISM, ANALYSIS

Alain Resnais: James Monaco; Secker & Warburg (Cinema Two), £7.95 hardback, £4.95 paperback O.U.P, New York, $14.95; pb, $5.95.
On the whole Mr Monaco elucidates this intriguing but not always crystal-clear director's work with clarity and vigour, though admittedly falling at times into both the garbled pretentious, and the painfully obvious. 'A film not shown is a film without effect'—how much deep thinking went into *that* startling revelation? 'Intellection' is not in my dictionaries—French, English or American. He also puts the

occasional claim for brilliance somewhat high: is the prosaic still of a door and doorbell on p. 91 really so striking? It is doubtful whether he makes the endlessly fascinating *Last Year at Marienbad* much more accessible; but that great film is probably best left unanalysed, to be appreciated in much the same way as a piece of 'pure' music or a recondite poem. Production of the book is well up to Cinema Two standards—with good documentation and well-produced stills.

American Silent Film: William K. Everson; Oxford University Press, £6.95/O.U.P, N.Y., $17.50.
The silent cinema has in recent years been receiving more of the attention it has so long deserved—perhaps in the hope that the television companies may decide to be a good deal more enterprising and considerate than they have been in showing these often wonderful old movies. Mr Everson is one of the foremost writers on film history and film by-ways; here he has conceived and delivered a first-rate survey, which is animated, knowledgeable, affectionate and scholarly. Obviously, those filmgoers fortunate enough to have known the silent film in its heyday will wish that this or that particular favourite had been given more (or this or that pet hate given less) prominence—but no one surely can quarrel with his suggestion that the greatest of them all was Murnau's *Sunrise,* a masterpiece which, if presented in a decent copy, has lost none of its power to delight and to move.

In a book of some 350 pages of text it is clear that many good pictures have to be accorded only a brief mention, but as an overall view this is a fine achievement. There are four thick sections of excellent illustrations, a useful appendix on other books dealing with the silent film, and a brief Chronology of Highlights. Strongly recommended.

The Ancient World in the Cinema: Jon Solomon; Tantivy, £9.50/Barnes $19.95.
Truly a film book with a difference, this fascinating volume is a study of the ancient historical, mythical and Biblical movies of various countries from the earliest years, written by an author who is an expert on the subject. He casts a piercing but by no means jaundiced eye over the numerous anachronisms and lunacies, but also appreciates the painstaking attempts to achieve historical accuracy in both detail and overall picture which so often went into the making of these famous and costly productions.

An enormous number of films are covered—not only the blockbusters, the *Ben Hurs,* the *Ten Commandments,* the *Lives of Christ,* the *Solomons and Shebas,* but also the fantasies proper, such as *Jason and the Argonauts,* the endless *Hercules* sagas (over thirty of them), horror films such as *The Mummy,* and comedies such as *Carry on Cleo* and *A Funny Thing Happened....* Even Felix the Cat and Popeye have their respective, and respected, places. One really cannot, in a brief space, do justice to the vast amount of information (historical and cinematic) with which these large pages are crammed—information always

lucidly and often very entertainingly presented. Among the most valuable pages are the Chronological Tables in which, in date order, the historical and/or Biblical events are listed beside the films dealing with such events.

The illustrations are excellent, in numerous cases comparing the actual (a vase, carved figures such as those on Trajan's column, buildings or ornaments) with the filmed reproduction. An excellent index rounds off what must surely be placed among the most useful, interesting and original film books of the year.

Aspects of American Film History Prior to 1920:
Anthony Slide; Scarecrow Press, Bailey Bros & Swinfen, £6.35
In this delightful little book with the disproportionately large title the author continues to pursue his engaging travels in the by-ways of early cinema history, leading us, fascinated, after him. Among his subjects are 'The Evolution of the Film Star', 'Forgotten Early Directors', 'Comediennes and Child Stars of the 1910s', and chapters on pioneer companies such as Thanhouser. His delightful final essay, 'Film History Can Also Be Fun', justifies all the

rest. The book is painstakingly documented, contains rare and excellent illustrations, and is as entertaining for the ordinary film enthusiast as it is valuable for the research worker.

Born To Lose—The Gangster Film in America:
Eugene Rosow; Oxford University Press, £10.75/ O.U.P. $19.95.
This splendid book is surely the most important study of the gangster film that has appeared yet, or that is likely to appear in the foreseeable future. Far more than an account of a movie *genre*, it is also a history of a notable American phenomenon, and can be read for its social history with equal profit—and above all, pleasure—as its film analyses. Fully documented, it is scholarly and authoritative, but also thoroughly entertaining and stimulating; pleasant to handle, easy reading, and excellently illustrated not only with stills but with historical photographs. In addition there is an admirable annotated filmography covering some eighty gangster films from the early years to the present, each with credits, full cast lists and an informative and illuminating comment. Unreservedly recommended.

The Cinema of Ernst Lubitsch—The Hollywood Films:
Leland A. Poague; Tantivy, £6.50/Barnes, $12.00.
Lubitsch has received disproportionately little attention compared with other (often lesser) directors about whom books pour from the presses. In the matter of stills (which are superb) and filmography (which is magnificently detailed and concerns itself with his *full* output) this book makes admirable amends. Unfortunately, however, the text is turgid and pretentious, full of the pomposities and absurdities which appear frequently to afflict proponents of 'higher criticism'. The author, who evidently does not undervalue himself (see the opening of his Preface) brings to bear the hammer of such weighty expressions as 'semiology' and 'meta-criticism', *et al.*, to crack the delicate nut of Lubitsch's exquisitely light and witty touch, and loads the films with ponderous 'meanings' which one feels would astonish that cunning creator of shrewd and often sharply-pointed entertainment.

A Critical History of British Cinema: Roy Armes; Secker & Warburg, £6.50 hardback, £3.90 paperback/O.U.P., N.Y., $17.50.
In this splendidly pithy, concise history Mr Armes traces the growth and development of British cinema against the political and cultural background of the country during the past eighty years. Into some 340 meaty pages he packs a wealth of fact, theory and comment. He corrects some mistaken impressions—Friese Green, for instance, comes out considerably smaller than he went in. His viewpoint would appear to be somewhat left of centre but he does not allow bias to distort his text to any undue extent, and he avoids the stridency (and carelessness) of Raymond Durgnat's *A Mirror for England*. Hundreds of films and dozens of directors are discussed with pointed brevity; there are

several pages of reference notes and a copious bibliography. After a slow start, British cinema is becoming one of the most handsomely represented of all in the reference libraries; this is an essential addition to the literature.
In so careful and well-researched a work it is odd to find a name as famous as C. B. Cochran mis-spelt, the error being dutifully reproduced in the Index—which also, incidentally, mis-spells my own name (correct in the Bibliography) and refers to a film called *Tawney Pippet*, going one better than a mis-spelling already in the text as *Tawney Pippit*. For the record, the title should be *Tawny Pipit*.

Federico Fellini—Essays in Criticism: Ed. Peter Bondanella; Oxford University Press, £3.25/O.U.P., N.Y., $12.00; pb, $4.95.
Quantitatively, Fellini has been well served in the matter of printed material, and this is a welcome addition. It is an interesting and varied collection of writings by more than twenty authors, approaching the work of this endlessly-intriguing director from many angles. Taken together, they form a valuable examination in depth. Names, from a number of countries, include André Bazin, Alberto Moravia, Stuart Rosenthal and Joseph McBride. In addition there are five sections—interviews and articles—by Fellini himself. A good bibliography and a full filmography are provided, but surely the blank pages at the end of the book could have been put to good use with an index?

The Filming of the West: Jon Tuska; Robert Hale, £11.50.
The Western has had good coverage in the literature of the cinema, but seldom so fully and entertainingly as in this large and handsome volume. Basing his history on almost one hundred 'representative' films (from *The Great Train Robbery* of 1903 to *The Cowboys* of 1972) Mr Tuska has written a lively, informative account in which popular presentation and scholarly research are nicely balanced. Key names such as William S. Hart, Tim McCoy, Buck Jones, writer Zane Grey, directors DeMille, Ford, Hawks and Peckinpah—together with fountain-head John Wayne—have sections to themselves, but part of the attraction of the book is the more than adequate coverage given to lesser (though not less popular in their day) lights. In particular a commendably large proportion of space is given to the silent productions and early sound productions, and to those famous—ultimately notorious—'B' Westerns. No filmographies are provided, but there is an excellent full index. Opulently produced and printed, with a wealth of fine (and often rare) illustrations, this is a 'must' for both student and enthusiast.

The Films of George Pal: Gail Morgan Hickman; Tantivy, £8.95/Barnes, $17.50.
Highly regarded in the forties for his original and entrancing Puppetoons, George Pal (from Hungary) has been less recognised (outside the 'buff' world) as the producer or director of such famous sci-fi and

fantasy films as *Destination Moon, When Worlds Collide, The Wonderful World of the Brothers Grimm* and his masterpiece, *The War of the Worlds.* All his work to date is covered here, title by title, together with secrets as to how he achieved some of his magical effects. There are many good illustrations, including some of the delightful Puppetoons(who, for instance, could resist the fascinating young Miss Judy on p. 27?), and the whole book is a useful and entertaining coverage of one more hitherto somewhat neglected corner of Hollywood.

The Films of Michael Winner: Bill Harding; Muller, £6.95
Following the arrangement, though smaller in size, of the coffee-table 'Films of . . .' series, this is a very useful introduction to a director whose work, as the jacket blurb says, has not received the degree of critical attention commensurate with the commercial success of many of his films. A lack of attention, it must be stated, due to no fault of his own! All the films are covered (from the reprehensible and feeble *The Nightcomers* to the powerful, if controversial, *Death Wish*; from the early *West 11* to the recent *The Big Sleep*), with cast and credits, synopsis, and lengthy commentary for each, and there are supplementary sections on 'Winner Talking' and 'Others on Winner'. In addition, there are good photographic sections and a full index. Mr Winner may not be everybody's favourite director but he certainly warrants (as well as invites) attention in this enthusiastic and nicely written first book, and he certainly, if somewhat belatedly receives it.

The Films of Shirley McLaine: Patricia Erens; Tantivy, £8.50/Barnes, $17.50.
Surprisingly, only four films and one 16-mm documentary are listed for Miss MacLaine in the past nine years. There were twenty-five before this, starting with Hitchcock's *The Trouble with Harry* in 1955; some were unmemorable, but others—such as *The Apartment, The Children's Hour, Irma la Douce* and the parody-filled *What A Way to Go* which wickedly upset some critics—make one wish she had not deserted the screen for so long. This 'Films of . . .' account is a welcome record and reminder of past pleasures. The Filmography, unusually detailed, is placed at the end instead of being spread through the book with each film, the more usual and possibly more convenient method in this particular series. The biographical section takes due note of Miss MacLaine's political activities, and includes a pertinent comment: 'Unlike Jane Fonda . . . MacLaine never alienated her public. Reflecting on this phenomenon, MacLaine stated recently, "For one thing, I've worked inside the Establishment, and always will . . . And another thing is, I don't hate anybody"'. It is a pleasant personality that shines through Miss Erens's pages.

A Film Trilogy: Ingmar Bergman; Marion Boyars, £2.95/U.S. title *Three films by Ingmar Bergman:* Grove Press (1969); pb $4.95.
Four Stories: Ingmar Bergman; Marion Boyars, £1.95/

Doubleday, $7.95; pb $3.50.
The first of these paperbacks was originally published by Calder & Boyars in 1967. Containing the scripts of *Through a Glass Darkly, The Communicants* (*Winter Light*) and *The Silence,* with sections of stills, its reissue is to be warmly welcomed, and indispensable for anyone interested in Sweden's most famous director. The Four Stories are *The Touch, Cries and Whispers, The Hour of the Wolf* and *A Passion.* They are presented, not as straightforward scripts, but as 'summary texts', with some dialogue passages. For some these may be easier to read than actual scripts, but they are obviously less useful for study purposes. The omission of stills and credits also seems a pity. However, they are all we have (except for those fortunate enough to own copies) of four of his most subtle films, and are thus of considerable value.

Future Tense—the Cinema of Science Fiction: John Brosnan; Macdonald & Jane's, £6.95/St Martins Press, $15.00.
In the same format as his books on special effects and horror, Mr Brosnan follows with an equally enjoyable study of sci-fi. Though the subject has been very fully covered elsewhere, the author brings to it a knowledge and enthusiasm (and, where necessary, a very critical eye—see his comments on *Planet of the Apes*) which make the result both stimulating and informative reading. He follows a strictly chronological order, with chapters headed by years, which, supplemented by a fine index, makes his book easy for reference. Not the least of its attractions is a concise and valuable survey of TV science-fiction. Harry Harrison contributes a Foreword which includes a virulent attack—with which many surely will disagree—on *Close Encounters of the Third Kind.*

Great Film Directors, a Critical Anthology: Ed. Leo Braudy & Morris Dickstein; Oxford University Press. £4.50/O.U.P., N.Y., pb, $7.50.
This is a huge (nearly 800 page) paperback anthology of essays on the work of twenty-three leading directors, by such writers of authority as Andrew Sarris, Pauline Kael, David Thomson, Roy Armes, Stanley Kauffmann and Graham Greene, together with one or two fellow directors, e.g. Lindsay Anderson and Luis Buñuel. The range of subjects is wide, if not unexpected, and includes discussion of the work of Griffith, Lang, Chaplin, Flaherty, Hitchcock and Godard. Films specially treated include *The Seventh Seal, Metropolis, Vampyr, College* (Keaton) and *Psycho* among numerous others. From all this it can be gathered that—despite the presence of other collections of critical essays—there is something here to interest, please, and perhaps healthily irritate, almost everybody. The selections have been garnered from both books and periodicals.
The Directors are listed alphabetically; even so, an index of film titles could helpfully have been provided to fill the blank pages at the end of the book.
This is an eminently recommendable collection, particularly in these days of high prices.

Harold Lloyd: Adam Reilly; André Deutsch, £7.50/ Macmillan, N.Y., $14.95; pb, $9.95.
At last, in this excellently-researched volume, we have a worthy tribute to one of the Big Four of the silent comedians. Sadly, few of his greatest films are to be seen complete today. The better-known compilations—excellent of their kind though they may be—are poor substitutes for the complete versions of, say, *Grandma's Boy, Why Worry?* or *Hot Water.* It is generally admitted that the later sound films were an unhappy come-down, in particular the sad finale, *Mad Wednesday.* In these pages, for those of us lucky enough to have seen, grown up with, and treasured the silent features when they were first shown, is a feast of memories. The book consists of a biographical sketch, a superbly complete section on the early shorts, full coverage of all the features, half-a-dozen essays by leading film writers, and a most welcome and splendidly detailed collection of biographical articles on stars and supporting players. The illustrations are lavish and very well reproduced, and there are many lesser-known ones among the old familiars. This will surely remain for long THE book on Lloyd.

The Heroine or the Horse: Thomas Burnett Swann; Tantivy, £8.95/Barnes, $17.50.
Perhaps the most surprising thing about this picture gallery of the Leading Ladies of the Republic Studios is its extensiveness. Among the exhibits are such eminent names as Joan Crawford, Myrna Loy, Jennifer Jones, Dorothy McGuire, Susan Hayward, Barbara Stanwyck and Maureen O'Hara. These, and very many others, are each accorded a brief biographical section, many of which are well illustrated. The author, who unhappily died in 1976, has a lively style and his comments are often trenchant. ('Cybill Shepherd, a shapely model with no discernible talent.') He is, in fact, sometimes less than kind. There is also the occasional questionable remark; he asks for instance, who remembers Ruth Warrick's debut in *Citizen Kane*—but surely the leading role of Kane's first wife in one of the most famous and revered pictures of all time is unlikely to be forgotten while cinema screens (and television sets) exist? His closing chapter is devoted (the apt word) to an actress who really *is* widely forgotten—Adele Mara—and it is always refreshing to find someone who has been unfairly neglected finding a champion at last. The book is exceptionally well illustrated, and a worthy tribute to Republic's noteworthy President, Herbert Yates.

Hitchcock's Films: Robin Wood; Tantivy, £6.50/ Barnes, $12.00.
Mr Wood's book, first published in small paperback format in 1966, has always been widely regarded as one of the very best on the subject, dealing with the eight films from *Strangers on a Train* to *Torn Curtain* in detail and with a brief introductory survey of the earlier ones. In this enlarged, hardback edition he has added a chapter, but has left his main text largely

unchanged. As he wisely remarks: 'A book necessarily belongs to a particular phase in one's evolution and a particular phase in the development of the tradition within which it was written. . . . Rather than tamper with what I wrote, I prefer to offer a fresh statement of my position with regard to Hitchcock.' The three recent productions, *Topaz, Frenzy* and *Family Plot*, are discussed briefly in this new chapter. The filmography contains all Hitchcock's films, but is very brief for the early British ones.

Hollywood According to Hollywood: Alex Barris; Tantivy, £8.95/Barnes, $17.50.
Mr Barris continues his exploration of Hollywood by-ways (*Hollywood's Other Men, Stop the Presses*, etc.) with a bright survey of the film capital's representation of itself on film, from the 1920s to the 1970s. He has amassed a wealth of detail, which he presents with a witty—indeed, sometimes a wicked—commentary. He has also collected a really splendid array of stills, many from the silent and early sound period, unfamiliar and doubly welcome on this account. He does not shirk a couple of chapters on the most depressing of all Hollywood genres—those terrible wartime 'cheer-'em-along' musicals, and the almost without exception ghastly 'biopics' on, for example, Harlow, Chaney, Barrymore and daughter, Cantor and Keaton—great personalities woefully misrepresented and belittled in almost gleeful tastelessness. Perhaps in his inclusion of nostalgic collections of old-film-extract anthologies he stretches his boundaries a little; these are simply reissues, not 'the cinema world seeing itself in its films'. Still, this is wholly enjoyable entertainment, with an index which demonstrates the vast coverage, and the painstaking work that must have gone into its compilation.

The Hollywood Studios: Roy Pickard; Muller, £14.95
Reviewing this splendid book of more than 500 pages posed a problem—should it be entered under 'History, Criticism, Analysis' or included in the 'Reference' section? In last year's *Film Review* I highly recommended Mr Pickard's book on *The Oscar Movies*. Here he has cast his net much wider, recounting the histories of the nine major Hollywood studios: Paramount, United Artists, Warner, Disney, Columbia, MGM, RKO, Universal and 20th Century-Fox. Each history is divided into two parts: a brief summary (about 10 pages) followed by a detailed Chronology (about 30–40 pages). After consideration it seemed most suitable to enter the book under 'History, Criticism, Analysis', partly because the Chronology is so much more than the word might imply and partly because the book can be read straight through with the greatest enjoyment, benefit and satisfaction. The amount of research and care that has gone into its compilation is staggering, and its accuracy is admirable. If the price looks at first glance a little formidable, the prospective buyer (and this is a book to

be bought, not borrowed) should realise that it is really nine books in one. Between two covers has been channelled a mass of information (and entertainment) from dozens of sources.

On page after page, among the cold lists of names, titles and statistics, one comes across fascinating details: e.g. how Paramount got its 'Mountain', why Veronica Lake's hair flopped over one eye, the original house of *Sunset Boulevard* and the reason for Joseph Cotten's tennis visor when an old man in *Citizen Kane*. There are gloriously dotty quotes from publicity-department extravagances; examples of personal wit, repartee, eccentricities and quirks; sad (but interesting) records of deaths and causes of death, and useful pieces of information such as the names of the singers and speakers in all the Disney animated features. A few illustrations precede each Chronology, but it is the words that matter here, not the pictures. The book is, in fact, a cornucopia of easily digestible information. With so much to applaud it may seem churlish to find fault, but it is often a reviewer's duty to administer reproof as well as praise and it must be admitted that Mr Pickard's style, though bright and lively in what must have been a most difficult task, has some unfortunate tricks and is occasionally careless. He indulges in the misuse of 'hopefully' twice in one paragraph in his Introduction; he refers to Douglas Fairbanks being completely 'disinterested' in *The Taming of the Shrew* when what he clearly means is 'uninterested'. On p. 152 is the surprising statement that 'whilst endeavouring to shoot his next film, *The Circus*, his [Chaplin's wife (the former Lita Grey) files suit for divorce'. He distorts 'debut' into a verb (pronounced . . . ?). But the worst fault is an irritating habit of starting a sentence with a transposed 'said': 'Says Harry Cohn . . .', 'Said Cukor . . .', 'Said Mamoulian . . .', 'Says slow-motion master Peckinpah . . .', 'Comments veteran Howard Hawks . . .'. The habit, indulged in on page after page, can become both trying and tiring.

In addition, more care in proof-reading might have avoided rather more misprints than are excusable, not only in words (extravagent, fiancée (Mae Clarke's!), potruding, re-occurring, phyisical, aposite, mony, nonchalent, eight eighty, for eighty eight, etc.) but also in names (Frank Finley, George M. Cahn, Lean Horne, Lupe Belez, Orsen Welles, Fay Wary (!), *Lethernecking, Harold Diddledock* . . .)

This is not to carp. It is precisely because the book is so valuable that such errors are worth pointing out. It deserves to become a standard reference work, with many years of life—with possible updating and amendment from time to time.

A final word of praise must go to the excellent index.

John Garfield—his Life and Films: James N. Beaver, Jr.; Tantivy, £8.50/Barnes, $17.50.

John Garfield will always be remembered as a fine actor whose career was ruined by the House Un-American Activities Committee. He made his first film in 1938 (with the three Lane sisters), his last in 1951. His penultimate one the previous year was titled, with

grim aptness, *The Breaking Point*—his final one, scarcely less aptly, *He Ran All The Way*. He died, from natural causes, at the age of 39. Despite all this he had, and deserved, a considerable share of success, appearing in such esteemed movies as *The Postman Always Rings Twice, Gentleman's Agreement* and *Force of Evil*, and winning awards and Academy nominations. Mr Beaver tells his story with sympathy and frankness, and the main section of the book—on the individual films—is well up to the usual production standards of similar large-format career picture books.

The Magic World of Orson Welles: James Naremore; Oxford University Press, £9.75/O.U.P., N.Y., $15.95.

Books on Orson Welles are starting to proliferate, but Mr Naremore's study is welcome on account of its freshness of approach. He has tapped little-known sources in placing the great director's films against a historical and political (and psychological) background. In so doing he has without any doubt enlarged the filmgoer's interest in, and deepened his appreciation of, the achievement of Welles. His book is scholarly without pedantry, lively and very readable. It is also very nicely produced and pleasant to handle. Documentation is excellent, e.g. the bibliographical notes. Illustrations (frame blow-ups), though not particularly generous, are adequate. The index is full but sadly lacking in sub-entries. *Citizen Kane*, for example, is given nine lines of page numbers without a single helpful sub-entry, turning what should be a help to a quick reference into a wearisome chore. This is unhappily far from uncommon practice, but a painstaking book deserves a more painstaking index.

The Martial Arts Films: Marilyn D. Mintz; Tantivy, £5.95/Barnes, $9.95.

Presumably a book on this subject had to be written, and this is quite well done and very well documented and illustrated. But it is an abysmally depressing experience to turn page after page and be confronted with glaring brawny figures (male and female) bashing, kicking, belting and slashing at one another, and generally behaving like hooligans—the whole thing being made even more wearisome by the knowledge that it is all faked anyway. Most repulsive of all are the kung-fu films, with their silly grunts and yelps, their puerile scowlings and jumpings about, their grim viciousness and total lack of humour. Altogether one is faced with a repulsive record of sub-civilised carryings-on, in one of the least admirable and most dispensable of film by-ways.

Movie Special Effects: Jeff Rovin; Tantivy, £7.95/Barnes $17.50.

Following John Brosnan's excellent study of the subject, *Movie Magic*, comes Mr Rovin's more recent survey. Its main advantage is the large format, enabling justice to be done to the many stills. These are, inevitably, much more plentiful when more recent years are reached, but the text contains interesting inside information on a number of silent and early sound classics. Chapters are mainly divided into

decades, but Ray Harryhausen, Disney and Pal have sections to themselves and there is a final brief word on television. 'Disaster' films such as *Earthquake* and *The Towering Inferno* receive particular attention. Mr Rovin's style is—still—not of the most polished, but he has much 'how-it-was' done' detail to impart, and is at his best when at his most technical.

Olivier—the Films and Faces of Laurence Olivier: Margaret Morley; LSP Books, £7.95./Citadel Press, $14.95.

Miss Morley has made a notable success into her 'first published essay into the field of filmography'—a worthy tribute to one of the great actors of our history. To start with she has assembled an impressive list of contributors to the opening section of commentaries, including Dilys Powell, Roger Manvell, Tom Hutchinson, Sheridan Morley and Michael Caine. This is followed by the films, set out in the customary 'Films of . . .' series format, with commendably full cast-lists, synopses and brief selections of press criticisms (but did Margaret Hinxman *really* describe Moriarty as 'Holme's' [sic] 'nemisis' [sic]?).

The illustrations are always a leading feature of the series. Here they are magnificent, and lavish to a degree—stills, personal portraits, dozens of production shots, and all well reproduced. A fine pictorial record of a great character-actor's film career; highly recommended.

Orson Welles—a Critical View: André Bazin; Elm Tree Books, £3.95/Harper & Row, $10.00; pb, $3.50.

The publishers have performed a service in now making available in English the updated version (1958) of Bazin's study. Apart from its intrinsic merits, it is interesting to read the views of a famous critic on a famous director after twenty years. Pride of place, as might be expected, goes to *Citizen Kane*, with *The Magnificent Ambersons* a close second. But Bazin has something stimulating and revealing to say on all the films up to *Touch of Evil*, bringing to the lay viewer's notice numerous points which will surely increase appreciation of at least two of the major achievements of the cinema. For a bonus there is a long Introduction by François Truffaut, bringing the book up to date, and fully as interesting—though not so long—as the Bazin essay. The original Profile by Jean Cocteau is also included.

It is interesting to note how inaccurate and careless a highly respected critic can be over details—duly recorded and corrected by the sharp-eyed translator, Jonathan Rosenbaum.

Raggedy Ann and Andy: Kathleen N. Daly; W. H. Allen, £2.95/Bobbs-Merrill, $8.95; Dell, pb, $2.95.

This charming little book is an adaptation of the animated film by Patricia Thackray and Max Wilk about the adventures of the two well-known dolls with pirates, a Loonie Knight and other engaging characters. Profusely and colourfully illustrated with frames from the film, it should entrance any child, whether reading or being read to.

Robert Mitchum on the Screen: Alvin H. Marill;
Tantivy, £8.95/Barnes, $19.95.
Despite the different wording of the title, this is really
another in the 'Films of . . .' genre, an up-to-standard
example of the apparently limitless series. It has the
usual ingredients: biographical introductory essay,
survey of all the films (with, in this case, commendably
full cast-and-credit lists), brief portrait gallery, and
good index. The film comments are, on the whole,
perceptive and fair, though occasionally odd, e.g. on
the unforgettably haunting *Night of the Hunter,* 'a
gripping if somewhat electric horror tale . . . bordering
somewhat on the arty'. What is an *electric* horror tale?
The films total 95, which may surprise some filmgoers.
How many, one wonders, could they name without
reference to the book? The illustrations are well
reproduced, and by no means all complimentary—see
p. 40, for example. Mitchum himself is frequently
quoted, often to sharp and witty effect.

The Shattered Silents: Alexander Walker; Elm Tree
Books, £7.95
The advent of sound was the most traumatic
experience to hit Hollywood and was far more
cataclysmic than the eruption of TV. Surprisingly for

the first time, a full study of those two or three
tumultuous years now appears, dealing with all its
effects—aesthetic, technical, financial, personal and
disastrous. It is fortunate that the period should have
as its detailed historian so informed, painstaking and
lively a writer as Mr Walker, whose book is a most
important, and entertaining account. There are also
numerous fascinating stills, some rare indeed. (Can the
illustration on p. 144 *really* be Nancy Carroll?)
I can remember well the impact of 'the talkies' on the
avid, if somewhat indiscriminate, filmgoer of the time;
an aspect not always sufficiently realised (particularly
by the sophisticated, satiated, understandably caustic
critics then writing) was the sheer *excitement*—for good
or ill—of hearing long-worshipped silent heroes and
heroines SPEAK.

The War, The West and the Wilderness:
Kevin Brownlow; Secker & Warburg, £15/Knopf,
$25.00.
This magnificent volume is a companion piece to the
author's highly regarded *The Parade's Gone By.* In
his Introduction he describes it as a 'journey of
discovery through archives, private collections and
stock shot libraries in search of history on film',
mentioning as key films Griffith's *Hearts of the World*
(war), *Isn't Life Wonderful?* (war's aftermath),
Cruze's *The Covered Wagon* (Western) and Cooper's
Grass (wilderness). In the brief space here available,
it is difficult to summarise or to convey the vast fields
which are covered, and with time pressing for
inclusion in this issue of *Film Review* (and such an
important book should not have to wait for over a
year) it is impossible to do it full justice. From the
earliest years of cinema to about 1930, Mr Brownlow
includes both fictional and factual films on all aspects
of his three subjects, and the result is engrossing
both as cinema and as history, well documented and
scrupulously researched. The stills and other
photographs, of the utmost rarity, are excellently
reproduced – set similarly to *The Parade's Gone By*
but avoiding the occasionally slightly confusing
pagination of the former book. With no doubt
whatever, this is a worthy companion to its august
predecessor.

REFERENCE

Close-Ups from the Golden Age of the Silent Cinema:
John R. Finch & Paul A. Elby; Tantivy, £14.50/
Barnes, $25.00
It was an excellent idea to produce a book of nearly
500 full-page and mainly rare photographs of stars
and character-players of the silent screen, and an
even better one to add brief biographical paragraphs
on all those represented. More's the pity, therefore,
that the result can be faulted in a number of respects.
A few careless name misspellings ('Corrine' Griffith,
Ronald 'Coleman', 'Marion' Nixon), though
surprising, may be excused; and the authors' honest
apologies for the omission of a large number of
names, though regrettable, must be accepted since no
photographs are in their possession. The real matter
for regret, however, is the very poor quality of many

(to be fair, not all) of the reproductions. This sort of
thing perpetuates the myth that has grown up from
the often muddy and mutilated film prints shown
today that the studio photography of the period was
of inferior quality. In truth, it often surpassed that of
today. The jacket blurb states that the majority of the
portraits are unfamiliar, indeed, some of them are
unrecognisable. They are certainly not, as is also
claimed, 'big and *clear* and intimate'.
The biographies themselves have some odd
omissions, eg in the matter of deaths, which could
have been discovered from Evelyn Mack Truitt's
excellent book *Who was Who on Screen.*
An enjoyable and useful volume in many ways,
therefore, but—as the examiner said—it could have
been better.

Those Fabulous Movie Years—the 30s: Paul Trent;
Orbis Publishing, £5.50/Barre Publishing, $14.95
This is a welcome and attractive picture book on a
key era of the cinema. In about 130 sections the
author has written brief articles on leading films,
leading players and occasionally a *genre* (horror,
musicals, etc). The articles are admirably succinct,
containing both information and opinion—the latter
often refreshingly frank, see for instance the final
comment on Bette Davis. The plentiful illustrations
include a number of early colour stills, as well as
posters and publicity shots, and are well reproduced.
A brief reference section give credits and cast lists:
the latter one might wish to have been fuller, but
indeed the volume as a whole can be regarded as a
useful reference book on a transitional and important
period which has not been as fully covered as others.
Recommended for both study and nostalgic
indulgence.

The Great British Films: Jerry Vermilye; Citadel,
dist. by LSP Books, £11.50/Citadel Press,
$14.95
It is very pleasant to see a warm, generous tribute to
the British from the USA, and much more so when it
is paid in so excellent a form as this. Ranging from
The Private Life of Henry VIII to *The Go Between,*
Mr Vermilye has selected some seventy films and
discusses them in brief articles full of discernment,
affection and interest. He praises but is never
fulsome—his comments, indeed, are as perceptive as
they are informed. (How welcome, incidentally, is his
staunch defence of black-and-white against the all-
pervading colour of today.) His choice of titles is
laudably catholic. As is to be expected, the big names
are present—*The Third Man, Brief Encounter, Great
Expectations, The Red Shoes, Room at the Top,
Rembrandt,* etc, etc—but he also includes a
considerable number of what he (rightly) considers
underrated films, or those which deserve to become
known to a wider public.
In such a collection, obviously, there are one or two
omissions (and inclusions) which might cause the
raising of a surprised eyebrow, but Mr Vermilye's
stated aim is to be as representative as possible, and
in this he is entirely successful. Thus, of the three

The Film Books of the Year

great British war pictures, *In Which We Serve, The Way Ahead* and *The Way to the Stars*, he selects the first, but the second receives honourable mention. All three Oliver Shakespeare productions are included. To the articles themselves (which often contain fascinating production details, eg *The Thief of Baghdad*) are added credits and excellently full cast lists, together with a lavish collection of splendid stills. Two minor points about the last-mentioned. Anna Lee has been unkindly lopped from that on p. 29, and the 'Queen' on p. 78 is, of course, the 'boy actor' at the Globe Theatre.

As a final charming touch to this altogether engaging book, the covers and jacket (designed by Janet Anderson) are resplendent in red, white and blue. Mr Vermilye's dedication is to four names—'Anglophiles all'—indeed, yes! Highly recommended, both for usefulness and for pleasure.

The Illustrated Who's Who in British Films: Denis Glifford; Batsford, £10.50/distributed by Hippocrene Books, $27.25.
Profiting from his labour on an earlier useful booklet on British players, and on his monumental and indispensable *British Film Catalogue*, Mr Gifford has produced an equally indispensable companion to the latter, in which no fewer than one thousand British stars, directors and characters through eighty years are presented, with brief biographical details and—all-importantly—with *complete* British filmographies. In addition there are nearly 300 well-reproduced illustrations, many of them appearing for the first time, some of them book jackets accompanying a full bibliography at the end of the book. Even with the groundwork of the previous two volumes the loving labour going to this compilation must have been Herculean. The result is particularly valuable for its wide coverage of the earlier years, where documentation has for long been so much harder to come by.

Presumably, in a task such as this the occasional slip or omission is almost bound to occur (eg Norman Wooland, the excellent Horatio, has Olivier's *Hamlet* missing from his credits), but the researcher can rest comfortably assured that in such painstaking hands these are absolutely minimal.

With its illustrations, clear and attractive layout and lower price than that of its august companion, this volume may well have a wider appeal; but to any enthusiast worthy of the name *both* books are—once again—indispensable.

International Film Guide, 1979: Ed. Peter Cowie; Tantivy, £3.75/Barnes, $6.95.
What can one say about this huge horn of cinematic plenty that has not been said already? It is a wide, concise survey of film information from fifty-four countries: from Algeria, through Bangladesh, England, Iraq, Italy, the Philippines, USA to Yugoslavia. It includes sections on every conceivable aspect of the film world—including books, music, animation, cinemas, and a video survey—in addition to pages of splendid advertisements and illustrations galore. This

year's five-character Director's Pantheon consists of Shyam Benegal, Werner Herzog, Márta Mészáros, Fons Rademakers and Martin Scorsese. A book with its greatest appeal to the specialist and superbuff, perhaps, with its many films that we are tantalisingly unlikely to see—but at 520 packed pages (stoutly bound in soft cover) for £3.75, there must surely be *something* for everybody.

The Non-Western Films of John Ford: J. A. Place; Citadel, dist. by LSP Books, £14.50/Citadel Press, $17.95.
Dr Janey Ann Place here follows up her earlier study of Ford's Western films. Her book is arranged in useful sections, rather than chronologically—Americana, War (comedies and documentaries), Irish, Action, 'Foreign'—which aids critical assessment, and is prefaced by a brief analytical study. Stills are lavish, credits full, and the analyses admirable. Well up to the general standard of this series, this volume, taken in conjunction with the author's previous one, must surely form a definitive survey of this outstanding film-maker's long and distinguished career.

Science Fiction in the Movies, An A–Z: Roy Pickard; Muller, £3.50
A very useful, concise handbook with brief details of films, directors, players, writers, technicians, etc—even includes a select list of the books burnt in *Fahrenheit 451*, under the heading 'Mein Kampf'. It does not pretend, in 120 pages, to be all-embracing, but within its limits—'a book of information to use in conjunction with the great new movies in the *genre* and those likely to be seen or reseen on television'—it is more than adequate. As might be expected from so painstaking an author (though not, unfortunately, quite painstaking enough to avoid the horrible and misleading misuse of the adverb 'hopefully') the alphabetical arrangement is not made an excuse for shirking an index. Twenty-six stills add to the attraction of a well-produced little book.

Screen World 1978: Ed. John Willis; Muller, £7.55/Crown, $12.95.
The highest praise one can give the latest issue of this long-running annual is that it is up to the standard of its predecessors, which is high praise indeed. The details of the year's releases (American and a number of foreign) with the fullest available cast-lists, the Academy Awards, select biographical paragraphs, obituaries, etc, plus the dauntingly enormous index are all features that reappear—embellished with hundreds of good stills. Though they have not come my way, I understand that the earliest volumes were re-issued some time ago as collector's items; anyone possessing the whole set would be advised to keep them well locked behind glass—and very thoroughly insured—should he or she be in the habit of admitting film enthusiasts into the room where these volumes are kept!

Who Was Who On Screen (Second Edition): Evelyn Mack Truitt; R. R. Bowker & Co, £21.50/Bowker, $29.95.
The first edition of this indispensable reference book

was highly recommended (unfortunately slightly mistitled as *Who was who on the Screen*) in a previous *Film Review*. The second merits even higher commendation. Entirely reset, in smaller but perfectly legible type, it contains an additional 3,000 entries in some 500 large pages (not 650 as in the publicity brochure, but this may have been estimated before the resetting), bringing the total to an incredible 9,000 names. So far as is humanly possible, a *complete* list of screen appearances is given in every case, the obituary limit being 1975. Brief biographical details are given (date and place of birth and death, often cause of death also, etc). Though concentrating mainly on American and British players, the new edition includes a large number of foreign names. Perhaps most valuable of all is the attention paid to small and bit-part players—details which are so much harder to discover than in the case of stars. Personalities such as Picasso, Maugham and Shaw, who have appeared on screen, are included; famous four-footed players such as Lassie, Tony and Rin-Tin-Tin (senior and junior) receive due respect. The sole criterion is an actual appearance *on*, not merely behind, the screen—see, for instance Cecil B. DeMille.

A jewel of a book, fashioned and polished with loving care and astonishing endurance!

The World's Great Movie Stars and their Films: Ken Wlaschin; Salamander, £7.95
In his Introduction to this handsome volume the author modestly states that it is 'not academic'; even so, it contains a wealth of reference material which it is very useful to have in one clearly set-out book. It is divided into three sections—Silent, Classic and Modern—each containing brief biographical and critical articles and a selected list of 'best' films, covering in all some 400 stars. Most interesting, perhaps, are the first and third sections, as so much is already available on the Classic periods, but all three are admirable. The emphasis, obviously, is on American and British players, but the content is by no means confined to these. French, Japanese and German, for instance, are here, and there is a special article on the Ingmar Bergman repertory company. Mickey, Felix, Tom and Jerry also find honoured places.

Ken Wlaschin writes in a lively, easy style (though he is guilty of that horrible error, the misused 'hopefully') and, as Director for some years of the National Film Theatre, is obviously well equipped for such a task as this. Clearly his omissions will be challenged by the occasional stalwart admirer of an absent name, and his list of 'best' films will be questioned; but this is, as he emphasises, a 'personal' selection, and it is sufficiently wide and varied to meet most of such challenges. Illustrations—colour, tinted and black-and-white—are lavish, generally well reproduced, and by no means all familiar.

A 'non-serious' book, perhaps, as Mr Wlaschin modestly states, but one which may well provide as much entertainment—and useful information—as many a graver tome.

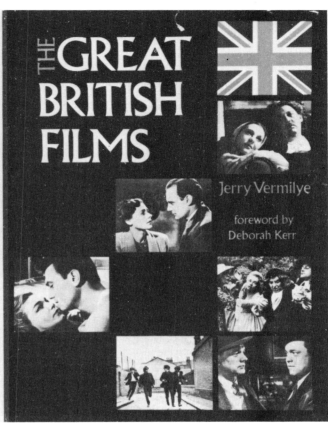

Children's Film Foundation

The two escaped convicts (Michael Elphick and Allan Surtees) and the two youngsters (Martin Murphy and Michael Salmon) who unwillingly share an otherwise uninhabited island with them in the Kingsgate Films production for CFF, *Black Island*.

Last year at this time the future of the Children's Film Foundation appeared somewhat in doubt, with stories being bandied around Wardour Street about the suggestions of some people within the industry that the financial support, without which the CFF would be unable to continue to make new product, should be restricted, severely reduced or even entirely withdrawn.

Fortunately such destructive efforts appear to have been abortive and, indeed, to have resulted in something of a backlash, with a stronger, renewed determination emerging from the film industry as a whole that the Board's great work should not only continue but also, if possible, be extended.

There is no doubt that the Wilson Committee, when enquiring into the whole of the British film industry, were considerably impressed both by the Board's own representations and by those made on its behalf by many other organisations who all praised it and suggested that the CFF had in fact become something of a modern social necessity.

An indicative of this new mood of optimism and determination was the raising of the Board's annual grant to a new high figure of £570,000 for one year—a much welcomed, and needed, increase in income.

But with all this reassuring good news the Board have not sat back and relaxed to carry on comfortably as before. Indeed, they are using the current climate to explore new ways and means of expanding their work. For instance, three committees have been set up to go into the possibilities of (a) the wider marketing and showing of children's films at points other than just the usual Saturday matinées; (b) the sponsorship, or partial sponsorship, of CFF films, and (c) the practicability of obtaining wider distribution by means of 16-mm films and by the new video cassettes. One of the less happy pieces of news to come from the Foundation during the year was the announcement of the decision by Executive Producer Henry Geddes to retire from his key post in the summer of next year, 1980. Since he joined the CFF in 1964, Geddes has been an untiring ambassador for, as well as chief working executive of, the Children's Film Foundation, having had overall responsibility during those sixteen years for the production of no less than 97 feature films, 73 serial episodes and 75 two-reel comedies! Even before he actually joined the Board, Geddes had made four features—as an independent writer–director– producer—for it and even during his term of office he has managed to continue to squeeze into his tight schedule the writing of a number of screenplays for children's movies. The resignation blow was softened somewhat by Henry Geddes's announcement that his stepping down from the CFF's top job would not mean his severing his connections with the organisation. In fact he has said that he will continue

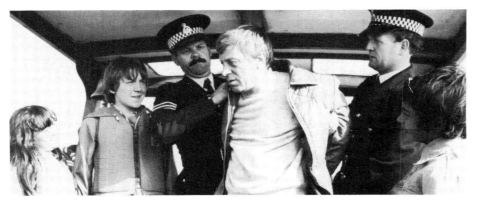

The illegal-immigrant racketeer (Ken Farrington) says he'll give up after losing a fight with small feminine opponent (Virginia Fiel) at the climax of the Eyeline Films–CFF production *Deep Waters*. Her brother (Luke Batchelor) is amused, not so the sergeant (Frank Jarvis) and the constable (David Millet). At extreme right, Raymond Persoud.

to act in a consultative capacity (with particular reference to overseas contracts and the wider marketing of CFF films) and will also concentrate on other aspects of the Foundation's work which have, unfortunately, because of pressure had to be rather neglected in the past.

Incidentally, in 1975 Henry Geddes was awarded the Mérite Cinématographique in the grade of Chevalier by the Fédération Nationale des Cinémas Français in recognition of his contribution to the International Children's Film Movement, and he is now serving the second year of his three-year term as President of the International Centre of Films for Children and Young People, of which some fifty countries are members.

To celebrate the International Year of the Child, taking place this year (1979), the CFF organised a blanket release (on 28 April) of five new CFF productions through some 200 cinemas throughout the UK. These films were shown at Saturday matinées from 28 April to 19 May during what was termed a 'Children's Film Month'. Full details of these and the other CFF releases during the year will be found below.

Black Island
The story of two boys who are washed out to sea in an old boat and end up on a small island on which two criminals are hiding, one of them a dangerously violent character. Made on location on Osea Island in the Blackwater Estuary, Essex, and at Burnham, Bucks. Cast: *Martin Murphy, Michael Salmon, Michael Elphick, Allan Surtees, Norman Tipton, Hugh Martin, Brian Osborne, Mike Savage, Anthony Powell, Simon Dawson.* Dir: Ben Bolt. Pro: Carole Smith. Screenplay: Peter Smith and William Humble; based on a story by Peter van Praagh. Ph: Ricky Briggs. Ed: Thomas Schwalm. Art: Bob Berk. M: Patrick Gowers. (Kingsgate Films for CFF.) 57 mins. Cert U.

Deep Waters
About a boy and his young sister on holiday at the seaside who ignore warnings and start off on an adventure which puts their own and other lives at risk, more so when they become entangled with a group of ruthless illegal-immigrant smugglers. Cast: *Virginia Fiel, Luke Batchelor, Raymond Persoud, Paul Hillman, Jonathan Burn, Ken Farrington, James Coyle, Renu Setna, Ahmed Kalil, Colin Rix, Jeremy Bullock, Frank Jarvis, Peter Theedom, David Millet.* Dir: David Eady. Pro: John V. Lemont. Screenplay & story: John V. Lemont. Ph: Ray Orton. Ed: Richard Mason. Art: Michael Pickwood. Assoc Pro: Harold Orton. M: Harry Robinson. Made on location in the Isle of Sheppey. (Eyeline Films for CFF.) 55 mins. Cert U.

The Electric Eskimo
Delightful little fantasy about an Eskimo boy who, becoming accidentally involved with an experiment to harness the electro-magnetism of the North Pole, becomes an enormous source of electricity and is brought to London to undergo tests, during which two crooks who find out his secret try to kidnap him and use him for their own purposes. Cast: *Kris Emmerson, Debby Padbury, Ian Sears, Derek Francis, Tom Chadbon, Diana King, Ivor Danvers, Madeleine Christie, David Rowlands, Victor Brooks, Richard Wren.* Dir, Pro & Screenplay (the last with H. MacLeod Robertson): Frank Godwin. Assoc Pro: Denis Johnson Jr. Ph: Ray Orton. Ed: Richard Mason. Art: Mike Pickwood. M: Harry Robinson. Filmed on location in Surrey. (Monument Productions for CFF.) 57 mins. Cert U.

A Hitch in Time
Humorous science-fiction adventures of two children who, on the way to school, rescue a professor trapped by his experimental time-machine and themselves become involved with trips into time. Cast: *Michael McVey, Pheona McLellan, Patrick Troughton, Geoffrey Rawle, Sorcha Cusack, Ronnie Brody.* Dir: Jan Darnley-Smith. Pro: Harold Orton. Screenplay: T. E. B. Clarke; from his own story. Pro Man: J. C. Wilcox. Ph: Tommy Fletcher. Ed: Gordon Grimward. Art: Michael Pickwood. M: Harry Robinson. (Eyeline Films for CFF.) 57 mins. Cert U.

Mr Selkie
Charming little fantasy about the gent of the title who is really a seal but changes shape in order to try to convince the Mayor and Councillors of a small

seaside town that it is time to halt pollution of the sea. Cast: *Samantha Weysom, Clark Flanagan, Michael Mannion, Peter Bayliss, Noel Howlett, Molly Weir, Zara Nutley, Derek Tansley, Christine Ozanne.* Dir: Anthony Squire. Pro: Jean Wadlow. Screenplay: John Tully, James Hill & Anthony Squire; from a story by Janey Eckford. Pro Sup: Ron Appleton. Ph: Norman Jones. Pro Man: Aivar Kaulins. Ed: Monica Mead. M: John Gale. Made on location at Brixham, Devon; Bracknell, Berks, and London. (Wadlow Grosvenor Productions for CFF.) 60 mins. Cert U.

Eskimo boy Poochook (Kris Emmerson) shows off his extraordinary electric powers by lighting up a light-bulb in the Monument–CFF production *The Electric Eskimo.*

The Professor (Patrick Troughton) explains his time-machine to curious callers Michael McVey and Pheona McLellan in Eyeline Films–CFF's *A Hitch in Time,* a Welles-like fantasy in which the trio travel backward through the years.

Conversation between seal-man Mr Selkie and the Ross children (Peter Bayliss, Samantha Weysom and Clark Flanagan) in the Wadlow Grosvenor–CFF production *Mr Selkie,* which at its centre is a plea for less pollution of our shores.

Index

Page numbers in italics indicate pictorial references; titles in italics indicate reference to books.

Index